Southern Living®

2001 Garden ANNUAL

A sweep planting of black-eyed Susans creates an impact of color. (See page 56.)

Southern Living.

2001
Garden
ANNUAL

Oxmoor House.

Southern Living
2001 Garden ANNUAL

©2001 by Oxmoor House, Inc.
Book Division of Southern Progress Corporation
P.O. Box 2463, Birmingham, Alabama 35201

Southern Living® is a federally registered
trademark of Southern Living, Inc.

ISSN: 1048-2318
Hardcover ISBN: 0-8487-2384-8
Softcover ISBN: 0-8487-2390-2
Printed in the United States of America
First Printing 2001

SOUTHERN LIVING

Executive Editor, Homes and Gardens: Eleanor Griffin
Senior Writer: Stephen P. Bender
Senior Photographers: Van Chaplin, Sylvia Martin, Allen Rokach
Photographers: Jean M. Allsopp, Ralph Anderson, Tina Cornett,
William Dickey, Laurey W. Glenn, Meg McKinney Simle
Associate Garden Editors: Ellen Riley, Charles Thigpen
Associate Garden Design Editor: Glenn R. DiNella
Assistant Garden Design Editor: Troy H. Black
Assistant Garden Editor: Liz Druitt
Production Manager: Katie Terrell
Editorial Coordinator: Bradford Kachelhofer
Editorial Assistant: Lynne Long
Production Assistant: Nicole Johnson

OXMOOR HOUSE, INC.

Editor-in-Chief: Nancy Fitzpatrick Wyatt
Senior Editor, Copy and Homes: Olivia Kindig Wells
Art Director: James Boone

SOUTHERN LIVING 2001 GARDEN ANNUAL

Editor: Susan Hernandez Ray
Copy Editor: L. Amanda Owens
Contributing Designer: Rita Yerby
Editorial Assistant: Heather Averett
Contributing Indexer: Katharine R. Wiencke

Director, Production and Distribution: Phillip Lee
Books Production Manager: Larry Hunter
Production Assistant: Faye Porter Bonner

We're Here for You!
We at Oxmoor House are dedicated to serving you with reliable
information that expands your imagination and enriches your life.
We welcome your comments and
suggestions. Please write us at:
OXMOOR HOUSE, INC.
Editor, *Southern Living 2001 Garden Annual*
2100 Lakeshore Drive
Birmingham, AL 35209

Cover: Red poppies, page 118
Back Cover: Reproduction gate, page 63

Contents

cut flowers

daffodils

Exbury azalea

peppers

I confess: I'm a thoroughly disorganized person. My office is smothered with books, magazines, envelopes, maps, writing paper, letters, boxes, newspaper clippings, catalogs, and packages of weird, alien fertilizer—all laid down in sedimentary layers from floor to ceiling. It wouldn't surprise me if years from now, some paleontologist digs his way to the bottom and discovers a pencil belonging to the Pleistocene Age.

How I wish I had more books like this one! This single volume contains all of the gardening stories that appeared in *Southern Living* this past year. I highly recommend this resource to you and all other gardeners. Now, rather than wade through a sea of various gardening books, you can simply leaf through these pages and find helpful information on a wide range of topics—from how to use color in the garden to growing cool-weather vegetables to putting in new stone steps. In addition to inspirational stories on the South's most beautiful gardens, you'll also find a plant hardiness map, source lists for featured plants and products, and a whole year's worth of garden checklists and letters to our garden editors.

So don't think a healthy interest in gardening means adding a library onto your home. All you need is a spare shelf for a few books like this one. Send that paleontologist home.

Senior Writer

A trio of pots fills a corner of the deck. The star of the show is the bougainvillea, one of many choices for the summer season. In the back are the supporting players, shrubs that remain season after season. (See page 53.)

Forcing branches into bloom (See pages 16–19.)

January

Checklist for January

EDITOR'S NOTEBOOK

Now that we've entered the 21st century, I am exercising my prerogative as editor of this page to select a new Plant of the Century. (For those of you who missed this column in January 1900, my last Plant of the Century was kudzu. See how popular kudzu became?) Requirements for this hallowed title are stringent. Said plant must be evergreen (Southerners love evergreens). It must have multi-season interest (which eliminates juniper, quince, mock orange, and Belgian endive). It must do equally well in sun or shade (unlike peach trees, which do well in neither). Most importantly, it must be so tough that unless your spouse digs it up with a backhoe and throws it away, it will be in your garden at the turn of the next century. Now for the moment you've been waiting 99 years for. The next winner is (drumroll, please): nandina. That's right—plain old nandina. Think I'm nuts? Fine—you can name the next winner. Call me with your nomination in December 2099.

Steve Bender

TIPS

◀ **Birds**—Keep your feeders filled. For birds, this is a critical time of the year. Suet-based food helps keep up their energy reserves during cold weather. It's also a good time to set out landscape plants—such as yaupon, American, and deciduous hollies in the Lower, Coastal, and Tropical South—that attract birds.

☐ **Fruit and nuts**—In the Upper South, mail-order plants, such as Montmorency cherries and Moorpark apricots, now for setting out in February. Apricots are excellent yard trees, although they may not produce fruit every year due to late freezes. Gala, Fuji, and Granny Smith apples are good choices for Panhandle gardens. Seibel 9110 (white) and Chambourcin (red) grapes may be grown on arbors or trellises. The best pecans for the area are Peruque and Kanza.

☐ **Mulch**—The coldest days are ahead, but you still have time to mulch. Apply pine needles, bark chips, or ground-up leaves to conserve moisture and insulate your soil from wide variations in temperature. As spring dawns, the mulch will also help keep down weeds. Many municipalities collect and shred Christmas trees, then offer the mulch to the public. This is a great way to recycle your tree, as well as to get some free (or very inexpensive) mulch for your garden.

☐ **Pesticides**—Remember to store these products in a locked cabinet in a place where they will not be exposed to freezing temperatures. In the future, minimize the amount of pesticides you have in storage by buying only as much as you need for one season.

☐ **Seeds**—If you buy seeds through the mail, this is a good time to order. Sometimes you get early-season bonuses, not to mention quick delivery. ▶

Dream of spring— Now is the time to keep warm in the house while going through seed and plant catalogs.

PLANT

☐ **Annuals**—In the Lower and Coastal South, this is a good time to set out Sweet William, calendulas, dianthus (pinks), ornamental cabbage and kale, violas (Johnny-jump-ups), and pansies. Select sunny areas, and add 3 to 5 inches of organic material, such as composted pine bark, sphagnum peat, or your own compost, along with fertilizer such as 17-17-17 as recommended on the label.

◀ **Herbs**—Many cool-weather herbs can be grown now in the Coastal and Tropical South, either from seeds or transplants. Try basil, dill, sage, catnip, borage, cilantro, or any of the mints. All of these herbs prefer a sunny location in the garden.

☐ **Lawns**—Lower South lawns can turn quite brown this time of year, especially if a freeze occurs. One way the lawn can be greened up is by overseeding with annual ryegrass. It will provide bright color in your yard until warmer spring weather, when the perennial turf is actively growing again.

□ **Poinsettias**—After enjoying your holiday poinsettia indoors, don't throw it out in the Coastal and Tropical South. You can plant it in a sunny spot in the garden. Be sure to avoid planting it in areas near streetlights or porch lights because long, dark nights will be needed to stimulate flowering next winter.

□ **Transplants**—A simple way to get a lot of new plants is from the old ones. Transplant suckers that pop up around the base of sweet shrub, forsythia, hydrangea, spirea, viburnum, and weigela. This transplanting method works for fruiting plants such as figs, blueberries, blackberries, and raspberries, as well. ▶

□ **Trees and shrubs**—In both the Lower and Coastal South, winter and early spring are ideal times to plant hardy shrubs and trees. Outstanding trees include live oak, Chinese pistache, bald cypress, Mexican plum, and redbud. It's also a good time to transplant trees and shrubs anywhere the soil is not frozen; the cooler weather and relative dormancy of the plants make it an ideal time. Keep as much of the root system intact as possible, and don't allow the roots to dry out in the moving process. After planting, water the soil around their root systems thoroughly. Mulch to ensure survival.

PRUNE

◀ **Annuals**—Cool-weather annuals, such as dianthus, snapdragons, petunias, and calendulas, can be renewed by simply deadheading. If the plants have become too leggy, prune the stems back to a desirable size and shape. They will reward you with more flowers within a few weeks.

□ **Shrubs**—This is a good time of year for you to prune damaged or overgrown shrubs. Remove stems that are dead or injured by storms, diseases, or insects. For a natural form, remove a branch at its point of origin. For sheared forms, cut below the outline of the plant to allow new growth to branch, and fill the hole. Delay pruning spring-flowering shrubs until after they have flowered.

CONTROL

◀ **Houseplants**—This is a good time to check your plants for spider mites. These pests prosper in the dry heated home. Spider mites live on the underside of leaves and suck the green juice from them. Affected foliage will appear stippled with yellow. Take plants outside on a warm day, or place them in the shower. When dry, spray with SunSpray Ultrafine Oil according to directions.

January notes:

TIP OF THE MONTH

Need a funnel, saucer for a pot, and some plant markers? Cut up and recycle an old bleach bottle. The top and handle make a funnel, the bottom makes a saucer, and the sides can be cut into about 45 triangular plant markers.

Mrs. Robert D. Zarr
Bay Minette, Alabama

Jewel orchids are prized for their colorfully patterned, often velvet-textured leaves.

Macodes marmorata

Ludisia discolor

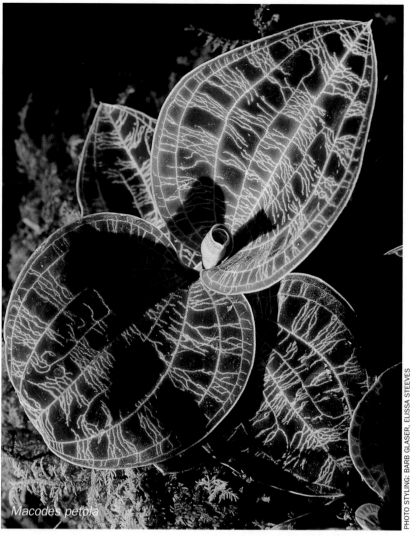

Macodes petola

PHOTO STYLING: BARB GLASER, ELISSA STEEVES

Meet the jewel orchids.
Year after year, these

VIBRANT
GEMS

bloom atop crowns
of colorful leaves.

BY LINDA C. ASKEY / PHOTOGRAPHY VAN CHAPLIN

Cystorchis javanica var. purpurea

Anoectochilus koshunensis

The name "orchid" brings to mind big corsages, greenhouses, and awkwardly shaped, difficult-to-grow plants. But seldom does it conjure memories of velvet foliage and easy care. That's the wonder of the jewel orchids. They'll be a welcome addition to your winter days indoors.

These tabletop favorites hail from the forest floor of tropical climates such as Indonesia and Malaysia, so they will not enjoy life outdoors in areas that are cold right now. But they will thrive in a heated home with no more than indirect window light. In fact, if that window is south-facing, pull the plant away a few feet or it may appear bleached from the overabundance of sunlight.

The jewel orchids are actually a group of genera, all of which offer handsome leaves and easy maintenance. The easiest of all is *Ludisia discolor,* an orchid commonly found in retail centers. Its greenish-bronze leaves are streaked with red veins. Most of us would be happy if it simply survived, but it grows well and blooms to boot.

According to Dwayne Louder of The Dowery Orchid Nursery in Hiwassee, Virginia, "*Ludisia discolor* will grow in Pro-Mix [or similar potting soil] just fine, and it will grow in plain water. If you take a cutting and drop it into a glass of water, it will root and bloom and grow like crazy."

Busy gardeners need agreeable plants, and this is a good one. Flowering is almost automatic. Cooler temperatures near a window and shorter days cause the flowerbuds to set in the center of the rosettes. Stems will grow to 12 inches and produce dozens of half-inch white flowers in the middle of winter.

After your orchid flowers, cut off the stalks. The plant will then begin growing, producing side shoots both above and below ground during the spring and summer. In fact, a small orchid is enough to make a showy specimen in only a year or two.

Feed your plants with a water-soluble fertilizer such as 12-12-12 mixed at half the recommended strength. Apply this instead of water once every three weeks.

As easy to grow, but with a distinctly different pattern on the leaves, is *Macodes marmorata.* With the texture of red-and-green mottled velvet, the veins are a net of red, silver, or green. Its close relative *Macodes petola* has velvet green leaves with a net of gold veins. Because of the look of these leaves, Virginia gardener Elissa Steeves calls the *Macodes* "Oriental carpet orchids."

Once you get hooked on these and want to enhance your collection, you might try to collect rarer jewels such as *Anoectochilus* sp., *Goodyera* sp., and *Cystorchis* sp.

Dwayne suggests top-dressing the plants with sheet moss. He collects his from the forest near his home. It helps give the foliage an attractive background while retaining moisture, much like a mulch does in a garden bed. "I would hesitate to use Spanish moss," Dwayne explains, "as it often contains spider mites, to everyone's regret." ◇

(For sources turn to pages 250–251.)

Remedies For Pansies

Winter's challenge is to stay healthy. Life is no easier for pansies. These garden jewels suffer the ills of unpredictable weather as much as we do and can struggle to hold their flower heads high.

These plants flourish with moderation—when temperatures balance between the 30s and 40s. They need sunny days with a minimum of four hours direct sunlight. But winter has fickle habits, with temperatures that change dramatically from noon to nightfall and cold gray rain that seems to last a lifetime. These unpredictable patterns can cause healthy pansies to become stressed. Here are preventions, symptoms, and sure-cure remedies to help them through midwinter blues.

A BIG CHILL

Occasional warm days lure pansies into a false sense of spring. They produce new leaves and bloom profusely. Then the thermometer threatens to drop rapidly, way below freezing. Pansies need help to cope with the fast change. First, head into the garden; remove all the flowers, and bring them indoors for miniature bouquets. Then cover the plants with a light pine straw blanket. Use enough to insulate plants and soil, but don't flatten plants with excessive straw. When the thermometer is again above freezing, pull back the pine straw to expose the foliage to warm sunlight.

Even with pine straw, damage may occur. This is evident when yellow leaves appear at the base of the plants. Pinch or clip off all discolored or mushy leaves, and put them in the trash to prevent further decay and bacteria.

FEED THE COLD

Lack of sunshine stops flower production. When winter skies stay gray for weeks at a time, pansies go into hibernation. Remove all spent blooms, and give them a fertilizer boost. Feed weekly with a liquid such as 15-30-15 to stimulate roots and produce new leaves and flowers. Continue this routine until winter weather stabilizes, usually by late February.

THE WARM SIDE

We take such delight in balmy days during winter, and pansies do also. Continuous unseasonably warm weather brings its own problems. A growth spurt produces tender stems, new leaves, and blooms like there's no tomorrow. Then the aphids arrive, with a feeding frenzy on every inch of lush new growth.

Act fast to save plants from these invaders. First, remove mulch that inhibits air circulation. Then saturate the leaves and buds with insecticidal soap. Pinch back leggy growth, and place insect-infested clippings in the trash. Once cool weather returns, feed pansies with a liquid fertilizer such as 20-20-20 to help them recover.

Ellen Riley

CONTAINER CARE

Pansies in pots suffer cold damage faster than those in the ground. Take these precautions to minimize problems when the weather gets tough.

- Cluster pots against the house for wind protection.
- Carry lightweight containers into an unheated garage for severely cold evenings.
- Water containers prior to a hard freeze.
- Large pots can be protected with a plastic trash bag. Tuck the bag's edges under the pot for a snug fit. Do not allow foliage to come in contact with the plastic. Remove it early in the morning, before sunlight heats the plastic.

Exotic Pitcher Plants

Pitcher plants *(Sarracenia* sp.) are a striking example of nature's intrigue. "These are not your everyday plants," says Dr. Larry Mellichamp, director of the University of North Carolina at Charlotte Botanical Gardens. "They are almost otherworldly in appearance, but they are very easy to grow."

Unfortunately, they have been largely unavailable in nursery trade, making wild collection a common practice and a problem. That has changed due to the efforts of Larry and Rob Gardner, curator of plants at the North Carolina Botanical Garden at Chapel Hill.

Pitcher plants are native almost exclusively to Southern bogs and wetlands. "They're uniquely Southern," Larry says. "These plants are accustomed to heat, full sun, and wet feet. They are also being lost in massive numbers due to habitat destruction and overcollection," he says. "Plants collected from the wild do not thrive. They don't adapt to cultivation, so it's a waste to collect them."

Larry and Rob have worked since 1984 to develop hybrid pitcher plants for home gardens, with three hybrids currently being mass-produced. "They are fancier than the wild species, with more interesting pitchers and colors. We're trying to remove any incentive at all to wild collect," Larry says.

FEED ME
The tubular pitchers, marked with colorful veins and ruffled edges, are endowed with a healthy appetite for insects. Add to their unique appearance the fact that they're carnivorous, and they instantly become more interesting. "They're not a substitute for a bug zapper," Larry says, "but they do attract moths, beetles, wasps, and similar insects. It's interesting to watch bugs being lured to the spots, colors, frills, and nectar of the pitchers. It all goes hand in hand to attract their prey."

UP CLOSE AND CONTAINED
Best viewed up close, pitcher plants are perfectly suited to dish gardens and containers. Larry recommends a pot with a drainage hole, along with a saucer underneath. Plant in half peat moss and half coarse white sand; keep water in the saucer for necessary moisture.

Cover exposed planting mix with fresh moss to help retain moisture. "The pitchers benefit from feeding, but it must be a light mix," Larry says. Use a well-balanced water-soluble fertilizer, such as ½ teaspoon of 20-20-20 per gallon of water. "Feed them twice a month during the growing season. Occasionally flush the container with clear water to prevent the soil mix from becoming stagnant," he says.

The containers will be attractive through summer and fall. Leave them outdoors in cold winter months; bring them in only when temperatures threaten to damage the pots.

These native Southern carnivorous plants have a breathtaking understated elegance. Purchase them from reputable sources; by doing so, you can help preserve those left in their natural habitat.
Ellen Riley

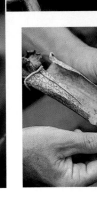

Content in containers, pitcher plants offer gardeners a fascinating look at a carnivorous Southern native. And they are surprisingly easy to grow.

PITCHER PERFECT

The three hybrid pitcher plants currently available are Ladies in Waiting, Flies Demise, and Dixie Lace. Purchase them only from nurseries that do not wild collect.

flirting
with spring

Branches coaxed into bloom bring a hint of spring to your windowsill.

ABOVE: *A saucer magnolia stem becomes a still life display under a bell jar.* RIGHT: *Forsythia and quince are a color burst. The tin-lined basket is filled with crumpled chicken wire to hold tall stems upright. Forsythia is one of the most vigorous candidates for cutting, with pruning necessary almost every year.*

In January, winter flirts with spring. Occasional warm days entice quince, forsythia, and pussy willow to emerge from dormant sleep. With the slightest swelling of buds, it's time to cut a few branches and invite spring indoors before winter turns its cold shoulder.

You don't have to prune heavily to have branches for forcing. A few cuttings can provide plenty of flowers for a small arrangement. Remember, any cut you make will alter the plant's appearance, so treat this as an opportunity to gently shape and trim trees and shrubs. A branch cut now will also lessen the show later, so avoid being heavy-handed. Cut branches headed in the wrong direction or crossing other limbs now. Major pruning should wait until after spring bloom. Choose twigs with rounded, fat buds. Leaf buds are usually smaller and pointed.

BY ELLEN RILEY / PHOTOGRAPHY JEAN ALLSOPP

Small arrangements can make a big impact. A simple trio of quince tips brings life to this windowsill.

A LITTLE PUSH

All it takes to coax budded branches into bloom is fresh water, moderate indoor temperatures, and patience. Cut each stem at an angle, and put it immediately into a container of water; indoors, make a fresh cut. Then place branches in a deep vase with tepid water. Keep the vessel in a cool spot out of direct sunlight. Change the water every three to four days, and recut stems once a week.

A bud that has begun to swell should begin to open indoors in one to two weeks. Dormant branches will bloom, but patience is necessary, as they may take up to four weeks to flower. The more dormant a branch is when cut, the more subtle the blossom's color will be. For vibrant color, wait to cut until buds are close to blooming outdoors.

When the first flowers open, cut stems once again and loosely arrange them in a decorative vase. In a large container, a needle holder or chicken wire can support larger branches. Avoid using florist foam with woody stemmed branches. It will inhibit fresh water uptake.

While masses of dayglow forsythia may light up a room, a few snips from a spring-flowering specimen can provide colorful blooms for a windowsill or small arrangement. If you would like a large display but don't have the materials in your garden, purchase tall branches from a florist.

This is a good time to have a dalliance with spring. A small vase filled with delicate blooms is not unlike a stolen kiss. There's surely more to follow, but for now, these few flowers will keep us going through winter. ◇

FAR LEFT: *Tiny cherry twigs and a star magnolia stem breathe spring's promise in a gentle manner. Cut branches take up large quantities of water, so small vases need fresh water added every day.*
LEFT: *Forsythia branches needn't be cut long and lanky. A small arrangement can highlight color in surrounding accessories and add a splash of sunshine to a room.*
BELOW: *Pale pink quince and Bradford pear twigs are a soft understudy to tall pussy willow branches.*

An inspiring makeover from the **Southern
Living Landscape Book** (See page 29.)

February

Checklist
for
February

EDITOR'S NOTEBOOK

Ours is a busy and complex world. Each day we're bombarded with momentous questions, the answers to which could alter the course of human evolution, such as: How many gold chains can I possibly wear before being hit by lightning? Is manure tea better served hot or cold? I can't answer these difficult questions, but I can help with one that's bugging many of you: Will that Boston fern I left out to die last winter miraculously spring back to life? The answer is yes. Just go to your nearest home-center and buy a can of green spray paint. Shake well, press the nozzle, and watch your plant instantly regain luster. Paint-restored ferns last for months and don't need water. Of course, this brings up another important question: If spray paint restores my Boston fern, will it also work on that African violet I accidently set on fire?

Steve Bender

☐ **Azaleas and camellias**—Make color choices while plants are in bloom and readily available in garden centers. That time is now for the Coastal South. Camellias and azaleas prefer slightly acid, organic, and well-drained soils. Shade from afternoon sun is recommended.

☐ **Water**—It may be quite dry this time of year, and unless your garden is designed to tolerate drought, it is important that your garden receive at least an inch of water per week. Soaker hoses are best on amended soils, and micro-sprinklers that deliver water under individual plants are better for native sand. Both are efficient ways to irrigate. How long you water depends on your soil and water pressure.

☐ **Wildflowers**—In the Middle and Lower South, this is the time wildflowers reawaken and many begin to bloom. A new guide, *Southeastern Wildflowers* by Jan W. Midgley (Crane Hill, 1999), is an excellent book for gardeners who want to grow, as well as know, the natives. ▶

☐ **Annuals**—You can begin planting coleus, impatiens, torenias, and caladiums in the Lower and Coastal South in areas that have at least a half day of shade.

Choices for sunny areas include zinnias, marigolds, celosias, sunflowers, cosmos, and coreopsis.

◀ **Bedding plants**—You can still plant pansies in the Middle and Upper South. Wait until the worst freezes have passed, and set them in full sun. Incorporate slow-release fertilizer pellets such as 14-14-14 at planting time. Other choices include violas, sweet William, calendulas, English daisies, and sweet alyssum.

☐ **Nasturtiums**—In the Lower and Coastal South, when freezing temperatures become less likely, plant nasturtiums from seeds or transplants. They will withstand the occasional late frost. Full sun or partially shaded locations work well for these annuals. Choose from bush or vining forms in a variety of colors.

☐ **Roses**—Plant in a spot that has at least five to six hours of direct sun and good drainage. If the soil is clay and compact or dry and sandy, add organic matter to improve the quality. Most shrub roses also grow nicely in containers.

☐ **Vegetables**—This is a good time to plant tomatoes, peppers, and other spring vegetables in the Coastal and Tropical South. In the Lower South, wait to plant until the danger of frost is over. Gardeners in the Middle, Lower, and Coastal South should plant their English peas and edible-podded peas (sugar snaps and their kin) this month. Other vegetables that can be planted from seed include lettuce, beets, mustard, radishes, spinach, and turnips.

☐ **Windbreaks**—If you live in an area buffeted by winter winds, plant a row of evergreens on the side of your garden that will buffer the prevailing breezes. Good choices are hemlock, Southern magnolia, and wax myrtle, depending on your area.

PRUNE

☐ **Fruit trees**—Annual pruning keeps fruit trees productive. The last few weeks before spring is the ideal time to prune. Cut out broken or diseased branches, as well as those that cross or grow toward the center of the tree, straight up through the center, or around the base of the trunk.

☐ **Overgrown shrubs**—Cut back misshappen summer-flowering shrubs now. Don't prune spring-flowering shrubs, or you'll remove potential blooms. In the Coastal and Tropical South, be sure to prune summer-and fall-flowering at the end of the month, when new growth signals the arrival of spring. Early pruning helps promote flowering in plants that bloom on new growth.

◀ **Roses**—Prune early this month in the Tropical South, but wait until late February in the Coastal and Lower South, March in the Middle and Upper South. This is the best time of year to shorten tall bushes. Remove all the dead canes, as well as those that are thin and weak, leaving only the strongest stems.

☐ **Trees**—Begin by removing dead or weak wood or limbs that cross. Balance the appearance and weight of the tree by removing excess growth where possible. Avoid topping, as it results in loss of the natural form of a tree as well as unsightly branching at the ends of limbs. Keep the natural form of the tree in mind as limbs are removed or shortened.

FERTILIZE

☐ **Greens**—As the day temperature in the South warms, greens such as kale and collards that have survived the winter need fertilizer. Apply granular 12-6-6 or similar formula to encourage new leaves to harvest next month. ▶

☐ **Iron**—Feed camellias and azaleas in your garden this month with a product that is labeled specifically for those plants. If they show symptoms of iron deficiency—yellow leaves with pale green veins—you should also sprinkle a cup of sulfur around the base of each shrub. You may experience a similar problem with iron deficiency on your ixoras and gardenias. If your soil or water is naturally alkaline, apply ½ to ¾ cup of sulfur under each bush to acidify the soil, make the iron more available to roots, and turn the leaves green again.

☐ **Spring growth**—In the Tropical South, it's just the right time for the first fertilizer application of the year on citrus, avocado, and other fruit trees, as well as landscape shrubs. For fruit trees, be certain to select a fertilizer formulated especially for them such as 12-5-8 (Vigoro's Citrus and Avocado food).

February notes:

TIP OF THE MONTH

After planting a rose, mound a hill of soil about 8 inches high around the base of the canes to keep them from drying out. When new growth appears, you know the roots are established and you can safely remove this extra soil.

SUSAN L. WIENER
SPRING HILL, FLORIDA

PAINLESS LOVE

Enjoying roses without thorns

Southern gardeners adore roses. And roses—lush, colorful, and fragrant—give some of their best performances in warm climates, whether nestled up to a 100-year-old veranda or gracefully "Southernizing" a brand-new chain-link fence. It's a nearly perfect relationship—and yet, as with so many relationships, there's been some thorny pain involved.

Every spring, rose-enamored gardeners go bravely out to prune and train their cherished darlings, only to end up scratched and bandaged. There are so many different sizes and shapes of rose thorns (more properly called "prickles") that it seems at least one manages to snag through protective clothing and draw blood. And how many times have you stopped to smell the roses, only to end up muttering and sucking a wounded finger?

If you're starting to feel you've donated one pint too many and if the sight of a vase full of roses no longer makes you think of romance but of suffering, take heart. There are actually quite a number of thornless or nearly thornless roses to fill your garden with kinder, gentler beauty.

BY LIZ DRUITT
PHOTOGRAPHY VAN CHAPLIN

LEFT: *Veilchenblau adorns the fence of a vegetable garden and poses no threat to the gardener.* ABOVE: *Smooth Prince*

ROSE TIPS

- Thornless or not, all roses will perform best with at least six hours of direct sunshine, rich well-drained soil, and plenty of fertilizer and water.
- Thornlessness is not a completely stable trait in roses. Cultural differences may cause your thornless roses to occasionally throw a cane with a few or even a lot of prickles. Remove the cane, or try a different thornless rose in that location.

Many gardeners are already familiar with some of the older varieties, such as the vigorous spring-blooming Lady Banks rose. Its cascades of clustered yellow or fragrant white flowers are an essential part of the Southern landscape. By April, they fill up treetops and joyously overwhelm fences. Veilchenblau, the "blue" rose, is another thornless spring-blooming climber, and it's a Southern hand-me-down. The tart apple-musk scent of its vivid gold-and-purple blossoms is as unforgettable as the color.

Classic, repeat-blooming climbers are just as easy to come by as these old, once-blooming favorites, especially now that more nurseries are selling great garden roses of the past. For an arbor over a high-traffic passageway, choose white Aimée Vibert, blush-pink Climbing Pinkie, or apricot Crépuscule. Any of these will bloom heavily in the fall as well as in the spring, with scattered flowers throughout the summer too. And the pleasure of being able to tie up the canes of a climbing rose without it attacking your hat is quite remarkable.

Thornless roses are obvious choices for narrow spaces, gateways, arbors, or anywhere they'll often come in contact with tender human flesh or expensive clothing. Planning a garden wedding? Trade in the veil-snatchers in your rose border for thornless beauties such as cabbage-flowered Paul Neyron, purple Reine des Violettes, citrus-scented Heritage, or classic red Smooth Prince. Line the herb garden walkways safely with dainty white Marie Pavié, which will release a light nutmeg scent, and dark pink Bayse's Blueberry, which sports bright gold stamens and fat orange hips.

There are even thornless roses for container plantings or tiny spaces. China Doll and Pinkie are small, constantly in pink bloom, and painlessly pickable. Golden Century is a soft gold, thornless miniature; Cinderella is a charming microminiature suitable as a gift for even the tenderest little girl.

It's such a relief to know that the romance doesn't have to end. You can plant roses, prune roses, decorate the house with roses, and even do the tango with a rose gripped in your teeth. With these thornless roses, love no longer hurts. ◇

(For sources turn to pages 250–251)

PHOTOGRAPH: JEAN ALLSOPP

Swamp rose

PHOTOGRAPH: EMILY MINTON

LEFT: *The smooth canes of Lady Banks rose are a Southern favorite.*

Smooth Angel

RIGHT: *Climbing Pinkie won't scratch passersby who stop to enjoy this rustic bench.*

MARY'S GOLD

The flowers of Calendula officinalis, *also known as Mary's gold or pot marigold, are a bright blessing for warm Southern winters.*

PLANTING TIP

Pair calendulas with other cool-season flowers such as pansies, stock, or snapdragons. Use them to highlight flowering quince or contrast with summer snowflakes and spring phlox. Edge a bed with calendulas and parsley, or scatter them through crimson poppies.

As Texas gardener Elizabeth Winston says, "Of all the herbs that grow in the garden, calendula is the flower I'd choose to heal both the body and the soul." Known as Mary's gold, these vivid annuals are supposedly named for the Virgin Mary and her golden halo. Now they are commonly called by their Latin name, *calendula,* and are also known as pot marigold to avoid confusion with the newer Tagetes marigolds. Calendulas are admired by gardeners for their silky, 2-inch-wide disks of gold, cream, and orange on 1- to 2-foot plants.

These annuals have many culinary and medicinal uses. They're also a good food source for butterflies and a charming vegetable garden companion plant that may help deter tomato hornworms and asparagus beetles.

Calendulas will withstand light frost (to 25 degrees) and will flower until a hard freeze knocks them back. In mild winters, they'll go from fall to spring if deadheaded to encourage constant bloom. They like full sun in winter but will appreciate afternoon shade as the weather warms. In the Upper South, plant them in March, and they'll blossom into summer. In the Lower South, set out transplants in February or October. They bring their glowing warmth to the garden during the coolest seasons, and help satisfy our color-starved hearts with their halos of gold. ◇

Fresh Look for Flowers

Transform a simple arrangement from so-so to so creative with this easy idea. Instead of discarding flower stems, use them to decorate a vase. We chose gerbera daisies because they typically have long, slender stems without leafy foliage. Other suggestions would be Asiatic hybrid lilies, iris, or other common daisies with their foliage removed.

Any smooth-sided glass container will work for this project—even a simple drinking glass. Just be sure you have enough flower stems to surround the vase completely. (Long stems can be cut into two pieces.)

The process is simple. First, place a rubber band around the container. Then remove each stem from its blossom, leaving enough stem so the flower heads can reach the water once placed in the vase. Slide the cut stems under the rubber band. Place stems around container until it is covered, and then trim them so they're even with the mouth of the container. Use a ribbon to hide the rubber band.

The result is a cheerful arrangement that makes a perfect centerpiece for a small table and brightens a room. ◇

The Garden Of Your Dreams

Close on the heels of the best-selling *Southern Living Garden Book* and the *Southern Living Garden Problem Solver* comes another book that every Southern gardener will want to have—the **Southern Living Landscape Book**.

This new book focuses on design. It explains in nontechnical, easy-to-understand language how you can create a garden every bit as beautiful as the ones that appear in *Southern Living* each month.

The book's opening chapter, "Gardens of the South," showcases 39 of the best designed gardens from every state of our region. Both inspiring and informative, it reveals the key design decisions that make each garden work.

Next comes "Planning Your Garden," a hardworking chapter showing how to make your dreams reality. You'll learn to see the world through the eyes of a garden designer as you establish goals, analyze your site, settle on a style, implement basic design principles, and sketch out a plan.

In Chapter 3, "Landscaping With Structures," you'll learn how to successfully integrate arbors, gazebos, fences, patios, water features, and other structures into your design. These components enrich the outdoors with form, texture, and color.

Choosing the right plants is the focus of Chapter 4, "Designing With Plants." It gives guidelines for selecting and placing trees, shrubs, annuals, perennials, herbs, bulbs, lawn grasses, and more. It also features more than a dozen beautifully illustrated plans, including designs for a perennial border, shade garden, cottage garden, herb garden, kitchen garden, and fragrant garden.

A landscape's personality doesn't come from plants and structures alone. Much of it depends on "finishing touches," the subject of Chapter 5. These personal touches range from formal and elegant (an antique olive jar and a lion's head wall fountain) to fun and folksy (pink flamingos and bottle trees).

Chapter 6, "Materials and Techniques," is for do-it-yourselfers. Clear, step-by-step instructions and diagrams show how to build decks, steps, retaining walls, brick walks, and much more. You'll also learn how to choose the right nails, screws, lumber, stone, tiles, and bricks for your project.

"Garden Makeovers," the book's final chapter, ties it all together. It highlights 20 outstanding before-and-after projects, reflecting both large and modest budgets. Subjects include creating curb appeal, updating a pool, detailing a deck, solving parking problems, and designing a welcoming entry.

Look for softbound copies of the new **Southern Living Landscape Book** at bookstores, home-centers, and garden centers. To order a hardbound copy ($29.95 plus shipping), call 1-800-765-6400. Or try visiting www.southernlivingbooks.com to order online.   *Steve Bender*

Inspiring and instructive, the new Southern Living Landscape Book *is exactly what you need to create the garden you've always wanted.*

BEFORE

Tapping Your Roots

PHOTOGRAPHS: VAN CHAPLIN

To take a soil sample, dig a hole about 8 inches deep. Cut a slice about 1 inch thick from one side. Make sure you get the top crust as part of the slice.

You brought them here. You volunteered to care for them. You know they're hungry. But your plants don't speak your language, and you're not sure what they really want. What can you do?

Take a soil test! As Sam Feagley of Texas A&M University says, "Until you know what you have, you can't put the nutrients you need back in the soil."

Never done it before? It's easy. If this is your first time, we suggest you contact your cooperative Extension. (Look in the blue "government" pages of the phone book, under "County Governments.") They'll tell you where to pick up one of their soil test kits, complete with how-to instructions, sample bags or boxes, an information sheet, and a mailing box. The information sheet is critical. On it you select which tests you want, list what you've been growing in the tested area, and indicate what you hope to grow in the future. It is important to note which fertilizers you've been using and what specific problems you have with that area.

To take the core samples for the test, you'll want a rust-free, nicely sharpened spade, a clean trowel, a plastic bucket (metal ones could contaminate your sample), a handful of sandwich-size zip-top plastic bags, and an indelible marker.

Then decide which portions of the yard you'll be testing and how many tests you will need. Flowerbeds, for example, would be one test area; vegetable beds would be another; and lawns should be tested separately from both of those. In an average suburban yard, count on taking four or five randomly spaced cores from each area to be tested, whether flowerbed or vegetable plot. If you're doing the lawn, take four or five cores from the front yard, the same from the backyard, and two or three on each side of the house. And if you're having real problems with some of your plants, sample those areas separately from the rest. In a large yard, plan on roughly eight cores per acre.

Remove all but the center core of the slice, about 1 inch wide. Pick out large rocks, hunks of grass, or big leaves.

To take a sample, dig a hole about 8 inches deep. Cut a slice about 1 inch thick from one side. Make sure you get the top crust as part of the slice. Dump the core into the plastic bucket. Refill that hole, and move on to a new spot; repeat the procedure about four times.

Testing once a year, or even once every three years if you experience no special problems, is often enough. Plan to do your testing in summer or winter, when labs aren't quite as busy as in other seasons. This will give you some time to work out and implement your new fertilization plan.

Start with the basic test. This usually includes pH, salinity, and N-P-K (nitrogen, phosphorus, and potassium—the most important plant nutrients) ratios. Organic gardeners or those with neutral to alkaline soils may want to have micronutrients tested as well. This should be done at least every three to five years.

A basic soil test takes from 5 to 10 working days, and costs from $7 to $30, depending on the tests, plus shipping. The results will include recommendations about fertilizers and pH adjustment and suggestions for problem solving. Most state labs send a copy of your test results to your local cooperative Extension agent when they send them to you. You can call for quick answers to questions.

A soil test is a terrific way to communicate more effectively with your leafy guests. It's like having your own United Nations interpreter. *Liz Druitt*

Blooming Beauties

Carter and Holmes offers visitors something that's hard to resist—some of the most beautiful orchids you've ever seen.

Mac Holmes holds a Brassolaeliocattleya Owen Holmes 'Mendenhall' AM/AOS, a cattleya orchid named for his father.

Phalaenopsis are the easiest orchids to grow as house-plants because they do not require cool night temperatures or as much light as many orchids.

It was love at first sight. At Carter and Holmes Orchids in Newberry, South Carolina, rows of Phalaenopsis orchids bloomed with graceful sprays of pink flowers. But the big question is how to get one of the fragile-looking beauties home on the plane?

"No problem," said Mac Holmes, head of one of the largest orchid growers in the country. "Select one with buds, and we'll pack it for travel just like we do the orchids that we ship to customers all over the world."

Mac is living proof that family roots run deep. Carter and Holmes was started by Mac's father and uncle more than 50 years ago. "My uncle, Bill Carter, was a high school principal and history teacher who came home to care for a family member and opened a florist shop," explains Mac. "My father, fresh out of the marines, came home for a visit and stayed to open a gift shop. They combined the two businesses and moved to the family homeplace where they'd grown up together. In the beginning they specialized in cut flowers, but for the last 30 or so years we've concentrated on orchid plants for hobby growers.

"This was my summer job when I was growing up. So when my father was going to retire, I moved back to help out." Mac, who gave up a law practice in Atlanta to return home and run the family business, is guiding the company into the next 50 years.

"Orchids make up one of the largest plant families on earth, and they're also the most varied," he explains. Carter and Holmes is an internationally recognized orchid hybridizer, known especially for its "art shade" cattleyas. Orchids are produced here from seed and from tissue culture. "We've been 'cloning' orchids for well over 20 years," says Mac.

And what about the Phalaenopsis I'd selected? "This is one of the easiest for the beginner to grow," Mac assures me. "Just remember the four mistakes many people make when growing not only orchids but other plants as well: not giving them enough light; overwatering; overfertilizing (less is more) or not fertilizing at all; and putting them in pots that are too large (orchids like to be tight in the pot).

So how's my orchid doing? It's blooming beautifully.   *Karen Lingo*

(For sources turn to pages 250–251)

Their Pioneer Spirit Blooms

These Texas farmers have built a life and a business growing and selling cut flowers.

I n the Hill Country near Blanco, Frank and Pamela Arnosky's small farm, once covered with rocks and cedar, now bears fields of flowers. And from their beautiful harvests, the couple has grown both a life for themselves and their four children and a flourishing business, Texas Specialty Cut Flowers.

On this spring "bouquet-making" day, Pamela stands under a tin shed surrounded by buckets filled with thousands of freshly picked flowers—delphiniums, cornflowers, larkspur, Queen Anne's lace, daisies, statice, and more. The long table before her holds piles of flowers, and the mixed blooms create a boisterous scent of the season.

"The bouquets' color scheme is entirely different in the spring and fall," she says as she chooses yellow, white, blue, and pink flowers and deftly assembles a bouquet. "In the fall it's deep maroons and oranges and reds. People love the bouquets because they have so many different flowers in them."

When the two Texas A&M graduates bought their 12 acres, the goal was to raise their children in the Hill Country and support the family with a bedding-plant business. "We were always growers of bedding plants," says Frank, stepping into the shade of the building. "We started the ¼ acre of flowers in front of the house as an experiment."

Their cut-flower experiment began seven years ago when friends planned to start an Austin farmers market for local growers. "The market never panned out," Frank says, "so there we were with a ¼ acre of flowers."

He took some to Central Market in Austin. "They were amazed the flowers were grown locally," he remembers. "They

sold out instantly and wanted more, more, more. By the end of that season we were doing 350 bouquets a week."

Last year their Texas Specialty Cut Flowers sold 16,000 garden bouquets and about the same number of single bunches of zinnias, marigolds, and snapdragons. "Now we are looking at doing 1,000 bouquets a week just for Central Market," says Frank. "They want to keep an exclusive, but it's not even an issue. We can't produce more than their stores in Austin and San Antonio can sell—even though we've doubled production every year.

ABOVE: *Seven years ago, the Arnoskys planted a quarter acre of flowers as an experiment. Now they are producing 1,000 bouquets a week.*

ABOVE, BOTTOM: *From their Hill Country farm, Frank and Pamela Arnosky continuously harvest crops of lovely flowers nearly year-round for their business, Texas Specialty Cut Flowers.*

ABOVE: *The first bunches of cut flowers that Frank took to Central Market sold out instantly. "By the end of that season we were doing 350 bouquets a week," he remembers.*

"The main problem we've had besides weather is worse weather," he quips. In the spring of 1999, they were rejoicing that the farm looked its best. "Then we had a 30-mph windstorm for two days straight. It blew down everything. The following night it froze. We were out there at 9:30 at night covering as much stuff as we could."

They have a system for such crises. "One of us is in control and the other is in panic mode. Then we change places," Frank allows with a wry grin.

Building their business has truly been a rugged labor of love. They moved onto the undeveloped farm with their children, a chainsaw, and $1,000, staking a tent-home at the back of the property. Soon after that they built a modest house and the greenhouses with little outside help. For seven or eight years they took baths in the greenhouse, which had both tub and water heater. "Our youngest still remembers when we didn't have hot water in the house," Pamela says with a broad grin. "There aren't very many kids that can say that."

Their biggest pest problem has been deer, which are now fenced out. In turn, they have almost no trouble with insects. "Once I counted five different beneficials (insects) on the sunflower leaves eating the aphids," says Frank. "By not doing anything we build up a balance."

Frank and Pamela employ a logical system to produce crops continuously on 8 acres, using their greenhouses as a production factory. They beat the Texas heat with cool-season flowers, planting in November those that normally grow in the summer of a cooler climate. "The delphiniums will take the winter cold and then bloom in April or May," explains Pamela. "By the end of May our greenhouses are full of transplants that can take the heat. When a bed is finished, we come out with plants from the greenhouse, stick them in the ground, and start all over."

They hand-transplant everything. "On a typical week we put out 3,000 sunflowers, 1,500 zinnias, 1,000 marigolds, 1,000 celosias, and another thousand odds and ends. We put out 16,000 delphiniums in the winter of 1999."

Hiring additional help has recently lightened their workload. "But no two years out here are ever the same," Pamela says with a smile of acceptance. "When the tornado hit Austin, the wind came here and knocked 14,000 sunflowers on the ground. We had to stand every one of those guys up and stomp them in. Three days later it happened a second time. Each sunflower was worth a dollar, so, of course, we're going to pick them up again."

Rain, windstorms, and hard work aside, the Arnoskys are living their dream and prospering. Lady Bird Johnson, who shares their love for flowers, has come to know the two and admire their efforts. "She calls us," Pamela says proudly, " 'real pioneers.' "

Rogayle Franklin

Snowdrops and bluebells that have flourished for years in a Verbena, Alabama, homestead (See pages 60–65.)

March

Checklist for March

EDITOR'S NOTEBOOK

Certain things invite criticism, like pink shag carpeting, bagpipe music, and any form of acting Bo Derek has ever attempted. But try as I might, I can't find a single thing wrong with pearl bush (*Exochorda racemosa*), one of my all-time favorite, spring-blooming shrubs. It gets its name from rounded, white flowerbuds that resemble pearls before they open. Though individual flowers last a short time, new buds open over a period of weeks, extending the show. Seedlings pop up like toast around a mature plant and are easy to share. In fact, my plant started as a seedling given to me by Celia Jones of Gibsland, Louisiana, a few years ago. I planted it in awful, rocky clay. Yet during the withering drought of summer 1999, it never wilted, and it grew several feet. For outstanding contributions to the world of horticulture, I rate pearl bush a "10." That's 10 points more than Bo gets for her acting ability.

Steve Bender

◄ **Birdhouses**—Set up houses now to attract those early birds. For information about selecting, building, and siting houses in your garden, visit the Audubon birdhouse Web site at www.bcpl.lib.md.us/%7Etross/by/house.html and follow the links.

☐ **Children**—Peanuts are a fun garden project for children. Buy some raw peanuts in the shell, and then help the kids carefully shell them without damaging the peanuts' red coat. Plant them in a sunny spot in the garden. Children are fascinated by the way the blossoms bury themselves and bear new peanuts underground.

☐ **Citrus**—Trees are blooming this month in much of the Coastal and Tropical South. Avoid using insecticidal sprays on flowering trees now. You may accidentally kill honey bees pollinating the trees, and plants won't bear any fruit.

☐ **Repot**—Vigorously growing foliage and flowering plants need a bigger container every year or two. It's time to repot when leaves are smaller on new growth, plants wilt soon after watering, lower leaves turn yellow, and roots are showing on the soil surface. Use a professionally prepared potting mix and a new pot that is about 2 inches larger. ►

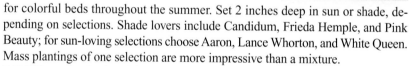

☐ **Annuals**—As threat of frost passes in the Coastal South, set out warm-weather annuals such as impatiens, begonias, petunias, geraniums, and coleus. Space them 8 to 12 inches apart in raised beds where 4 to 6 inches of organic material such as sphagnum peat moss, composted pine bark, or compost has been tilled into the existing soil. ►

☐ **Caladiums**—Plant tubers now in the Coastal South for colorful beds throughout the summer. Set 2 inches deep in sun or shade, depending on selections. Shade lovers include Candidum, Frieda Hemple, and Pink Beauty; for sun-loving selections choose Aaron, Lance Whorton, and White Queen. Mass plantings of one selection are more impressive than a mixture.

☐ **Edibles**—Beginning this month, plant frost tender vegetables such as corn, beans, cucumbers, squash, and eggplant after the last expected frost in your area. This is also a good time to set out basil, rosemary, and sage.

☐ **Fall flowers**—Chrysanthemums, Mexican bush sage (*Salvia leucantha*), aromatic aster (*Aster oblongifolius*), lemon marigold (*Tagetes lemmonii*), and Mexican firebush (*Hamelia patens*) can be set out after the danger of frost has passed now for display this fall. Existing clumps may be dug, divided, and reset into prepared beds as new growth begins.

◄ **Figs**—This is a good time to plant these old Southern favorites in the Lower and Coastal South and in sheltered locations in the Middle South. Popular, time-tested selections include Brown Turkey and Celeste. New choices include LSU Everbearing, LSU Gold, and LSU Purple.

☐ **Tomatoes**—A few well-tended plants can provide more fruit than a number of neglected ones. Select a site that receives at least six to eight hours of direct sunlight and that has rich organic soil and good drainage. Choose the best producing selections in your region, and work a half cup of balanced fertilizer such as 10-15-10 into the hole at planting. Then feed with water-soluble fertilizer such as 20-20-20 twice per month. Stake or cage plants for easy harvest. Be prepared to cover in case of a late freeze. Watch closely for insect or disease damage, and get ready for those first luscious tomatoes by late May or early June.

☐ **Vegetables**—Cabbage and its relatives—broccoli and cauliflower—are usually set out as transplants so that they mature before hot weather arrives. Other cool-weather vegetables, including beets, spinach, English peas, edible-podded peas, turnips, Swiss chard, kohlrabi, radishes, and carrots, can be sown directly into the soil.

PRUNE

☐ **Last call**—Major pruning of trees, shrubs, and roses should be completed this month. However, you should wait to prune climbing and once-blooming roses until after their spring flowers fade.

☐ **Liriope**—Hard winters can leave your ground cover beds looking ragged. Raise the cutting height on your mower as high as it will go, or get out your nylon-string trimmer. Then remove the damaged foliage before the new growth begins to emerge. Within a few weeks, your beds will have the fresh look of new spring growth.

FERTILIZE

☐ **Lawns**—Feed warm-season grasses, such as improved Bermuda, St. Augustine, and Zoysia, when they begin to green up. Choose a high-quality product such as 16-4-8 or similar formula that contains slow-release nitrogen to prevent burning and ensure good growth over the weeks and months to come. If you have centipede, apply a fertilizer that contains iron. For more on making lawn maintenance easy, turn to page 38.

☐ **Perennials**—As new growth begins to emerge, feed established beds with 12-6-6 or a similar formula at the rate recommended on the label. Water well to wash granules from leaves and down through the mulch to the soil.

CONTROL

☐ **Lawns**—If you notice yellowed or dead patches in your St. Augustine lawn in the Coastal South, you probably have chinch bugs. Treat the lawn with Dursban or Diazinon insecticide in either granules or liquid. Be sure to keep pets and children off the lawn until sprays have dried and granular products have been watered into the turf and allowed to dry.

☐ **Palm problem**—If your sago palm (*Cycas revoluta*) is showing brown, dead leaflets in the top center of the plant, it is suffering from manganese deficiency. Apply a general fertilizer containing manganese, or better yet, add ¼ to ½ cup of manganese sulfate to your fertilizer application. The damaged leaves will not improve, but the next growth will be healthy. ▶

March notes:

TIP OF THE MONTH

When planting mustard and turnip seeds, mix some radish seeds in with them. The radishes will grow right along with the greens and keep aphids and other insects from getting on them.

LOUISE MCPHERSON
CUMMING, GEORGIA

N o one wants to spend weekends doing battle with an unmanageable lawn. A well-planned design and a few maintenance tips can make your lawn easy to maintain and cut your work time. As a bonus, your yard will look more attractive.

One of the best ways to reduce time spent cutting the grass is to reduce the size of your lawn. Large turf areas require hours of watering, fertilizing, weeding, and mowing. If you're redesigning or getting ready to install a new landscape, create large natural areas and use low-maintenance ground covers such as liriope, mondo grass, juniper, Japanese pachysandra, and vinca. If you need to add a parking court to your front yard, it will help reduce your lawn area while accommodating guests. Also, don't scatter trees or shrubs all across the lawn; group them together in masses. Mowing around each individual plant is difficult. And avoid planting narrow strips of grass.

Another way to reduce maintenance is to keep your grass healthy. A sick lawn is more susceptible to weeds, diseases, and pests. A good fertilization and pre-emergence program helps keep your grass thick and block out the weeds. Warm-season grasses (except centipede) like a steady supply of nitrogen during the growing season for a lush and green look. In the spring and summer, use fertilizers that contain two to four times the amount of nitrogen as they do phosphorus or potassium. Avoid over-fertilizing; this makes your turf disease-prone.

Also, don't be tempted to overwater. Grass that stays too damp will be susceptible to fungus and disease. Turf that's kept too dry will have a poor root system and poor coloration. Most lawns need between 1 to 2 inches of water per week during the growing season. In

BY CHARLIE THIGPEN
PHOTOGRAPHY VAN CHAPLIN

As the soil warms and the grass greens up, turn your lawn into an emerald island without becoming a slave to yard work.

Tame Your Turf

extremely dry climates, twice a week waterings should be adequate. If you have a timed irrigation system, shut it off during the rainy periods and while turf is dormant. Water only when needed.

MAKE MOWING EASY

There was a time when everyone had a square or rectangular lawn. Now smoothly curved bed lines are used in informal landscape designs. These curves create an attractive, flowing effect, and they allow lawnmowers to maneuver easily. If you have an established lawn, change your bed lines to make them more contoured for mowing. Then fill in tough-to-mow spots with ground covers and shrubs. Grass is much easier to maintain on level ground, so try to eliminate any turf on slopes.

Use a well-maintained mower with a sharp blade. A dull blade will cause the mower to bog down and the tips of your grass to have broken or tattered edges. This will give your lawn a brownish appearance. Mow grass frequently, and never remove more than one-third of a leaf blade per cutting. Limb up trees and cut back shrubs that create obstacles while mowing. Shovel cut a large ring or square around the base of trees, and cover the area with mulch or low-growing plants. Use a nylon-string trimmer to help maintain a crisp edge, but be careful not to nick trees. Wounds are inviting to borers that can enter the trees and weaken or eventually kill them. ◇

ABOVE: String-trimmers are great for keeping a clean edge, but don't use them too close to the trunk of a tree where they can cut into the bark and weaken it. ABOVE, RIGHT: Parking courts help reduce the size of your turf while solving your parking woes.

SOUTHERN LAWNS AT A GLANCE

Common Bermuda and Bermuda Hybrids (Zones MS, LS, CS, TS)
Tolerant of drought and most soil types. Bermuda spreads rapidly and is highly resistant to wear. Requires full sun, moderate feeding. Bermudas will not tolerate shade. Established by seed, sod, or plugs. Mow to ½ to 1½ inches.

Buffalo Grass (Zones US, MS, LS)
Low-maintenance, drought-tolerant grass with moderate wear resistance. Once established, requires little feeding or watering; will not thrive in shade. Tolerates alkaline, salty, and sandy soils very well. Established by seed, sod, or plugs. Mow from 3 to 6 inches.

Centipede (Zones LS, CS)
Although fairly shade tolerant, centipede grass cannot tolerate much wear. It prefers poor, acid soil and needs little fertilizer. Established by seed, sod, or plugs. Mow from 1 to 2 inches.

Cool-Season Blends (Zone US)
Blends are good in areas that have a variety of sun and shade. Beautiful, but high-maintenance turf; require average feeding and plenty of water. Will tolerate moderate traffic and light shade. Establish by seed or sod. Mow from 2 to 3 inches.

St. Augustine (Zones LS, CS, TS)
Shade tolerant and able to withstand salt spray by the coast; also moderately drought resistant. Requires average fertilizer. Susceptible to chinch bug and grub damage. Should be monitored and insecticide applied as necessary. Established by sod or plugs; spreads quickly. Mow from 2 to 4 inches.

Tall Fescue and Blends (Zones US, MS, LS-upper half)
This cool-season turf can grow in shade or full sun and is very drought tolerant when established. Should be overseeded periodically to maintain dense turf. Requires little fertilizer and is fairly wear resistant. A good alternative to bluegrass or ryegrass. Established by seed or sod. Mow from 3 to 4 inches.

Zoysia (Zones MS, LS, CS, TS)
Extremely drought tolerant and tough, this dense, slow-spreading turf can be established by sod or plugs. Tolerates some shade and requires regular watering; chokes out weeds. Mow from 1 to 2 inches.

CS=Coastal South, LS=Lower South, MS=Middle South, TS=Tropical South, US=Upper South

Japanese sweet flag looks right at home with pansies and mazus. The selection shown, Ogon, sports vibrant gold and green stripes.

Foliage With Flair

Flowers make the garden, but foliage holds it together through the seasons. That's where Japanese sweet flag *(Acorus gramineus)* comes into play. The bright sprays of foliage light up the garden. Japanese sweet flag complements flowering annuals and perennials, but it really shows its stuff when blooms are sparse.

Its straplike foliage is green with yellow or white stripes, depending on the selection. Some selections have solid gold or green foliage. The flowers are insignificant, with small spikes and no petals. Established plants send out underground creeping rhizomes that allow the perennial to spread. They can be divided every few years or left alone to create a thick mat.

Sweet flag has been a mainstay in Japanese gardens for years, but it has just recently become popular in the U.S. It ranges from 3 inches to 3 feet in height. The plant prefers damp soil and

grows well in bog gardens. It's great for edging ponds, and some selections will even grow in shallow water. If you don't have a soggy spot or a pond, don't worry—it will also thrive in loose, fertile soil as long as it receives partial sun to light shade.

The versatility of sweet flag makes it useful in the landscape. You can substitute it for mondo grass and liriope. In containers, it can be mixed with flowers or stand alone to make a bold statement. The spiky texture provides an interesting look when planted with large-leaved hostas or ferns.

Karin Purvis, of Greenville, South Carolina, dug a clump and placed it in a shallow pot two years ago (see photo at left). She has never fertilized, divided, or cared for the plant; it seems to thrive on neglect.

Sweet flag also likes the weather in the South. It takes the South's winters very well, even in pots, and the foliage is rarely damaged by the cold. If the leaves do look ragged, cut them back to the ground in the early spring. New growth will quickly appear and give plants a fresh new look.

Try Japanese sweet flag this spring and see how lovely it looks nestled among the flowers; then watch it shine in the winter when most plants have gone to sleep. ◇

A Cherry for the South

From blushing spring blooms to sweet fragrance to fall color, Yoshino has it all.

YOSHINO CHERRY
At a Glance

Habit: spreading tree with rounded top

Features: mildly fragrant pink to white blooms, fall colors of gold and orange

Bloom: early spring

Hardiness: Upper, Middle, and Lower South

Culture: sun, average soil, good drainage with medium moisture. Prune suckers off trunk.

Use: specimen garden tree or fast shade tree

Problems: subject to borers, stem canker, and bacterial canker

Imagine yourself on a fine, early-spring day when the lawn chair beckons insistently. As you sit reading a book, you notice a light fragrance in the air. Tiny, translucent, pale pink petals are drifting down onto the pages. It's like being in a wonderland.

How can you put yourself into this picture? Just plant a Yoshino cherry tree.

Yoshinos became popular in this country after the Japanese government presented a gift of their nation's favorite tree to the people of the United States in 1912. Pictures of Yoshino cherry trees blossoming along the Tidal Basin in Washington, D.C., soon became an annual harbinger of spring for all Americans.

Yoshino cherry *(Prunus yedoensis)* blooms in early spring with the forsythia. Slightly fragrant, ethereal, white blooms with a pink center usually appear before the leaves, giving the effect of a pale pink cloud. They are followed by inconspicuous purplish-black fruit. Ranging in size from 20 to 30 feet (with a possibility of 50 feet) in height and a spread of 20 to 30 feet, Yoshinos will give you shade in a very short time. Smaller selections are available, so it's important to know the ultimate size of the one you choose. Trees can have multiple trunks

or a single one with a canopy that spreads out like an umbrella. The blooms look especially pretty with a tall evergreen background. In summer, the tree's deep green leaves fade into the background until fall, when its leaf colors of gold and orange put on another show.

Full sun, a moderate amount of moisture with good drainage, and pruning to remove any deadwood or suckers on their trunks are all that Yoshino cherry trees ask in return for their spring extravaganza. If your soil is very acidic, adding some lime would help. A soil test can tell you how much lime you need. Because it tolerates pollution, Yoshino makes a good city or street tree.

You can grow this cherry in the Upper, Middle, and Lower South. Bill Welch, an Extension landscape horticulturist at Texas A&M University does not recommend it for Texas gardeners, nor does Kristin Pategas of the Disney Institute in Orlando suggest it for Florida gardeners. There's just not enough cold to set blooms. Elsewhere in the South, Yoshino thrives.

John Ruter at The University of Georgia Coastal Plain Station in Tifton, Georgia, is conducting a trial of cherry trees. He says, "The Yoshino requires around 900 chilling hours to bloom reliably. That means it will not bloom well in the warmest parts of the South, but I would grow it here in South Georgia just for its fall color."

In the central South Carolina city of Orangeburg, former city horticulturist Jon Mason, who oversaw the care of a large citywide planting, says, "If I were going to plant a cherry tree, I would choose Yoshino."

If you've always wanted an allée of trees but can't wait for live oaks, this cherry tree may be your answer. It won't live as long as an oak, but it grows up to 2 feet a year. In 8 to 10 years you will have a canopy you can walk under. Be the envy of the neighborhood at cherry blossom time. Plant your dream.

Orene Stroud Horton

YOU HAVE A CHOICE

Akebono (also known as Daybreak) Single, soft pink flowers; 25' high x 25' wide

Shidare Yoshino White flowers and weeping habit. 20' high x 30' wide, this is the tree known as the weeping Yoshino.

Cascade Snow Pure white flowers; more resistant to disease; 25' high x 20' wide

Creeping phlox (Phlox stolonifera) *provides a natural ground cover of woodland foliage. In spring, blooms emerge in shades ranging from light to dark pink with orange stamens.*

Spring's
Bashful Beauties

Drop in on Harry and Betty Casto in early spring, and you're most likely to find them strolling along the paths and bending low to get a bird's-eye view of wildflowers on the hillside behind their home. Charleston, West Virginia, is a wildflower haven, and the Castos' hollow is sanctuary to no less than 80 different woodland jewels of the Appalachian ridges and forests.

Before the Castos moved into their present home and broke ground for the garden, they pursued their love of forest-floor bloomers through Harry's hobby of photography. "We have slides of every wildflower in West Virginia," he says. Betty rejoins with the family joke: "That slide collection is why we had to move into this new house!"

Building the house entailed moving a stand of showy orchis, among other flowers, from the construction site to the hillside. And so the garden began. It stretches out across two acres of West Virginia woodland, perched on a steep mountainside. A ribbon of pathways—wide enough for one foot only—weaves through the trunks of established oak, hickory, and hemlock trees. "We started with a few stepping stones, and every year Betty would say to put a little more loop in that path," Harry remembers. "Now, we have about a mile of trails."

All along the trails thrive the ephemeral flowers of a woodland spring. Some bloomers came from other places on the Castos' property; others originated from natural habitats that were slated for construction.

The tightly curled leaves of bloodroot (Sanguinaria canadensis) *unfurl to reveal bulging buds that open into flowers of purest white with gilded centers.*

A colony of swamp buttercup (Ranunculus septentrionalis) *came from a tiny green sprig that Harry tucked into his creel during a trout fishing trip.*

With the ballet of bloom that unfolds each spring, it is hard for Harry and Betty to choose their favorites. Betty loves the bloodroot. "When they come up, everything is still brown; the ground is covered with dead leaves," she says. "Their beauty is stark and striking." She also likes the absolute showiness of the white trillium, but "by the time it opens, it signals that it's time for the spring show to wind down."

Harry cherishes each of his tender bloomers, but he is partial to the celandine poppy. "I rescued three from a dump," he laughs. That was 15 years ago. "Today we have literally hundreds of them, and I've easily given that many away." He is proudest of the blue-eyed Mary, because the Castos' corner of Charleston is the eastern-most place this flower grows.

The joy of wildflower gardening is that, following nature's lyrical lessons of love and species dispersal, the native flowers reproduce like crazy. "The caveat to growing them is that you can't have a neat garden," Betty says. "You have to let things go to seed in the summer." The result is twofold. "First, you can't go onto the hillside in summer. It's like a Brazilian rain forest."

The second result appears in spring, when the flowering beauties pop up in the hollow in different places than they were growing the year before. "Our flowers thrive because they are in a natural state," Harry says. "It's a wonderful habitat."

Julie A. Martens

(For sources turn to pages 250–251.)

Blushing spring-beauty (Claytonia caroliniana) *embodies the innocence of spring, with its bashful flowers that open only in sunshine. The pink-striped petals draw closed at dusk.*

GETTING STARTED

If you appreciate wildflowers, you have a dilemma. You don't want to dig up plants in the wild, but where else can you get them? Fortunately there are a number of mail-order nurseries that are growing plants from seeds and cuttings, rather than collecting them. Like the Castos, you can also rescue plants from construction sites where they would otherwise be destroyed.

For information that will help you get started, check your local botanical garden or Extension service, or contact with your state wildflower society. Also consult *Growing and Propagating Wild Flowers* by Harry R. Phillips, University of North Carolina Press.

Fragile blossoms of rue anemone (Anemonella thalictroides) *dance above a skirt of scalloped leaves, whispering promises of sunny afternoons to come.*

Better Blackberries for Your Garden

They may not be famous like Lewis and Clark. But for people who love blackberries, Jim Moore and John Clark of the Arkansas Agricultural Experiment Station have blazed a trail just as important. They've developed new blackberry types that are ideal for the home garden. Some don't have any thorns. And one produces fruit so big that a falling berry could dent your car.

Why grow blackberries at home? Well, for one thing, blackberries sold at the supermarket cost about the same as cosmetic surgery. For another, picking berries in the wild means cloaking yourself in long sleeves and pants in the heat of summer to ward off ticks, chiggers, and mosquitoes.

So let's talk about homegrown blackberries. The three Moore and Clark selections currently generating the most buzz are Arapaho, Navaho, and Kiowa. Arapaho and Navaho are thornless, grow well as far south as northern Florida, produce upright canes for easy picking, and show good disease resistance. These and other thornless selections don't spread as aggressively as thorny types. Jim rates Navaho as the best-tasting new blackberry. Arapaho runs a close second, but it ripens earlier and has smaller seeds.

Kiowa, a thorny, upright type, may very well be the biggest blackberry in the world. To give you some idea of the size, it takes more than 400 Navaho blackberries (the ones shown in the photo above) to make a pound. It takes only 70 from Kiowa. Kiowa also appears to need even less winter chilling and fruits well in Central Florida.

BERRY BASICS

Blackberries are easy to grow, requiring only sun and well-drained soil. Upright types don't need staking and generally do better in the South than

Navaho is widely considered the best-tasting, new thornless blackberry. In our Southern Living *garden, six plants produced enough fruit for a half-dozen cobblers the second year after planting.*

trailing ones. Late winter and early spring are good times to plant. Space plants 3 to 4 feet apart. A half-dozen plants are plenty to start with for a family of four. Keep them well watered the first year. After that, they tolerate drought, but benefit from moist soil while bearing fruit.

Blackberry canes are biennial—they grow the first year, flower and fruit the second, then die. Dead canes can harbor disease, so prune any fruiting canes to the ground as soon as you finish picking the berries. New canes will soon replace them. Jim also recommends spraying the bushes with lime-sulfur at bud break each spring to prevent disease. *Steve Bender*

(For sources turn to pages 250–251.)

Blackberry canes are biennial plants—they grow the first year, flower and fruit the second year, then die and are replaced by new canes. Thorny selections spread much more aggressively than thornless types.

color
in the garden

Welcome to our Southern Gardener special section. Color is like icing on a cake—it's the finishing, personal touch that pulls the landscape together. We show you how to make every effort count and use color to its best advantage. Look for extra tips throughout the section to help you grow color-confidant.

Southern Living
SPECIAL SECTION

Color Where It Counts

Color is the finishing touch to a landscape, adding polish and personality. It takes time and a bit of money, but the results are worth the effort. But because of busy lives, opportunities to plant can be a luxury. So plan color for maximum impact with minimal expense and effort.

DESIGN: JANIE SINGLETARY, GREENVILLE, SOUTH CAROLINA

FRONT AND CENTER

"Put flower color where you want to focus your attention," says landscape designer Randy McDaniel, owner of McDaniel Land Designs in Mountain Brook, Alabama. "The entryway or front door is many times the most important focal point in the landscape."

Begin by looking at both sides of the front door. "Then, take steps back and look for places to put color that will lead your eye along a path to the entry. The goal is to bring your eye ultimately back to the front door," Randy says. "Walk halfway through the yard and look; then walk out to the street. You might even go further, into a neighbor's yard, and look at your entrance from their vantage point." "It helps to see your landscape from a distance for a little objectivity."

An entryway is not always visible. The door may be set back or positioned to one side. "If the front door is hidden from view, flowers can be used as a directional element," Randy says. "Put a little punch of color in an urn or in the ground to highlight the area."

The most pleasing landscapes are those where color is uncomplicated. Too many

COLOR TIP

To make a small space feel larger, place warm colors (red, orange, and yellow) in the front of a garden and cool colors (blue, green, and purple) in the back.

shades and hues do little to enhance a house. "Keep the color planting in your front yard simple," says Barbie Tafel Thomas, a landscape designer with Webb-Thomas in Louisville. "Generally, a lot of busy color in the front is not a good feeling. Use a single color for a calm appearance."

Flowers are not unlike a painting. A masterpiece is lost without the proper frame. The same is true in a garden. "Color is most effective when snuggled in next to something green," Barbie says. "Color needs that green backbone behind it to work well, and it should enhance your shrub base."

"Don't float your annuals out in the middle of the yard. They will get lost without a green backdrop, and the appearance is unorganized. Keep color concentrated by the front door and maybe by the mailbox," she suggests.

PHOTOGRAPHS: JEAN ALLSOPP / OWNERS: MARCUS AND ZOE CASSIMUS

LEFT: *You don't have to plant large beds to make a statement. All eyes go to the front door with this vibrant pansy display. The containers provide impact and require minimal care.*
BELOW: *Crepe myrtles frame this entrance, and the color is mirrored in containers near the door. White petunias and caladiums lead your eye up the front walk and complete this welcoming combination.*

LEVEL THINKING

Plan color on more than one level. "Don't think of color on only one plane," Randy says. "Typically, people plant seasonal color in the ground and in a container or two. Layer it for more impact and bigger bang for your buck."

The Mediterranean-style house pictured below provides a good example of layering. Crepe myrtles planted along the sidewalk frame the entrance and introduce color at street level. That color then reappears on another plane, near the front door, in containers. In between, white caladiums and petunias add another color tier designed to draw your eye to the front door. The flowers are layered, from the street to the front entry.

BROADEN YOUR FOCUS

Look beyond your front door for other areas to use color effectively. "Windows are like steps between indoors and out," Barbie says. "A window box can add a terrific amount of softening. You can keep it pretty 365 days a year, and it will provide color and greenery where there is no other planting pocket."

A patio or deck can be another good place to focus color. "A terrace is a place to relax. Keep your color simple and easy to maintain," Barbie advises. "You don't want to feel compelled to deadhead and maintain when you really want to rest." Place color in containers for reasonable care requirements. "Do color on your own terms. You don't want to be a slave to what you've created," says Barbie.   *Ellen Riley*

DESIGN: RANDY MCDANIEL, MOUNTAIN BROOK, ALABAMA / OWNER: ANN HUCKSTEP

The Southern Gardener Special Section was coordinated by Ellen Riley and designed by Amy Kathryn R. Merk.

How to Choose Color

It's overwhelming and intimidating. Stop by a garden center in spring, and you're visually assaulted with color. There are so many shades to choose from, and each becomes a favorite. Whether or not those preferences are the best choice for your landscape is another matter. Many plantings miss the mark with color that's not quite right.

COLOR TIP

Warm colors are effective accents. Use them in small amounts to brighten up a cool color scheme.

"Color unifies the house with the land-scape," says Catherine Bowen Drewry, a landscape designer in Crawford, Georgia. "People spend a lot of time thinking about the colors inside their home and on the exterior. They need to factor landscape colors into the equation."

CHECK IT OUT

Take cues from your architecture. Roof, trim, and house colors are all factors in determining the best palette. Make note of mature trees and shrubs that bloom throughout the year. Their flowers should complement the overall scheme as well. "If your house is orange-based brick, ask yourself how that hot pink crepe myrtle is going to look against it," Catherine says. "Is it going to pick up a little pink in the brick, or is it really going to clash with it?

"A lot of the landscape is seen from indoors. If the dining room is soft yellow and you're looking out into the garden, you might want to see more soft yellow repeated outdoors. It helps make the garden feel like it's part of the house," she says.

ABOVE: *White flowers are the best choice for this crisply trimmed bungalow. The appearance is inviting and ample without overpowering the entry. Green ferns on each side of the door add warmth.*

THE BIG PICTURE

An effective way to illustrate color is by example. The bungalow shown at left gets its color cues from crisp white trim. White flowers present a cool, unified look. They add ambience without being a distraction and complement the simple, elegant scheme.

In the charming Victorian cottage pictured at right, the front door and brick dictate the color palette. "The door is a rich color, chosen to work well with the old brick. We had to find flowers to complement both and not compete," says Bill Nance, a garden designer in Huntsville, Alabama. "The salmon impatiens lead your eye up the stairs to the door and mirror its shade. The green ferns add inviting texture and prevent color clutter." The brick, door, copper light fixtures, and flowers are all planned to present a pleasing, unified presence.

A MYSTERY SOLVED

One of the most illusive color concepts is working with brick. Many homeowners struggle with the perfect palette to complement this popular facade. "With brick, you need to determine its base color," says Bill.

"Take red brick—some of it has an underlying yellow base. This makes the brick color go toward orange. Other red brick has a blue cast. You must look for the base color and see if it goes to the orangy side of red, or the blue side."

"If your brick goes toward orange, choose warm-colored flowers such as oranges and yellows. If you have blue-red brick, go toward the blue and blue-violet flower family. It's when you combine the red-orange flowers with the red-blue flowers that you get into visual trouble," he says.

"When you have a brick home, be careful using azaleas as a foundation planting," Bill says. It is difficult to find a blooming shrub that works well with brick. Instead, he suggests planting boxwood or another evergreen as a buffer between the brick and azaleas. "I like azalea color against green. It doesn't compete with the brick, and green makes everything look good." *Ellen Riley*

FROM LEFT: *Red, orange, and yellow flowers complement brownish brick with yellow undertones. Neutral purple pulls the others together. Rose, blue, and soft yellow work in harmony with pink-based brick. This blue-gray facade can handle bold yellow and purple. The soft yellow prevents harshness.*

PHOTOGRAPH: VAN CHAPLIN

ABOVE: *Drought-tolerant lantana provides color through the hottest summer.*

COLOR TIP

Red dominates—
use it to
draw the eye and bring
objects closer.

Long-Lasting Color

To get the most out of your color beds, select plants that bloom for long periods. Installing annuals and perennials can be back-breaking work; digging each individual hole, watering, weeding, and fertilizing isn't easy. When you go to the garden center this spring, make it easier for yourself: Choose flowers or bright foliage plants that will shine for months at a time.

Before you buy anything, make sure you have a prepared area. Plants won't perform well in poor soil. To amend beds, add organic material such as leaf mold, soil conditioner, or mushroom compost; then till thoroughly. For heavy clay soils, you may want to incorporate coarse sand or a clay conditioner to help improve drainage. The soil should be loose and fertile and easy to work with. Add a long-lasting slow-release fertilizer to boost plants through the season.

The least expensive way to achieve long-lasting color for sunny locations is to throw out cosmos seeds after the last frost. Cosmos come up quickly and offer colorful spring and summer blooms. They need little care or water.

If you want a faster means of achieving color, look for cell packs or small containers of begonias, impatiens, lantana, petunias, melampodium, and narrowleaf zinnias. These tried-and-true flowering plants are tough and have a lengthy bloom period.

There are also numerous foliage plants that produce long-lasting color. Caladiums, coleus, hostas, ornamental grasses, and purple heart add vibrant hues to the garden.

GOOD BETS FOR COLOR

This dirty dozen should be on your most wanted list.

Begonias—These dependable annuals offer green or copper foliage with red, white, or pink blooms. The angel wing type, Dragon Wing, is not so compact and is an impressive bloomer. Most begonias prefer full sun, but some selections will take a little shade.

Caladiums—Choose from large pink, red, or white arrow-shaped leaves. These shade lovers mix well with ferns. They need warm nights and a soil temperature of 70 degrees to grow, so don't put them out too early.

Coleus—This foliage plant comes in many colors from chartreuse to burgundy to multi-colored types. Most take the shade, but some new coleus are sun tolerant.

Cosmos—Dazzling blooms range from white, pink, red, yellow, and orange. Plants vary in size, depending on selection. They like well-drained soil and lots of sun.

Hosta—This showy-leaved perennial can range from blue-green to chartreuse. Variegated types have swirls of cream, gold, and white. They like shade and filtered light.

Impatiens—This shade-loving annual blooms from spring till first frost. White, pink, lavender, orange, red, and purple flowers are available with minimal care.

Lantana—This sun-loving plant thrives in summer droughts. Its large mounding form is topped with yellow, rose, lavender, and orange clustered flowers. It grows 1 to 4 feet tall.

Melampodium—This underrated annual takes sun and light shade. Yellow to gold, daisylike flowers cover it from spring till frost.

Narrowleaf zinnia—Both *Zinnia angustifolia* and *Z. linearis* come in white, yellow, and orange. This is one of the most carefree long-blooming annuals. It grows 12 to 16 inches tall and needs a sunny, well-drained site.

Ornamental grasses—Miscanthus and pennisetum are good for hot, dry, sunny areas. They range in height from 2 to 6 feet. Some pennisetums have burgundy foliage, and many of the miscanthus have showy white to cream stripes. Both grasses are topped with plumes in late summer and early fall.

Petunias—Old-fashioned petunias are tough, but new selections such as Madness and Wave seem to be very hardy also. Colors range from purple, white, red, pink, blue, lavender, salmon, and bicolored. Petunias prefer a sunny site with well-drained soil.

Purple heart—*Setcreasea pallida* has showy purple leaves that are tipped with tiny pink flowers. These plants like full sun and a well-drained site.

Charlie Thigpen

Easy Does It Color

Gardening on a deck has its limits. It takes effort to carry supplies up the steps. You need big pots, bags of soil, plants, and sufficient water to start your container garden and keep it looking good. Here's one way to have an abundance without breaking your back.

ABOVE: *When the seasons change, it's time to replant. Two bromeliads, underplanted with asparagus fern and variegated ivy, anticipate the colors of the approaching autumn.*

ABOVE: *A trio of pots fills a corner of the deck to perfection. The star of the show is the bougainvillea, one of many choices for the summer season. In the back are the supporting players, shrubs that remain season after season.*

In the corner of this deck are three pots. Shrubs grow year-round in two of them, creating a green frame for the third pot, the one that changes with the seasons.

The tallest of the three is Chinese abelia *(Abelia chinensis)*. It blooms in clusters at the ends of its branches continuously through summer. This shrub is a magnet for butterflies, adding a little living color to the composition.

A large-leaved evergreen, Japanese fatsia *(Fatsia japonica)* lends an element of simplicity to the trio. In the Upper South and cooler regions of the Middle South where it is questionably winter hardy, substitute another evergreen such as an azalea or conifer.

The main attraction is front and center. Planted for immediate impact, this pot is just the right size to hold a mature hanging basket such as this bougainvillea. Just take the plant out of its plastic container, and slip it into the deeper pot half filled with soil. Set it so that the surface of the root ball is slightly below the rim of the pot. Then fill around the edges with more potting soil. The plant will flourish with the extra legroom. When the color wanes, you can replace it for the price of another hanging basket.

LIGHT ON YOUR FEET
Consider using plastic containers. They are lightweight, easier to transport, and less likely to break from winter freezes. No matter what type of containers you choose, use pot feet to elevate them and prevent moisture from marking your deck. *Linda C. Askey*

Foliage as Color

It's easy being green, if you're a plant—maybe too easy. It seems as if a lot of leaves must have gotten bored with the basic color of chlorophyll because everywhere you look in nature there are different shades and blends. Foliage colors shift from the nearly black of some taro plants and mondo grass, through steel blue hostas, burgundy cannas, and the bleached blondes or silver-whites of countless variegations. And this is their everyday wear during the growing season.

So how does all this colored foliage stack up in the garden? Can it really make much difference when compared to the potent color supplied by flowers?

To Phillip Watson, owner of Watson Designs, Inc., in Fredericksburg, Virginia, there's no question about the high value of lovely leaves. "Colored foliage carries the color throughout any season when I can't count on an abundance of flowers."

"When blooming slows down due to summer heat, all those marvelous cannas, hostas, and variegated grasses keep a border full of interest with or without the presence of flowers," he continues. "Having golden and blue and variegated conifers and hollies in the garden is a real plus for winter decorations."

LIGHT AND DARK

There are also places in any garden where the light is not quite perfect, too strong or too weak. Phillip adds, "I started thinking about how light and shadow work in design, which is all about creating pleasing and memorable patterns.

"I use the bright foliage to create artificial light, to lighten dark corners. Or for backlighting something that is dark, I use a lot of

LEFT: *Using only foliage, this garden gives the effect of waves of light flowing past the base of a lone Japanese maple. It is a lush presentation where flowers would diminish the impact of the foliage.*

LEFT: *The blue-gray agave in the container is surrounded by a ground-hugging blanket of golden creeping Jenny, which glows brighter than any flower.* BELOW: *Layered shades of green need white flowers to create a dramatic container. Plants include (clockwise from top) Japanese fatsia, asparagus fern, Marguarita sweet potato vine, English ivy, and white impatiens in the center.*

variegated grasses (miscanthus for example) as backdrops for daylilies or tiger lilies. Dark tiger lilies and *Verbena bonariensis* really show off against that white grass.

"Dark foliage," he continues, "creates artificial shadows, and I can paint with these shadows to give texture to an overly bright area. Sometimes I've gone the opposite way, using superdark foliage in a shadowy area to intensify an existing effect."

For people who don't have room for major plantings, or for people who think they simply don't care for variegated foliage, Phillip offers easy advice: "Start with something fairly quiet. A lot of common variegated plants, such as aucubas, crotons, and euonymus, knock you over the head with flashy patterns that can be too strong unless they're surrounded by moderating plants.

"Variegated Leyland cypress, on the other hand, seems to have just a little bit of dappled light all over it. It has a soft, silver glow that makes a nice backdrop for spring flowers and helps the black and white of winter brighten up."

Showy foliage may not quite replace colorful flowers in the hearts of most gardeners, but it clearly holds an important place in that intricate pattern of beauty we call a garden.   *Liz Druitt*

Making Arrangements

Phillip Watson notes, "If you've got a small garden, you don't have to cut all your flowers at one time for arrangements. You can cut colorful foliage, add just a few flowers, and not strip your garden. Usually the foliage will outlast the flowers and be good to use for several arrangements. Imagine some leaves from a long-stemmed purple-leaved shamrock in an antique bottle with one pink rose—as elegant as anything you could buy from a florist."

COLOR TIP

Green is restful to the eye. It's the color for all seasons.

Arrange Color Carefully

Once you've decided where to put color and which colors work best in your landscape, you must decide how to arrange the plants. When arranged properly, color flows through a garden like a well-orchestrated piece of music. In reality, there are numerous pitfalls to placement that can ruin a harmonious planting. Here are things to avoid and ways to go with the flow.

PHOTOGRAPH: VAN CHAPLIN

LEFT: *Instead of stopping with a spot of color, plant a sweep. These black-eyed Susans were planted as if they were painted by the stroke of a brush.*

PITFALL #2: SOLDIERS
Don't arrange bedding plants like soldiers, arms length apart. When planting annuals, space them evenly, usually about 3 to 4 inches apart. This way, they will fill out and cover the bare bed in the first month or so. This ideal spacing prevents competition between plants and will shade the soil to keep out weeds. The flowers grow together to present a seamless, unified appearance.

PITFALL #3: DUCKS IN A ROW
Avoid planting annuals in neat and tidy rows all in perfect alignment. Plant in a staggered grid. Set out the first row, and then position your second row behind the first, but aligned between the ones in front. The third row will be directly behind the first row and so forth. Use the length of your trowel, or a portion of it, as a gauge to keep the spacing constant.

COLOR TIP

Add cool colors to a warm-color planting for balance.

PITFALL #1: DOTS AND SPOTS
Avoid alternating colors, one by one. A mass of one color creates more impact and is less confusing to the eye than a mishmash of different plants. A collection of one color is referred to as a sweep. Garden designer Fred Thode of Clemson, South Carolina, likes tadpole-shaped beds of each flower type. Thicker at one end than the other, these sweeps naturally provide a sense of movement in the border. It's easy to achieve this shape. "Simply use a garden hose to lay out your color," Fred suggests. Make a big loop, and then pull it so that it's longer than it is wide. Where the ends cross will be narrower than the curved side of the loop. If you plant several tadpole-shaped sweeps of color together, the garden will have an organized, tapestry-like appearance.

PITFALL #4: PERFECTION
Don't make things too perfect. The difference between a home garden and a commercial one is the element of surprise. Garden designer Ruthie Lacey in Columbia, South Carolina, says, "I mass plants and use curves. But then I like to put one plant out of place, so it looks natural." Add a visual blip to the garden to keep it from becoming static. A pot placed in a bed gives an unexpected thrust of height. Flowers spilling into a walkway soften a hard edge. *Linda C. Askey*

Making Shade Shine

To many gardeners, a shady garden means a green garden. But it doesn't have to be that way. Plenty of annuals, perennials, ground covers, bulbs, and shrubs combine colorful flowers or foliage with a love for shade.

COLOR TIP

Use cool colors in shaded areas for maximum impact.

ABOVE: *The rosy-purple leaves of Persian shield, Little Miss Muffet caladium, angel-wing begonia, trailing variegated greater periwinkle, and pink impatiens fill this pot.* LEFT: *Impatiens are the first plants most folks think of when adding color to shade.*

But before we list some lesser-known choices, let's get the obvious ones out of the way. Impatiens bloom from spring to frost, come in a rainbow of colors, and flower profusely in shade. Similarly, gaudy foliage and a hankering for shade place hostas, caladiums, and coleus among our top picks.

If you use just these four plants in your shade garden, you'll have lots of long-lasting color. But if you'd like to try new things, you've got plenty of options. Tom Mannion, a garden designer in Arlington, Virginia, touts some less common candidates.

For dry shade, he likes Lenten rose *(Helleborus orientalis)*, hardy begonia *(Begonia grandis)*, and money plant *(Lunaria annua)*. Money plant offers white or purple flowers in spring, hardy begonia sports pink blossoms in late summer and early fall, and Lenten rose blooms white and rose in winter. For moist shade, Tom extols purple-leaved golden ray *(Ligularia dentata* Othello and Desdemona*)*, the feathery blooms of astilbe, and the golden, grassy leaves of Bowles Golden sedge *(Carex elata* Bowles Golden*)*.

Keep in mind when choosing plants that not all shade is created equal. For example, although flowering plants grow in deep shade, few actually bloom in it. Light shade, punctuated by dappled sunlight, produces more flowers. And like Tom, you also need to consider whether you're gardening in dry or moist shade. Woodland gardens are typically quite dry, because tall trees suck up all the rain. Plants that require constant moisture wither here. Having moist shade usually depends on two things—a spring, stream, or pond nearby, and trees or structures providing shade from some distance away.

Shallow-rooted shade trees, such as maples, beeches, and Southern magnolias, challenge even the most accomplished shade gardener. Few flowering plants will grow beneath them. So plant a shade-loving ground cover with colorful foliage instead. Good choices include variegated liriope, variegated English ivy, Beacon Silver dead nettle *(Lamium maculatum* Beacon Silver*)*, and bishop's weed *(Aegopodium podagraria)*.

Of course, you can avoid the whole dry shade versus moist shade dilemma by growing shade-loving plants in containers, like the ones shown here. You can give plants just the right amount of water and the number of plants you can grow will skyrocket. For an extensive list of shade-loving plants of all types, see "Plants That Tolerate Shade" on pages 73–77 in *The Southern Living Garden Book.*

DON'T FORGET FOLIAGE

It's natural to think of flowers first when adding color to a shade garden. But don't overlook plants with handsome foliage. One of Tom's favorite shade combinations is Nellie R. Stevens holly paired with Bowles Golden sedge. "The dark, dark green [of the holly] makes the bright, golden yellow [of the sedge] look fantastic," he says.

Steve Bender

Plant Ahead for Color

Probably the greatest advantage Southern gardeners enjoy is the potential to have something blooming outdoors nearly every month of the year. However, realizing this potential means planting ahead.

Depending on where you live, spring is either in high gear now or nearly upon you. So there's not much you can do to embellish this particular spring, beyond sticking in some potted pansies and snapdragons at the last minute. But you can start planning for future seasons. This timetable will help.

LATE SPRING

■ Set out annual transplants for summer color before the weather gets hot. They'll become established quicker and give you a better, long-lasting show. This means replacing cool-weather annuals while they're still blooming, but the results are worth it.

■ For an informal, cottage-style garden, sow seeds of quick-germinating annuals, such as cosmos, zinnias, spider flower *(Cleome hasslerana),* marigolds, common sunflower, and Mexican sunflower *(Tithonia* sp.), directly into the garden. Barely cover with soil. They'll bloom throughout summer and into fall.

■ Plant summer- and fall-blooming bulbs, such as glads, cannas, callas, dahlias, spider lilies *(Lycoris* sp.), and ginger lilies. And don't forget caladiums for spectacular summer foliage.

■ Set out shrubs and perennials that add blooms to either the fall (roses, sasanqua camellias, Mexican bush sage, ornamental grasses, asters, mums) or winter (winter honeysuckle, winter daphne, common camellia, Lenten rose).

SUMMER

■ Midsummer isn't too late to add fall-blooming plants to your perennial border. Good choices include asters, joe-pye weed, Mexican bush sage, pineapple sage, ironweed, mums, and goldenrod (no, it doesn't cause hayfever). Look for plants with healthy roots growing in 1-gallon pots. After planting, be sure to water daily for two to three weeks until the plants are established.

■ In late summer, sow seeds of cosmos and large-flowered zinnias directly into the garden for an easy color display throughout the fall.

FALL

■ Get out to your garden center early for the best selection of winter- or spring-flowering bulbs, such as daffodils, tulips, hyacinths, snowdrops, and crocus. Plant by early December. If you live in an area with short, mild winters, chill bulbs in the refrigerator for 8 to 10 weeks before planting.

■ Set out transplants of cool-weather flowers that will bloom next spring. Good choices include foxgloves, pansies, violas, snapdragons, stock, and sweet William.

■ Sow seeds of spring-blooming annuals, such as poppies and larkspur, directly onto bare soil, and barely cover.

■ For winter flowers in Florida and the Tropical South, plant petunias,

pot marigold *(Calendula officinalis),* pansies, Drummond phlox *(Phlox drummondii),* snapdragons, nasturtiums, and violas.

■ Fall is a great time for planting hardy trees, shrubs, vines, and perennials to supply colorful flowers and foliage next year.

Peg's Picks

Peg Moore, owner of one of Charleston, South Carolina's most beautiful gardens, says, "Thinking ahead is important. I like to have color going constantly." To that end, she employs a couple of uncommon plants for flower-challenged months. The first is tatarian aster *(Aster tataricus),* which grows 6 to 7 feet tall with showy blue flowers. "It blooms nonstop for two months beginning in late August," she notes. The other is Bowles Mauve wallflower *(Erysimum Bowles Mauve),* a short-lived perennial with gray-green leaves and abundant lavender flowers. It blooms all winter and through the spring.

Go With What Works

Once you find the perfect color scheme for your landscape, stick with it. It's possible to stay focused on a particular palette from one planting to the next, even if you have to fudge a bit on specific shades. Refer to the list below for seasonal options. All plants mentioned bloom for a month or more.

ORANGE
Spring—English wallflower, nasturtium, pansy, poppy, pot marigold *(Calendula officinalis),* snapdragon, sweet pea
Summer—canna, cosmos, daylily, gerbera daisy, impatiens, lantana, marigold, Mexican sunflower, zinnia
Fall—chrysanthemum, cosmos, dahlia, marigold, pansy
Winter—nasturtium*, pansy*, pot marigold*, snapdragon*

YELLOW
Spring—daffodil, English wallflower, pansy, pot marigold *(Calendula officinalis),* snapdragon, sweet pea, viola
Summer—allamanda, black-eyed Susan, canna, common sunflower, daylily, gerbera daisy, hibiscus, lantana, marigold, melampodium, yellow shrimp plant, zinnia
Fall—chrysanthemum, cosmos, dahlia, pansy, viola
Winter—nasturtium*, pansy*, pot marigold*, snapdragon*, viola*

RED
Spring—pansy, poppy, snapdragon, stock, sweet pea, sweet William
Summer—caladium, canna, coleus, geranium, gerbera daisy, globe amaranth, hibiscus, impatiens, pentas, petunia, scarlet sage, verbena, wax begonia, zinnia
Fall—chrysanthemum, coleus, dahlia, petunia, pineapple sage, viola, wax begonia
Winter—pansy*, petunia*, snapdragon*

PINK
Spring—English daisy, foxglove, larkspur, pansy, peony, poppy, snapdragon, stock, sweet pea, sweet William, viola

Summer—caladium, cosmos, geranium, gerbera daisy, globe amaranth, impatiens, mandevilla, pentas, petunia, purple coneflower, spider flower *(Cleome hasslerana),* verbena, wax begonia, zinnia
Fall—aster, chrysanthemum, cosmos, dahlia, hardy begonia, Japanese anemone, pansy, petunia, wax begonia
Winter—Lenten rose**, ornamental cabbage and kale+, pansy*, petunia*, snapdragon*, viola*

BLUE, PURPLE, LAVENDER
Spring—blue phlox, forget-me-not, larkspur, money plant, pansy, stock, sweet pea, sweet rocket *(Hesperis matronalis)*
Summer—ageratum, bachelor's-button, balloon flower, browallia, cape plumbago, impatiens, lily-of-the-Nile *(Agapanthus africanus),* petunia, verbena, Victoria Blue salvia, wishbone flower *(Torenia fournieri)*
Fall—aster, dahlia, hardy ageratum, Mexican sage, mum, pansy, petunia, viola
Winter—Bowles Mauve wallflower+, pansy*, petunia*, snapdragon*, viola*

WHITE
Spring—English daisy, larkspur, money plant, pansy, snapdragon, stock, sweet pea, sweet rocket *(Hesperis matronalis)*
Summer—caladium, geranium, gerbera daisy, impatiens, lantana, moonflower, morning glory, petunia, phlox, spider flower *(Cleome hasslerana),* verbena, wax begonia, zinnia
Fall—cosmos, dahlia, ginger lily, Japanese anemone, pansy, petunia, wax begonia, viola
Winter—Lenten rose**, ornamental cabbage and kale+, petunia* *Steve Bender*

* Blooms in winter only in the Coastal and Tropical South, ** Blooms in winter in the Middle and Lower South, + Blooms in winter in the Lower, Coastal, and Tropical South

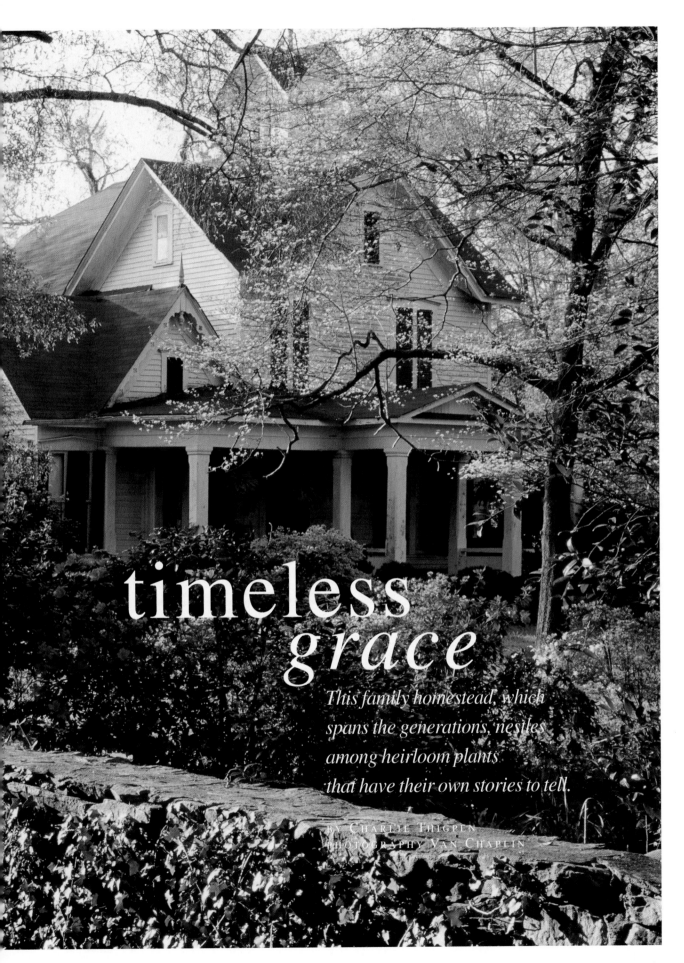

timeless
grace

*This family homestead, which
spans the generations, nestles
among heirloom plants
that have their own stories to tell.*

BY CHARLIE THIGPEN
PHOTOGRAPHY VAN CHAPLIN

In front of this fair house where two roads meet
And come together as good friends would greet
Two sweetheart oaks grow, pressing lip to lip
And join their leaves in happy fellowship

from "Oakside" by Clifford Lanier

They are to this day the sure image of the South: grand old homes graced by glorious gardens. Such seasoned homesteads still anchor our region, in big city and small town alike. Most contain heirloom plants that have endured the elements—and possibly neglect—yet they flourish every spring. When they do, they serve as windows through which we can see the past and glimpse our heritage.

Mrs. Gertrude Gibson McGehee has invited me to look back in time by strolling the grounds of Oakside, her

childhood home in Verbena, Alabama. Her grandfather, Major Joseph Carr Gibson, built the house in 1873. In later years, her father, Sidney Lanier Gibson, and mother, Mary Lee, lovingly planted the gardens. Mrs. McGehee's aunt Mrs. B. B. Comer assisted in the planning. Together the three, none of whom had any formal training, fashioned a timeless garden that complements the fine home. Today, Mrs. McGehee and her sister, Judith Gibson Robinson, maintain the home and garden.

ABOVE, LEFT: *Azaleas and dogwoods cover the landscape and wrap around the old well.* INSET: *Mrs. McGehee and her mother in December 1971*
ABOVE: *A reproduction of the original gate makes an inviting entrance when surrounded by spring flowers.*

A lichen-covered rock wall that is nearly consumed by English ivy surrounds the property. Mrs. McGehee's father pulled the stones from a nearby creek and used a mule to deliver them to the front yard. The wall must have been built well, for it is very much intact. Massive roots from large trees nearby have heaved it up in places, making it tilt, but it refuses to tumble.

Once through the waist-high walls and past the oversize finials I look beyond the boxwoods and see the stately home towering majestically over the flowers and shrubs. As I admire the massive oaks that frame the house, I realize where Oakside got its name.

A train whistle blows in the distance and the rumble grows louder until it's so close, I can feel it underfoot. Major Gibson intentionally built the home near the tracks because, at the time, rail was the only means of transportation other than horse and buggy.

An old well lies directly outside the front door. Not just a garden ornament, it was where water was drawn for cooking and cleaning. I can't imagine how many buckets of water it took to fill a bathtub.

The distinct odor of boxwoods permeates the garden, but tea olives, winter honeysuckle, roses, and numerous bulbs help sweeten the earthy smell. Bulbs bloom so thickly that a visitor once asked Mrs. McGehee how in the world her mother planted all of them. Mrs. McGehee chuckled and replied, "Mother didn't plant all those bulbs; they have multiplied over the years."

Many of the things her family planted are still popular today. During the dead of winter the dark green boxwoods form the bones of the garden, creating little hedged rooms across the yard. In January the camellias and quince buds burst open on sunny days. There is a collection of camellias that nestles quite happily underneath long-armed water oaks. February reveals tuliplike blooms that unfurl on the stems of sprawling, deciduous magnolias. Winter honeysuckle's discreet flowers scent the chilled air.

As the soil warms in spring, daffodils, narcissus, snowdrops, and bluebells fill the beds. White and purple iris blooms pop out from clumps of fanned, swordlike foliage. Pink, red, and white azaleas look like blotches of watercolors dabbled across the landscape. Numerous dogwoods grace the air with starry blooms.

This third-generation house and garden become harder to maintain as the years pass. Painting, replacing rotting wood, tugging on the escaped wisteria vine, and weeding are never ending. The little imperfections around the 127-year-old Southern home and garden add character and charm.

As I talk with Mrs. McGehee about growing up in this beautiful place, she smiles. Her stories are filled with fond memories of a simpler time. Afternoons weren't spent in front of the TV—they were spent relaxing on the front porch where the landscape could be admired and the children could be seen.

Fridays were always special because her father would hire a young lady to tell stories and play games with the children in the village. The young ones would gather at Oakside to romp around on the grassy lawn.

As I walk around the garden, I imagine them playing hide-and-seek, peeping out from behind a tree trunk, or balancing atop the stone wall with arms spread like an airplane. I can even picture a young Mrs. McGehee grinning as she presents her mother with a handful of freshly picked daffodils. It is a beguiling image of her and of this garden's past. ◇

The little imperfections around the 127-year-old Southern home and garden add character and charm.

ABOVE, LEFT: *Quince puts on a show in early spring.*
ABOVE, RIGHT: *Snowdrops and bluebells are so content, they have multiplied beyond their original boundaries.*
ABOVE: *Stones from a nearby creek form a low wall that surrounds the homestead.*

*Golden iris flourishing in
a Mississippi garden
(See pages 88–91.)*

April

Checklist for April

EDITOR'S NOTEBOOK

I know your bathroom tissue is squeezably soft. But what about your soil? This is of utmost importance when you're getting ready to plant. If your soil is still wet from winter rains then, digging, cultivating, or walking on it will compact it, transforming it into something nearly as hard as sitting through the Pokémon movie. So how can you tell if your soil is too wet? Try the squeeze test, the first trick I learned as a young gardener. Pick up a handful of soil and squeeze it. Then move your thumb and fingers back and forth, as if you were trying to crumble up dry cornbread. If the soil crumbles easily and falls through your fingers, it's dry enough to work with. But if it holds together in a sticky clump, you need to wait a week or two. How can you occupy yourself while you're waiting for it to dry? Well, I hear the Pokémon movie is out on video now.

Steve Bender

☐ **Moss**—Contrary to popular belief, Spanish moss and ball moss do not damage trees. So leave them if you like the old Southern look, or remove them if you don't. A buildup of ball moss in a tree often indicates that the tree is not healthy for some other reason, however. ▶

☐ **Mower safety**—Always wear sturdy shoes, preferably with treaded soles if you have to cut a slope. Always push, never pull, the mower. Wear safety glasses to protect your eyes. Send family and pets indoors before you crank the engine. Never allow a child to be a passenger on a riding lawnmower.

◀ **Seeds**—Soak seeds with hard outer shells overnight in a saucer of water to speed their germination. Candidates include morning glories, moon vine, and okra.

☐ **Thinning**—If you let closely spaced flowers and vegetables continue to grow, they will be too crowded and never develop to their potential. Read the seed packet for recommended spacing when you are sowing green beans, radishes, zinnias, and cosmos. Sow twice as many seeds as needed, and then pull out half. That way you get a full row, even if some of the seeds don't germinate.

☐ **Annuals**—After the danger of frost has passed, plant beds of summer annuals such as marigolds. Work the soil first to loosen, and incorporate organic matter and timed-release fertilizer. Rake the bed smooth, and apply mulch before you plant. Then lay out your transplants in a staggered grid on top of the mulch, and work your way across the bed with a trowel to plant. Water thoroughly. Sunny areas provide ideal exposure for marigolds, zinnias, celosia, cosmos, and petunias. For shady areas consider impatiens, begonias, pentas, coleus, and caladiums. Arrange in drifts (elongated masses) of at least a dozen or more individual plants. ▶

☐ **Cut-flower garden**—In the Middle, Lower, and Coastal South, select a sunny, well-drained area of the garden, and devote it to flowers suitable for cutting and bringing indoors. Zinnias are the all-time favorite with the large and intermediate types preferred. Marigolds, celosias, and nasturtiums are all well adapted to the area and are easily grown. They also tend to produce over a fairly long season if blossoms are harvested every few days.

☐ **Fall flowers**—Mums, aromatic asters *(Aster oblongifolius)*, Mexican bush sage, goldenrods, swamp sunflower *(Helianthus angustifolius)*, and obedient plant *(Physostegia virginiana)* are all dependable. Bulbs to plant now for fall bloom include white rain lily *(Zephyranthes candida)*, oxblood lily *(Rhodophiala bifida)*, and spider lily *(Lycoris radiata)*.

☐ **Papayas**—These trees are easily grown from seeds collected from fruit in the Tropical South. Remove the jellylike membrane around seeds, and dry them for a few days. Plant them a half-inch deep. Keep moist and fertilized, and you can be picking papayas in less than a year.

☐ **Tomatoes**—Wait until all danger of frost has passed before planting summer crops such as tomatoes. Stretch your harvest by choosing several selections with staggered maturity dates. Set plants deeply in enriched soil so that the lowest leaf is about 2 inches above the level of the soil. Set in stakes, cages, or trellises now to avoid disturbing plants later.

☐ **Vegetables**—In the Lower and Coastal South, plant peppers, beans, cucumbers, and squash. Peppers are readily available as transplants, while cucumbers, beans, and squash are best started directly from seeds planted in the garden. Be sure to spade or till the soil to a depth of 8 to 10 inches and form rows to facilitate drainage.

PRUNE

☐ **Espalier**—Select and begin training an espalier (pronounced es-PAL-yay) on a wall or fence. Espaliers require little horizontal space while softening walls and adding interest. Begin by selecting a plant with a central leader and several horizontal branches. Fasten the stems at approximately 1-foot intervals with plant ties secured by mortar nails, eye screws, or lead-headed nails. Consider pyracantha or an alternative such as sasanqua, kumquat, holly, and other plants adapted to your area that respond well to training. For large and tall wall areas (15 feet or greater) try Southern magnolia and Nellie R. Stevens holly.

☐ **Roses**—Repeat-blooming roses should be pruned early this month in the Upper and Middle South. Remove dead or weak canes. Shorten healthy canes to 18 to 24 inches. For climbing and once-blooming roses, prune after spring bloom.

FERTILIZE

☐ **Lawns**—Wait a couple of weeks after your warm-season lawn turns green; then apply a quality fertilizer such as 29-3-4 or 27-3-4 that will feed over several months. Timed-release products are less likely to burn grass or have their nutrients washed away in heavy rains.

CONTROL

☐ **Orchids**—Check orchids for scale insects. Boisduval scales are tiny greyish insects that look like flakes of dried oatmeal on the bulbs and leaves. Remove as many as possible by wiping them with a damp cloth; then spray or dip the plant in a solution of Cygon 2E according to label directions. Repeat the treatment in 10 days.

☐ **Palms**—Palm trees show two common nutrient deficiencies. Orange freckles on the lower leaves and a narrowing trunk signal a potassium deficiency. Apply a fertilizer high in potassium, such as a 4-8-8. Frizzle top, in which the newest leaves in the top center of the crown are dwarfed and distorted, is caused by a lack of manganese. It can be corrected by the addition of manganese sulfate to the soil. Both of these problems may take a year or more to correct.

☐ **Thrips**—As roses, gardenias, and other flowering shrubs bloom this month in the Coastal and Tropical South, they may become heavily infested with thrips, tiny yellow-to-black insects that feed on the petals and cause ugly brown spots. Their population explodes when oaks and citrus bloom; then they move to your flowers. Spray the buds with Orthene 75S to control.

April notes:

TIP OF THE MONTH

Over the years, I planted eight rhododendrons, only to have most of them turn yellow and die. Then two years ago, a friend told me to put pine needles around them. I placed pine needles under each rhododendron, about 3 to 4 inches deep, out to the ends of the branches and about 3 inches away from the trunk. In three weeks, the change was dramatic—lots of new, green growth. Now my rhododendrons are thriving.

STEWART N. CHRISTNER
SENECA, SOUTH CAROLINA

Clean out the kitchen cabinets, and plant a culinary collection. Colanders and strainers provide perfect drainage, so water these plants every day.

Thyme To Sit Around

These fun and easy containers prove that herbs are willing to grow almost anywhere.

Even if you don't have a square foot of garden soil, you can grow herbs. Agreeable to almost any type of container, they have only a few requirements. Drainage is essential; herbs cannot tolerate soggy roots. If the perfect vessel does not have a way for water to escape, add one large drainage hole or several small ones around the bottom. This is your best insurance for success. But remember, well-drained soil must be watered frequently when temperatures soar in the summer.

When planting containers, always use a good quality potting soil. There are numerous types available and several things to consider. Cheap is not always the best choice. Choose soil that is light in the bag; heavy sacks can indicate soil that may not drain well. If your containers are small, consider a potting mix with moisture-retaining polymers already included.

Place the soil in a clean bucket, and add water to thoroughly moisten. Loosely fill your container with the damp dirt, and add a well-balanced, timed-release granular fertilizer to the mix.

PERFECT FRIENDSHIP

Herbs get along beautifully in container combinations. Most have compatible light and water requirements. Choose tall herbs for height, shorter selections to fill mid-range, and trailing ones to spill over the side. Take into account the container size, and pick plants that will mature to complement the pot's dimensions.

BY ELLEN RILEY / PHOTOGRAPHY JEAN ALLSOPP

Thyme and oregano soften the edge of a container with cascading foliage. Parsley and small basil selections such as Spicy Globe and Minette are good midsize choices. Taller options include sage, rosemary, and basils such as Siam Queen, African Blue, and Thai. Chives and fennel add textural diversity.

A great-looking container is chock-full of plants. Snuggle root balls together, and fill the pot with herbs. It will start out fat and full, and get better with age.

NEEDS AND NOURISHMENT

Herbs are sun lovers. Be sure to place your containers where they will soak up at least four hours of sunlight daily. Water them in proportion to the amount of heat they receive and the pot size. (Keep in mind that small containers should be checked daily.) They generally will forgive a little bit of dryness, but too many days of drought will damage even the toughest planting.

Frequent watering and heat will quickly deplete the timed-release fertilizer. By midsummer, feed your containers every other week with a water-soluble, well-balanced fertilizer, such as 20-20-20. To avoid fertilizer burn, always wet the soil with clear water prior to feeding.

Herbs are meant to be picked and enjoyed. Harvest them frequently for use and to prevent containers from becoming overgrown. Allowed to flower, many herbs will quickly set seed and die. Pinch buds as they appear for sustained growth throughout summer. ◇

A child's antique shopping cart puts herbs on wheels. Roll it close to the kitchen for easy access, or move it around to follow the sun.

HAVE A SEAT

Flea markets and yard sales are good places to find old, inexpensive chairs. If the finish is not to your liking, paint it to complement the garden's decor.

MATERIALS

OLD CHAIR

CHICKEN WIRE

WIRE CUTTERS

STAPLE GUN

SHEET MOSS

POTTING SOIL

THYME OR OTHER LOW-GROWING HERBS

Step 1: Remove the seat from the chair, if still attached. Cut chicken wire several inches larger than the seat's frame. Staple the wire's edges to the chair, allowing excess wire to sag inside the seat.

Step 2: Cover chicken wire with sheet moss, and fill the planting area with moist potting soil.

Step 3: Plant herbs, placing some near the edges so foliage will tumble over the sides. Water gently, and feed every other week with a water-soluble, well-balanced fertilizer.

No Sting to Scorpion Weed

This white-eyed wildflower is painless to grow since it's self sowing.

PHOTOGRAPHS: TINA CORNETT

Scorpion weed naturally forms drifts in moist woodlands. Lavender-blue flowers appear in spring. Though small individually, when massed they put on a show.

SCORPION WEED
At a Glance

Height: 1 to 2 feet
Light: shade
Soil: moist, well-drained, acid, lots of organic matter
Pests: none serious
Range: Upper, Middle, and Lower South
Expect to pay: about $3 for a packet of seeds

W ho says weeds have to be ugly? Here is one of the prettiest weeds I know. Despite its name, scorpion weed doesn't come with a sting. Year after year, you'll get all of the flowers you're due.

Actually, scorpion weed *(Phacelia bipinnatifida)* is a biennial. It spends the first part of its life as foliage, then blooms, sets seed, and dies. But the seeds germinate so reliably, once you have this plant in your garden, it's likely to hang around forever. In most gardens, the foliage appears in late fall and winter and then slowly grows into a mound 1 to 2 feet tall. Lavender-blue flowers appear in early spring, about the same time as azaleas bloom. The plant dies when warm weather arrives, but don't feel cheated. Next fall, the dozens of seeds it dropped will sprout.

Native to the Eastern United States from Virginia to Missouri and down to Arkansas, Alabama, and Georgia, this wildflower is easy to grow. It prefers moist, acid soil that contains plenty of organic matter. Shade is a must. Sow seeds in summer or fall onto bare woodland soil. You can sow them in a cold frame in fall (barely cover them with soil) or sow them in a flat indoors in the winter.

Scorpion weed makes a fine addition to a woodland wildflower garden. It enjoys the same growing conditions as blue phlox *(Phlox divaricata),* wild columbine *(Aquilegia canadensis),* trillium *(Trillium sp.),* bloodroot *(Sanguinaria canadensis),* and foamflower *(Tiarella cordifolia).* Individual flowers are small, so plant a drift for better effect.

So far I've avoided addressing the obvious question: Why is this plant called scorpion weed? The answer is that Reinhold Phacel, the 18th-century botanist who first cultivated it, was killed and eaten by scorpions. Okay, I made that up. But it's an interesting story. And until somebody comes up with the real reason, I'm sticking to it.

Steve Bender

(For sources turn to pages 250–251.)

Shop for Color

Nurseries are filled with temptation. Go with a list and ask for advice if you're overwhelmed.

PHOTOGRAPHS: JEAN ALLSOPP

Beautiful flowers are available everywhere you turn. It's easy to pick up one of this and one of that on every outing from grocery stores to discount chains to garden shops. Suddenly, you are faced with a hodgepodge of mismatched colors and plants—all impulse purchases. "Before you head out to shop, have a plan," says Jimmy Collier, owner of Collier's Nursery in Vestavia Hills, Alabama. "Keep in mind the colors you want to work with, and then stick with them."

Color isn't the only consideration. "Do your homework before you shop. Know the areas you want to plant and how much sun each spot gets. Know the size of your beds and containers," Jimmy advises. When deciding where to shop, consider good information and healthy plants in addition to price.

BE INFORMED

For the time and dollars invested in planting, you want to begin with the best materials. Follow Jimmy's suggestions for an educated purchase.

■ Choose plants that are compact and have few blooms. Also look for dark green foliage with no yellow leaves. Your annuals should look as if they've just come off the truck.

■ Slide a plant out of its container. Roots should be white, thin, and fibrous. The root ball should not crumble when the plant is gently handled. Avoid plants with brown roots.

■ Check soil moisture. A dry plant is stressed.

■ Purchase only labeled plants. Without a label, there's no sure way to identify what you're bringing home.

■ Annuals come in packages that hold three or four small plants, permitting you to purchase small quantities. For

convenience, packs are sold in larger containers, called flats. Each flat will usually hold 36 small plants, and the price is slightly discounted. "Choose flats that are complete," Jimmy says. "If there are partial flats, they've been raided by other shoppers and picked through. If flats are full, employees have been restocking and giving the plants the attention that they need."

PLANTING TIPS

Jimmy offers this advice for planting seasonal color.

■ Pinch back most of the flowers at planting time to encourage new growth and healthy roots.

ABOVE, LEFT: *Choose plants that are compact and show no signs of yellowing foliage.* **ABOVE:** *Don't be afraid to slide the plants out of their containers to check the roots.*

■ Amend the soil seasonally with combinations of topsoil, peat moss, manure, and soil conditioner.

■ Plant annuals with a balanced timed-release fertilizer such as Osmocote (14-14-14), and follow up with a liquid food such as 15-30-15 every two weeks.

■ Soak the soil after planting; then let the garden dry out slightly between waterings. Containers require water more consistently than flowerbeds.

Ellen Riley

Spreading wider than it is tall, weigela offers a fine display of spring flowers, as it has for generations of Southern gardeners.

Good Old Weigela

Those who appreciate a fine antique will love old-fashioned weigela. This shrub has been flowering in Southern gardens for more than 100 years with little more to recommend it than its flowers and its hardy nature. In shades from white to pink to red, it carries on, spring after spring.

Weigela *(Weigela florida)* makes a statement in bloom. Depending on the selection, it will grow 3 to 9 feet tall and 4 to 12 feet wide. Give it full sun to partial shade and well-drained soil; then stand back. It will be a gratifying grower.

Because weigela recedes into the green backdrop of summer once flowering ceases, plant it as a background feature or in a mixed border of shrubs and small trees. It does not have a lot to offer in the other three seasons, so don't make it a focal point of the garden. Let it be, and when it blooms, weigela will call attention to itself.

In addition to a variety of flower colors, some selections offer plants with colorful foliage. This can be an asset in shrub borders where plants of varying

WEIGELA
At a Glance

Light: full sun to partial shade
Soil: well drained
Form: spreading 3 to 9 feet tall, 4 to 12 feet wide
Range: all South
Expect to pay: $7 to $20
Sources: See pages 250–251.

textures need to stand out from one another. For variegated foliage, try Variegata or Variegata Nana. Golden-leaved forms include Rumba and Rubidor. Keep in mind that burgundy-leaved plants such as Java Red, Minuet, or Alexandra will develop their best color in full sun.

For white flowers, look for selections such as Candida or White Knight. Red selections are much more plentiful, with names such as Evita, Minuet, Bristol Ruby, Red Prince, Rumba, and Nain Rouge. For pink blooms, plant Pink Princess, Polka, Java Red, or Variegata.

To keep your plant vital and attractive, lop out the oldest canes immediately after flowering. This will thin the plant, encourage new growth, and keep it flowering. While you're at it, cut away any dead wood. It is typical for some branches to die from time to time.

A little pruning isn't much to ask. The rest of the year, weigela takes care of itself. And for your trouble, you'll have flowery rewards, generation after generation.   *Linda C. Askey*

(For sources turn to pages 250–251.)

PHOTOGRAPHS: VAN CHAPLIN

Tiny but Unique

This lush front yard packs a lot of color in a little space.

With a front yard this small, most homeowners would settle for a grass panel with a few shrubs along the front of the house. This postage-stamp garden in the Grant Park neighborhood of Atlanta showcases the talent of its owners. David Dempsey and Lawrence Adkins of Viridis Garden Design, Inc., have transformed the small space into a colorful and creative garden.

In spring, flowering roses and pastel perennials give the home a distinct look. Although the border is dense, passersby can still see the house from the street. Sidewalk views allow an irresistible peek over the border and into the garden.

From the driveway, enter the garden through a simple arbor flanked with two common boxwoods clipped into conical shapes. A potted variegated agave provides a focal point at the other end of the yard.

Because both David and Lawrence are garden designers, it is especially interesting to see some of the other plant material they used. To stop your eye from going past the entry along the drive, they planted a mass of windmill palms. The palms also signal the entry to the front porch. A backdrop of green behind the potted agave emphasizes it as an accent. A large Ballerina rose gives outstanding color in the corner along the sidewalk. The planting is stair-stepped down along this side of the garden with lime-colored Japanese barberry, La Marne roses, and old-fashioned dame's rocket *(Hesperis matronalis)*. Along the porch, the

LEFT: *Flanked by two clipped American boxwoods, the entry to this tiny front garden frames a potted variegated agave as a focal point.* ABOVE: *Along the sidewalk, the border provides a foreground for the house. The layered planting allows passersby to peek into the garden.*

foundation planting is highlighted by several sheared American boxwoods.

To accomplish this look, the owners spend much of their gardening time in winter. That's when they plant, prune, and fertilize the garden. (They use liquid 20-20-20 fertilizer three or four times in the winter.) Then they enjoy the beauty delivered in spring.

John Alex Floyd, Jr.

Storage Bench

Nancy Porter of Little Rock discovered a great way to hide the uglies in her garden. She designed a small wooden bench that backs up to a water spigot. The bench can be used both as a nifty place to hide a hose and a place to stop and take a rest.

Nancy is lucky enough to have a handyman husband who enjoys taking on projects. So she drew up a plan, and her husband, Duncan, went to work in the wood shop. He cut a small square in the back of the bench allowing access to the spigot. This way the bench can sit flush against the house.

The seat is hinged so it can be raised and lowered. While Nancy waters the garden, the bench remains

Hinges allow the seat to be raised, accessing the storage area below.

open. Once finished with the hose, she rolls it up and tucks it under the seat. Then she lowers the seat, and the hose is completely out of view.

The way the bench is boxed around the spigot helps insulate the pipe, keeping it from freezing in cold weather. This is a good place to store a trowel or other frequently used hand tools as well. Nancy says her bench also makes a nice home for toads. They like to crawl inside where they enjoy the shade and moisture.

A hose stretched out through the garden not only looks bad, it can also be a hazard. If you're tired of tripping over hoses, build a little bench for storage. ◇

Save the Seedlings

PHOTOGRAPH: TINA CORNETT

PHOTOGRAPH: VAN CHAPLIN

LEFT: *All of the little Japanese maple trees in pots were collected around the mother tree in the background.* ABOVE: *The seedlings are easy to scoop up with a hand trowel.*

In the early spring, countless little Japanese maple seedlings meet their untimely death. They are cut down, sprayed with herbicides, and even smothered by loads of pine straw or bark. Most people don't notice the little plants that pop up around the mother tree. Each year I try to rescue a few of these baby plants so they may live on to become attractive specimens.

Many Japanese maples produce flowers around April, May, and June. The delicate flowers will later turn into small winged seeds. The seeds ripen in September or October and twirl down to the ground. They lie dormant throughout the winter; then begin to sprout in the early spring. The seedlings are small—only 3 to 4 inches tall—but they still have that distinctive Japanese maple leaf.

There are numerous selections of Japanese maples, but not all have viable

The seeds have little wings that whirl like helicopter blades as they fall.

PHOTOGRAPH: TINA CORNETT

seeds. Some selections produce abundant seeds that are sterile. If you are lucky enough to find a mature tree with productive seeds, you can dig plants from around it. Remember that seeds won't sprout in areas that have been treated with pre-emergence herbicide or that have been heavily mulched.

If you find small seedlings, scoop them up with a hand trowel and relocate into 1- or 2-gallon containers filled with well-drained potting soil. Water immediately. Then set the seedlings in a shady spot to root out for a year or two. The little trees are tough and will need minimal care. Keep them watered during dry periods, and give them a little all-purpose fertilizer to keep them healthy.

Once rooted and not so tender, they may either be planted in the yard or given away to a friend. The seedlings aren't reliable as far as looking like their parent. They each take on different growth habits and many will vary in leaf and stem color. In the trade these seedlings aren't considered valuable, but I've never had anyone turn them down when given as a gift.

So look before you mow, spray, or mulch. Little seedlings may grow into treasured trees.   *Charlie Thigpen*

*Dripping with sweet-smelling blooms, wisteria is one of our showiest vines.
Though bluish-purple flowers are the norm, white-flowering ones are common.*

Beauty and Beast

"Wisteria," says Art Mullen of Oklahoma City, "is one of those plants that, before you commit to planting one, you'd better have a *firm* idea of what you want to accomplish and how to go about it. It's kind of like getting married in that regard."

Well, far be it from me to compare the blissful ties of matrimony to the clinging, grasping, constricting stems of wisteria (you can lower that frying pan now, dear). But Art has a point. Despite its unparalleled beauty, wisteria isn't something you can plant and forget.

You see, wisteria grows and grows and grows some more. Its slender, twining tendrils eventually become thick, muscular limbs that wrap around trees, fences, and arbors like the coils of a python. Wisteria makes shredded wheat out of lattice and bends iron railings like taffy. And if it escapes to the woods, look out. Around my Alabama home, whole forests turn blue with it in April. Its weediness leads Lucky Pittman of Hopkinsville, Kentucky, to declare, "I think kudzu has more redeeming qualities."

The two species of wisteria with the prettiest and most fragrant flowers are also the most aggressive—Japanese wisteria *(Wisteria floribunda)* and Chinese wisteria *(W. sinensis).* The easiest way to tell them apart is that the former twines clockwise and the latter counterclockwise. Their native Southern counterparts, American wisteria *(W. frutescens)* and Kentucky wisteria *(W. macrostachya),* are far less rampant and destructive. But because their blooms are smaller and less fragrant, hardly anyone plants them.

How can you safely enjoy wisteria in your garden? First, forgo the notion of low maintenance. This is a high-maintenance plant that needs weekly pruning throughout the growing season. An easy way to control it is to pinch the tips out of runners soon after they sprout. Without the tips, the runners can't climb or twine. Of course, new runners sprout about every 15 minutes.

Proper placement is critical. If you can't keep a constant eye on it, plant it far away from anything it can strangle or destroy. A wisteria "tree" in the middle of the lawn is a common sight in the country. To make one, tie the vine to a 4-foot stake, trim off the lower branches, and let it sprout from the top. Matt Morrow of Guntersville, Alabama, also suggests growing wisteria "on an old water well or something, where it can just go wild."

Training wisteria to drape an arbor, fence, or doorway requires planning. Begin by tying the vine to a stake or wire, letting it wrap around this support only. When it reaches the desired height, place the canes atop a horizontal support, and let them wrap around each other. Never allow them to twine around lattice, pickets, downspouts, gutters, dogs, or anything else you value. As Matt notes, "[Wisteria] climbing up a tree or house is, frankly, very frightening." *Steve Bender*

All It Took Was a Look

Today, azaleas fill the garden with color each spring. The structures behind a massive triple-trunked ash are a toolhouse and greenhouse Bill built by himself.

On the cusp of a new year, almost four decades ago, Irene Mansfield found a sunken treasure.

New Year's Eve, 1964. Bill and Irene Mansfield, recently engaged, are out prospecting for a home on this snowy afternoon. Driving through Towson, Maryland (just north of Baltimore), they spy a house for sale beside a sunken lot. The site boasts a spring-fed stream—also old car batteries, bottles, discarded tires, and other trash. "That's the house," Irene declares to Bill. "Oh, what a fantastic lot."

Irene had a vision. What most people dismissed as a soggy pit, she perceived as a perfect spot for a sunken garden. Now each spring this lovely dell literally stops traffic. Neighbors admire banks of azaleas, drifts of wildflowers, and stacked-stone walls. But mostly they admire Bill and Irene, who have done every bit of the work.

She supplies the artistry; he provides the labor. (Lest you think we're slighting Bill

Pink wild geraniums, blue phlox, white doublefile viburnum, and dogwoods form a curtain of bloom beside the greenhouse.

ABOVE: *Japanese primroses thrive in the moist soil beside a small, spring-fed stream.*
RIGHT: *Irene and Bill Mansfield discovered their future garden in Towson, Maryland, on a snowy New Year's Eve more than 30 years ago.*

here, we need only note that he built all of the garden's structures, including the greenhouse, toolhouse, springhouse, and stone walls.) One of their first tasks after cleaning up the lot was deciding on something to plant on the slopes. As it turned out, the highway department decided for them.

A road was being cut through a landscape nursery owned by a friend of Irene's. Many old azaleas were too big to dig and sell, so the owner offered them to the Mansfields for free. "He said, 'Take as many as you want, and I'll show you how to trim them back,' " Irene recalls. Today, azalea blossoms of pink, rose, white, and purple smother the shaded hillsides.

Probably this garden's most winsome feature is a gurgling stream that springs up from beneath a massive white ash and flows through the lawn to a creek below. The wet soil around the stream supports moisture-loving native plants, such as ferns and skunk cabbage. But the star of the show is an import—the spectacular Japanese primrose *(Primula japonica)*. Irene started with six plants. Constant moisture and filtered

shade made them so happy that they seeded themselves around the yard.

Huge hardwoods drop truckloads of leaves each fall, but the Mansfields don't mind. They compost them and use them to enrich the soil. Judging from the way wild geraniums, blue phlox, bloodroot, marsh marigolds, Virginia bluebells, mayapples, and other wildflowers have colonized the hillsides between the azaleas, the soil is pretty good.

Irene will never forget the snowy day that she chanced upon her new home with Bill. She really didn't care what the house looked like inside—whatever was wrong, she knew they could fix. But to her, the sunken lot was a diamond in the rough that would shine if carefully polished. She and Bill have been polishing that gem for more than 30 years.

"When I come home from work at night," she says thoughtfully, "I'll say to Bill, 'You know, the yard's talking to me again. It says I need you.' I guess that's what it said to me that very first time I saw it."

Steve Bender

Probably this garden's most winsome feature is a gurgling stream that springs up from beneath a massive white ash and flows through the lawn to a creek below.

A Garage in Keeping

Like most additions, this one started as a simple need—a place to put the automobiles. But the owners also had several requirements: The garage could not block the views of the garden from inside the house; it should match the original house; and it should enhance, not detract from, the rear landscape. "I didn't want to tear up my yard to put in a garage," says one of the owners.

Working with Winter Park, Florida, architect Stephen Feller and local landscape designer Bob Heath of Garden Arts Designs, Inc., the owners got the garage and the garden they wanted.

A wide arbor creates a shaded walk from the garage to the house. Honeysuckle and Carolina jessamine were planted to vine over the arbor.

This addition to a 1920s house does more than provide a place to park cars. Planned carefully, the garage enhances both house and garden.

PHOTOGRAPHS: JEAN ALLSOPP

The garage addition at left was detailed to echo the original house. Careful site planning leaves much of the original garden undisturbed, while the new structure helps screen the area from a side street.

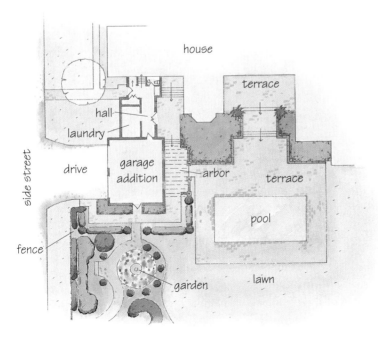

Hidden behind the garage and screened by a solid board fence, the garden becomes a private retreat.

A two-car garage is, by necessity, a good-size structure. (This one measures 23 x 26 feet.) To minimize its impact on the site, the garage was pulled as close as possible to the side street. "We didn't want it any farther into the backyard," says Bob. Steve adds, "We had to get a 5-foot variance so we could be closer to the street." (The minimum set-back is 20 feet from the side property line; the variance places the garage at 15 feet, which lines up with the end of the original house, built before the current setback.)

The garage also needed to seem an integral part of the house, not an addition. To that end, the architect used the original house as a pattern book for the new garage, repeating materials, colors, textures, and details. "The more you can match, the better," says Steve. Of particular importance was repeating the 12-in-12 pitch of the existing roof. "It's a real steeply pitched roof," he says. Although the roof pitch could be matched, the material could not. The owners decided to reroof the house and the garage in slate.

On the exterior of the garage, the architect had the builders repeat the stucco exterior finish of the house, carefully matching the texture. The garage dormers were copied from the ones on the house. "We matched them exactly," says Steve. Although the dormers were not needed for light, they help visually break up the expanse of roof.

As part of the addition, a connector links the garage to the house. This also provides space for other needed features, including a powder room and a laundry. Originally the laundry was in the basement. (Yes, there are a few basements in Florida.) "Access was just awful," says the architect. The new laundry is generously sized, with room for a refrigerator and ice-maker, and convenient to both the kitchen and the pool.

The architect recalls that they considered

a second-floor connector as well, linking the garage's attic to an upstairs office in the house, but head clearance in the connector presented a problem. "We talked about trying to connect the upstairs, but it would have been a hard connection. The roof would have gone up another 3 to 4 feet," he says, "and we didn't want to raise the roof." In the end, they decided to use the garage attic only for storage, accessible by pull-down stairs.

Instead of making the connector a simple rectangle, the architect broke it into two sections, offsetting one slightly from the other. In part, this was done to allow one end to center on existing steps from the kitchen. The other portion of the connector, which contains the laundry, sits back about 3 feet from the corner of the garage. (Without the offset, the connector would have been flush with the garage, creating a long, awkward wall.) "Little offsets give it character," says the architect. "New houses don't have the little nooks and crannies that give character."

To further reduce the scale of the garage, the landscape designer created an arbor that attaches to the end wall of the garage. "It softens that whole facade," explains Bob. In effect, the 10-foot-deep arbor creates an outdoor room. "We wanted to provide a seating area," he adds. The 6-inch-square posts supporting the arbor rest on brick piers. Low brick walls run between the piers, helping separate the brick terrace beneath the arbor from the adjoining planting beds.

One of the challenges was to make the new terrace match the existing brickwork around the pool and on an existing terrace at the rear of the house. "We ordered more brick than we needed," says Bob. "Then we picked out the ones that were way off." **Note:** Brick often comes in a range of tones, with some lighter and some darker than most.

But when it was all finished, the effect was just what the owners wanted. The new garage seems as if it has been there forever, and the landscaping looks established. Most importantly, the addition helps shape and define the site. "This has closed us in in a very nice way," says one of the owners. "It's a very private place."

Louis Joyner
(For sources turn to pages 250–251.)

The landscape designer created this simple potting bench from two 4 x 4 treated-pine posts, metal brackets, and cedar boards.

Easter Garden Centerpiece

MATERIALS

2 NONPARTITIONED FLATS

GREEN SHEET MOSS

GLUE GUN

FOIL

SCISSORS

FLOWERS, HERBS, AND VEGETABLES

Our centerpiece is a celebration of spring flowers, vegetables, and herbs. This arrangement is as simple as a trip to the garden shop. Follow our instructions for materials and assembly.

SHOP FOR COLOR

Choose a color scheme that complements your table linens and decor. Select bright flowers in cell packs and several 3- or 4-inch pots. This will provide diversity in height and fullness. Check out herbs and vegetables as well. Pots of fresh lettuce, parsley, and fennel make good choices for texture.

Purchase enough flowers, vegetables, and herbs to fill one flat. Many flats have built-in dividers; use one without partitions for this project. To add extra stability, place one flat inside another.

PUT IT TOGETHER

Use a glue gun to carefully attach sheet moss to the flat's outer edge. Trim the bottom of the moss with scissors so the flat will sit evenly on the table.

Line the container with foil, covering the bottom in one continuous sheet; press foil up the sides. We used florist's plant wrap foil with a plastic backing, but aluminum foil works just as well. Tuck edges down so the foil is not visible over the flat's edge.

Water all plant material prior to arranging. Choose a starting point in a back corner of the flat. Place the tallest flowers and herbs in this location, and arrange the others, stepping down in height to the edges of the container. Bedding plants may be cut apart or removed from their containers to snuggle roots more closely. Be sure to cluster flowers of like kinds together, adding lettuces and herbs intermittently for textural interest.

AFTER THE PARTY

The arrangement may stay in the flat for several days. Then you can transplant the contents into the garden. Keep in mind the individual light and water requirements for each seedling, and plant them in the appropriate place.

The flat and foil may be used again. Repair any moss that has come loose, and store it away from direct light. It will be ready to fill for the next occasion. *Ellen Riley*

PHOTOGRAPHS: TINA CORNETT / STYLING: BUFFY HARGETT

LEFT: *Our spring centerpiece includes small calla lilies, dianthus, stock, sweet alyssum, violas, lettuce, parsley, and fennel. The container on the cake pedestal is a plastic strawberry basket laced with ribbon and filled with sweet alyssum.* INSET: *Cover the outside of the flat with sheet moss, and line it with foil to protect your table from moisture.*

Quench Their Thirst

That's one of the keys to growing astilbe as a perennial in the South.

I reserve the right to grow wiser with age and occasionally change my mind. Therefore, I must confess that a story I wrote in 1986 was pure organic fertilizer. It concerned astilbe (pronounced as-TILL-bee), that wonderful perennial that performs so admirably in the North. I contended that, given reasonable care, astilbe would also grow well over large parts of the South.

Having nursed astilbe on life support during the following years in Birmingham, I now realize my head was up my leaf blower. But that doesn't necessarily mean astilbe is a bad choice for you. In fact, its spectacular plumes of red, pink, white, salmon, and violet are common in Maryland, Delaware, Virginia, West Virginia, Kentucky, Missouri, the Appalachian and Blue Ridge Mountains, as well as southern Ohio, Pennsylvania, Indiana, and Illinois. But if you plant astilbe in the Lower South, you'd better be prepared to do six things—water, water, water, and pray, pray, pray.

John Elsley, director of horticulture at Wayside Gardens in Hodges, South Carolina, concurs, particularly regarding the Arends hybrids that comprise most of the available selections. These German hybrids dislike the long, hot summers and short, mild winters that characterize much of the South.

"They struggle," states John. "They don't like humidity and cannot tolerate drought. I had a group of them in my yard for eight or nine years. Some years they did better than others. But they never really flourished."

However, astilbes often thrive in the Upper and Middle South. They produce feathery plumes from 18 to 48 inches tall atop deeply cut leaves in spring and early summer. Among the Arends hybrids, bright-red Red Sentinel and carmine-rose Federsee appear somewhat more drought tolerant.

Less thirsty yet are selections of *Astilbe chinensis.* Adventurous gardeners in the upper half of the Lower South might try these. Blooming in July and August, they include Davidii (deep rose-pink), Finale (soft pink), Visions (glowing raspberry), and Pumila (mauve). The latter selection, which grows only 12 inches tall and spreads slowly by stolons, makes a nice ground cover.

Of course, when speaking of astilbes,

"drought tolerant" is a relative term. "They all require constant moisture, moisture retentive soil, and good drainage," warns John. "They're also surface rooted, so you have to mulch. And before planting, you've got to cultivate down to a good foot or more and incorporate a lot of organic matter."

Afternoon shade is another must. The farther south you are, the more shade astilbes need. Planting beneath tall trees supplies the requisite shade, but keep one thing in mind—during a drought, no soil is drier than that beneath big trees because trees suck up every molecule of moisture available. So you'll have to water your astilbes even more.

I hate to water, which is why I've replaced my astilbes with a bench. But if watering is what makes your pot simmer, by all means give them a try.   *Steve Bender*

ASTILBE
At a Glance

Size: 12 to 48 inches (with blooms)
Light: light shade
Soil: acid, moist, well drained, lots of organic matter
Range: Upper and Middle South
Expect to pay: $4 to $8

ABOVE: *Low-growing Astilbe chinensis* Pumila *needs less water than other types and forms a nice ground cover.*
ABOVE, LEFT: *White Gloria sports fragrant, creamy-white plumes that stand 24 inches tall.*

With proper care, pink impatiens, maidenhair fern, rabbit's foot fern, and variegated creeping fig vine will last all summer.

Brighten Your Table

MATERIALS

1 (4-INCH) TERRA-COTTA
SAUCER

1 (12-INCH) TERRA-COTTA
SAUCER

POTTING SOIL

3 IMPATIENS PLANTS

3 (4-INCH) FERNS,
SUCH AS MAIDENHAIR OR
RABBIT'S FOOT

2 (4-INCH) TRAILING PLANTS,
SUCH AS IVY OR
CREEPING FIG VINE

1 HURRICANE GLOBE

1 PILLAR CANDLE

Dress up your outdoor table with an easy centerpiece planted in a terra-cotta saucer. The candle nestled in the middle adds an inviting touch to summer evenings and keeps the arrangement compact. Experiment with different candle and plant combinations to fit your tablescape.

Center the 4-inch saucer, upside down, in the larger one. Fill around it with potting soil about a half-inch deep. Gently loosen root balls, and arrange impatiens and ferns toward the inside of the saucer. Place low-growing and trailing plants near the edge.

Slide the hurricane globe on top of the small saucer. Add additional potting soil around the outside edge to cover roots, and water gently to settle the plants and soil. Place a pillar candle inside the globe. **Tip:** The small saucer serves as a base for the candle. If your globe does not fit over it, remove the saucer and position the glass without it. Keep the hurricane globe in place to prevent potting mix from soiling the candle.

CARE AND FEEDING

We used shade-loving ferns and impatiens for our plant assortment. Soil in a shallow saucer dries out quickly, but these plants require less water attention than those that need full sun. A good drink every other day was sufficient for our arrangement.

The terra-cotta saucer does not have a drainage hole, so water carefully. After rain, gently tip the arrangement to pour off excess water. Feed with a flower-boosting, water-soluble fertilizer, such as 15-30-15, every other week.

As the impatiens mature, they will become too large for the centerpiece. When they become leggy, pinch them back to half their height. You will need to do this only two or three times over the summer. Always cut directly above a set of leaves. New blooms will appear within a week.   *Ellen Riley*

A PROPER

Hard work pays off for Margaret Sanders, who plants, pulls the weeds, and keeps on smiling.

Gardening is a religious experience for Margaret Sanders. It must be, because every time you visit her garden in Columbus, Mississippi, you find her down on her knees—planting, dividing, weeding, deadheading, and thanking the heavens no armadillos invaded during the night.

Actually, a rampaging armadillo would be only a temporary setback. Thanks to stacks of mail-order catalogs, neighborhood plant swaps, and an inability to sentence any living plant to the compost, Margaret always has more than enough bulbs, perennials, and vines to repair the damage. Plants jostle for every inch of space, like commuters on the morning train. But lest you think her garden is as random as a lottery, take a closer look behind all the flowers, stems, and leaves. You'll discern a meticulous plan that has been years in the making.

The garden consists of two main sections. The first, a rectangular formal garden, sits just off to the side of the house. Though Margaret insists she's no good at designing with "stakes, strings, and geometry," you'd never guess. Straight brick walks separate azaleas,

Separated from the cutting garden by a lattice fence, the formal garden sits just off the side of the house. Its centerpiece is a lovely fountain Bill and Margaret gave each other for their 36th wedding anniversary.

GARDENER

BY STEVE BENDER
PHOTOGRAPHY
VAN CHAPLIN

hydrangeas, and perennials in the outer beds from a central bed of variegated liriope edged with clipped boxwoods. At the heart of the central bed, a fountain and pond sit on axis with a bench and arbor at the bed's far end.

A few steps away, a vine-draped archway in a lattice fence bids you enter the cutting garden. Awash in climbing roses, snaking vines, spires of larkspur, and mats of sedum, its plantings seem as free and heaven-sent as a daydream. Yet, underlying structure exists here, too, as gravel paths link rectangular planting beds.

> ## My garden is like a fruitcake. If you stick a shovel in, you hit a lot of things.
> *Margaret Sanders*

One path stretches beneath echoing arches draped with muscadines. To its left, a path lined with dwarf apple trees leads to a gazebo. Margaret explains her design: "I like to give the garden shape, then just let the plants be exuberant."

"Exuberant" is the perfect word. Each season, Margaret's garden sees a procession of foliage and flowers. "My garden is like a fruitcake," she says. "If you stick a shovel in, you hit a lot of things. I tend to plant plants on top of one another. One bed starts with hardy gladiolus, then it'll have poppies and Dutch iris, and after that, I plant zinnias. I really hate to see a piece of ground that's not doing anything."

While Margaret's plantings lean heavily toward tried-and-true Southern favorites, such as pearl bush, pussy willow, and Seven Sisters rose, an insatiable curiosity keeps this gardener experimenting. "Whenever I'm away from home and see something new and interesting, I burn with a desire to have it," she says. This year, for instance, she will be trying out the summer-blooming plumleaf azalea *(Rhododendron prunifolium)* she and her husband, Bill, admired last year at Callaway Gardens in Pine Mountain, Georgia.

Pressed to name a favorite flower, Margaret eventually settles on iris. "You just can't get too many kinds of iris," she says, ticking off the many types of irises that flourish in her garden—bearded, Siberian, Japanese, Dutch, Louisiana, spuria, and Japanese roof. Among the beardeds, her best performers continue to be the unidentified solid golds she and Bill inherited when they moved here decades ago. (She gave some to me; they bloomed and multiplied like crazy with absolutely no care.) Over time, she added many named selections that proved their mettle for the South. They include Beverly Sills (coral-pink), Blue Luster (violet-blue), Camelot Rose

Margaret uses pressure-treated 2 x 12s to edge her cutting beds. Flowers that reseed in the gravel paths are given to friends. "I can't stand to throw a flower away," she says. "I have to find a good home for it."

LEFT: *Margaret and Bill inherited these unnamed golden iris when they moved here years ago.* ABOVE: *A pussycat and pussy willows make fine companions on a garden bench.*

(orchid and burgundy), Laurel Park (peachy-orange), Snowmound (white and purple), Song Of Norway (ice blue), Vanity (medium pink), and Victoria Falls (medium blue).

Though Bill lends plenty of moral support ("He's a big encourager. He finds sources for plants, and he buys me good tools."), Margaret shoulders the garden's day-to-day upkeep with no outside help. "I've worn out several sets of knee pads," she reveals. "My children know that even though they gave me new ones last Christmas, I'll probably ask for them again next Christmas."

Mass plantings and mulch reduce maintenance in the formal garden. But because she can't mulch in the cutting garden for fear that larkspur, poppies, love-in-a-mist *(Nigella* sp.), "ragged-robins" (bachelor's-buttons), and other reseeding annuals won't come up, legions of seedlings greet her most spring and summer mornings. The flower seedlings she digs up and gives to friends. As for the weeds, she doesn't really mind pulling them. She knows this duty comes with the territory.

"You know what Kipling said about a gardener?" she asks. I nod as she quotes the verse: " '...Adam was a gardener, and God who made him sees / That half a proper gardener's work is done upon his knees.' " ◇

A garden of memories.
(See pages 116-119.)

May

Checklist for May

EDITOR'S NOTEBOOK

Anyone can grow big, bold, glorious, long-stemmed tulips. But it took a real expert—yours truly—to produce flowers so short and puny that gophers used them for corsages. I accomplished this by waiting to buy bulbs until mid-November, thus securing only the finest, picked-over merchandise. Next, I totally disregarded the need that tulips have for winter chilling. You see, tulips produce about 1 inch of flower stem for each week of chilling below 40 degrees. So for 10-inch stems, they need 10 weeks of chilling. We often don't get that much cold in Alabama, which is why folks around here chill their bulbs in the fridge for about six weeks prior to planting. That's their big mistake. That's what produces beautiful tulips like everyone else's. My advice—leave your bulbs in the garage until February. Not only will you stand out from the crowd, you'll make some gophers feel mighty special.

Steve Bender

☐ **Accent with foliage**—Buy caladiums, amaranthus, and coleus for foliage color through the summer months. The brilliant leaf color and bold texture of these plants are especially effective in masses of at least a dozen spaced 8 to 10 inches apart. ▶

☐ **Staking**—Tie tall plants to supports as they grow. If you let them get ahead of you, vining plants such as tomatoes could droop and break off when you finally get around to pulling them upright and tying them. Flower spikes such as foxgloves and delphiniums could break off in a spring storm if not tied to a support.

☐ **Tarragon**—If you are buying tarragon, look for plants labeled "French tarragon." These will give you the best flavor. Mexican mint marigold is a good tarragon substitute, particularly in the Middle, Lower, and Coastal South gardens where French tarragon is taxed by the heat.

PLANT

☐ **Annuals**—Sunflowers, French marigolds, salvia, impatiens, purslane, and dusty miller are just a few of the annuals that can be planted now in the Lower and Coastal South. To attract butterflies to the garden, plant porterweed *(Stachytarpheta* sp.), pentas, and bloodflower *(Asclepias curassavica)*.

☐ **Chayote squash**—In the Coastal South, buy chayote at the grocery store, and plant the whole fruit, stem end up, burying the lower half of the fruit. It will make a vigorous climbing vine, so put it near a tree or large fence that you want to cover. In November, the plant will flower, and it will produce fruit all winter long.

◀ **Daylilies**—As the daylilies begin to bloom in the Lower South, choose colors and sizes that best fit into your garden. Consider dwarf ones for borders and masses. Use larger types as pockets of color among evergreen shrubs. Masses of single colors are particularly effective. Daylilies prefer at least a half-day of direct sunlight and loose, well-drained soil. They should be divided in the fall every two to three years.

☐ **Mexican sunflowers**—Also called tithonia, these heat-loving annuals attract butterflies and create a tall background (up to 6 feet) for a flower border. The new selection called Fiesta Del Sol features saturated reddish-orange flowers atop 2½- to 3-foot plants that are as easy to grow from seeds as old-fashioned ones. It is an All-America Selection for 2000. For info on other winners, go to www.all-americaselections.org on the Web. ▶

◀ **Tomatoes**—Set out your tomatoes now. In fact, it's just the right time in the Middle South and perhaps even a little early in the Upper South. These summer-loving plants balk when placed in cold soil. It's always best to wait two weeks after the last expected frost date in your area to set them in the garden. Carnival, Spitfire, and Merced are good choices for home gardens in the Upper South. A few well-tended tomato plants can produce large quantities.

□ **Turf grass**—Right now is an excellent time of year to set out either sod or plugs of warm-season turf grasses in the Middle, Lower, and Coastal South. St. Augustine, Zoysia, and Bermuda grass are well adapted for this. For partially shaded areas, St. Augustine makes a good choice, although you'll find that it is not as drought resistant as Bermuda or Zoysia. Common Bermuda may be established from seed at this time, which is much less expensive than sod. Be prepared to irrigate newly planted turf every two to four days if there isn't sufficient rainfall.

□ **Vegetables**—Plant Southern peas such as black-eyed peas and Zipper Cream crowders in the Lower South. If you have plenty of space, you can also sow seeds of melons and okra now that the soil has warmed. Replace earlier cool-weather vegetables such as broccoli and cabbage with cucumbers, squash, and beans.

PRUNE

□ **Azaleas**—If azaleas need pruning to control their size or shape, do it this month when flowering has finished. Waiting until midsummer may prevent flowering next spring.

□ **Deadheading**—Remove spent blooms from cool-weather annuals such as pansies, stock, sweet peas, calendulas, and larkspur to prolong their flowering and to keep the garden tidy.

◄ **Grapefruit**—Trees that have limbs hanging all the way to the ground may be made more attractive by pruning off the lower limbs up to a height of 18 inches. This allows for good air movement under the tree and reduces the chances of foot rot and other trunk rotting diseases.

□ **Peaches**—Thin fruit on trees about two months after they have bloomed, leaving about 4 to 6 inches between peaches. You will have bigger fruit, and the tree's limbs will be less likely to break from the weight.

□ **Shrubs**—Now that spring-flowering shrubs have finished blooming, cut back any that are oversize or in bad shape. Try to maintain their natural form by removing entire limbs to their point of origin. Avoid sheared balls of forsythia, spirea, and azalea except in the rare case where a formal design dictates.

FERTILIZE

□ **Fruit trees**—Citrus, avocados, and mangoes should be fertilized three times per year. This is a good time for the second application of the season. Use a fruit-tree special such as 12-5-8 (for young, growing trees) or 18-5-18 (for older, full-size trees) at the rate recommended on the label. Broadcast evenly under the tree out to the edge of the canopy; then water it in. Avoid piling fertilizer against the trunk.

CONTROL

□ **Roses**—This month is the start of the rainy season, so black spot disease is likely to reappear. Prevent it by spraying plants every 7 to 10 days with a fungicide, such as Funginex, Manzate 200, or Dithane M-45. Be sure to coat both the upper and lower surfaces of the leaves.

May notes:

TIP OF THE MONTH

I use a video camera to aid in the design of my garden. All year I videotape my plants when they're blooming and record the dates. I review the tape in winter before I order new plants. It helps me remember color schemes and times when little was blooming.

GLEN W. PRILLAMAN
FAYETTEVILLE, NORTH CAROLINA

ELEVATING
vegetables

F rank Fleming seemingly began life in a garden. "From as early as I can remember, we helped take care of the farm and especially the vegetable garden. We all helped tend it, and we canned a lot of things. That's where I got my early start growing vegetables," he explains.

But gardening took a backseat to Frank's career for a number of years, as he became a nationally recognized sculptor. Now he draws from his early days in the soil to translate the magic of flora and fauna into his intricately detailed works. While sculpting is his occupation, Frank is quick to point out that gardening is his heart and soul. "When I moved to my present location, about 20 years ago, I started seriously growing again," he says about his garden in Homewood, Alabama.

The garden is a labyrinth of raised beds designed for maximum production in a confined space. Perched on top of a steep incline, the garden takes center stage in a portion of his front yard. From the street, passersby are unaware of the manicured beds above. "One reason I wanted raised beds was to keep things organized," Frank says. "The good topsoil had been washed away, so raised beds gave me control over the soil."

BY ELLEN RILEY
PHOTOGRAPHY JEAN
ALLSOPP

"This is a most effective way to control moisture," Frank adds. The beds confine soil, and water is limited to specific growing areas, with little wasted runoff in walkways. Many mornings he waters each bed by hand, inspecting his crops early in the day.

THE SETUP
Constructed from pressure-treated 2 x 12s, the beds have narrow passages between them. Frank's priority is space for cultivation rather than wide paths to accommodate a wagon or wheelbarrow. In addition to elevating the soil, he has devised a method to raise crops in a neat, vertical manner. "I put trellises in most beds so I can rotate crops and not worry about staking. They work for everything I grow that requires support," he says. The permanent wire walls are built with steel fence posts, hog wire, and bamboo across the top. When these materials are

lashed together, they will support a massive wall of pole beans or a crop of tomatoes.

Air circulation is another trellis benefit. Crops grown in close quarters suffer fewer disease and insect problems when air moves easily among foliage and fruit. By growing vertically on a sturdy, large support, the plants spread out and breathe easy.

GROWING SOIL

Placing good dirt in raised beds on top of a steep incline was no simple task. "Most of the soil in the beds is store-bought topsoil," Frank says. "Living on a hill like I do, it was impossible to have a truckload brought in. It was easier to get the bagged dirt into the garden. Then I began adding compost. I've added lots of it over the years, and I've experimented with all kinds of things in the soil.

"In some of my early beds, I put down a thick layer of leaves before adding the soil. In these beds, my tomatoes now have a hard time with a blight. I've had to grow them in other beds to combat the problem. Other vegetables don't seem to be affected."

FRUITS OF LABOR

This garden yields an extraordinary amount of produce. "I love harvesting in these raised beds. I don't have to bend over very far, and the trellises make it easy to gather from both sides," Frank says.

A quick spin through the garden shows Frank's passion for the tried-and-true vegetables of his childhood. He also loves to experiment. Last year's trial was a new, dwarf red corn. "I suppose it would have been great, but the raccoons came through one night and stole every ear," he says. This year he'll skip corn. There's always a new squash selection, an interesting eggplant, and a healthy dose of parsley and basil. "If something is successful, it can stay. I'll try anything that's new, but if it fails, I don't try it again," Frank says. ◇

STILL LIFE

Frank occasionally turns his garden into a studio. "I use a lot of vegetables for meals. Others I turn into art. I pick certain vegetables and make rubber molds of them, and then cast them in bronze," he says. For information on Frank's sculptures, see his Web site at www.rookids.com or E-mail him at artflem@ bellsouth.net.

The beauty of a raised bed is perfectly planned soil. Frank harvests potatoes by reaching down into the dirt and pulling what he needs for dinner.

New Hampshire Purple, a selection of bloody cranesbill geranium, will grow in sun or part shade, supplying bright blooms right through the hot months.

Try This Geranium

How anyone could look at such a lovely plant and name it bloody cranesbill geranium is beyond me. The tiny beaklike fruit it produces is said to be the inspiration for this injustice. Overlook the gory adjective and you'll find an enthusiastic little bloomer that comes back each year on its own.

Bloody cranesbills *(Geranium sanguineum)* are not what most gardeners think of when they hear the word geranium. The more familiar zonal geraniums sport clusters of flowers held aloft on stalks above rounded leaves. The blooms of bloody cranesbills are buttercup shaped and dot the foliage with color.

Flower hues range from white, pink, and red to the bright fuchsia blooms of the New Hampshire Purple selection (shown). Though all bloody cranesbills bloom from early summer until frost, New Hampshire Purple is known for nearly nonstop color during the hot months. Plants form low mounds of dense greenery about 1 to 2 feet high. Add bloody cranesbills to the front of your flower border for best viewing. Or try them along paths, tucked between stones, or creeping over the edge of a large container.

These plants can take the heat of summer, but they do need moist, well-drained soil. They'll bloom equally well in full sun or part shade. Blooming stops with the first cold snap, and leaves blush red before disappearing for the winter. New foliage will emerge in spring. Try bloody cranesbill. It's easy to grow, and the name is hard to forget. *Jo Kellum*

BLOODY CRANESBILL GERANIUM
At a Glance

Size: mounds about 1 to 2 feet high and 1 foot wide
Light: full sun to part shade
Soil: moist, well drained
Range: all South

low stress & COLORFUL

BY JOHN ALEX FLOYD, JR.
PHOTOGRAPHY VAN CHAPLIN

TOP: *Pink Flower Carpet roses provide color from late spring through fall.*
ABOVE: *Lilies dot the landscape in summer.*

I am an avid gardener who doesn't have time to garden. So when we built a new house five years ago, it was time for a reality check. How can I have a beautiful yard, still basically do it myself, and balance work as well as family issues that always seem to cut into my gardening time? There were some simple solutions.

First, I didn't try to do everything at once. I developed the garden over a period of years. (Even after five growing seasons I have some rough areas.) Next, I simplified most of the landscape and concentrated my efforts where I receive maximum benefit and enjoyment.

After I hired a contractor to build a retaining wall, add soil to the garden, and install a fence, I was ready to make the 30- x 80-foot space my garden. With these elements in place, I could start thinking about planting.

At our old home, we enjoyed the garden more in late April through June and again from mid-September through October. So I planned the new garden to be at its peak during these times.

As I started the design process, I remembered some advice from friend and retired landscape architect Fred Thode of Clemson, South Carolina: "Always define your garden edge." With that in mind, I chose yellow daylilies to form the border. I knew I wanted a clear yellow lily that blooms all at once in late spring, but I needed help choosing a selection. André Viette, owner of André Viette Nursery in Fishersville, Virginia, recommended 100 Suzie Wong daylilies. They bloom late May to early June. When the flower stalks fade, I cut them off and have lush green foliage as my edge until frost each year.

Because I didn't have a lot of time and it was late in the planting season, I set out color behind the daylilies the first year. It was a mixture of 10 flats (640 plants) of melampodium and narrow-leaf zinnias, but that was too much work. As fall rolled around, I knew

BEFORE

LEFT: *In late spring as the daisies and foxgloves fade, daylilies and Japanese iris become the flower show.* BELOW, LEFT: *Spikes of foxgloves break up the mass planting of daisies.*

from a maintenance standpoint that I needed to limit annuals to a few plants each season. Most of my color would have to come from shrubs, perennials, and reseeding annuals.

In the fall I planted three flats (196 seedlings) of reseeding Alaska daisies. Randomly placed throughout the daisies are 64 foxglove seedlings. I also planted 5 (1-gallon) containers of Japanese iris, 25 lily bulbs, and 25 (4-inch) pots of Newport Pink sweet Williams. I knew that I could depend on color year after year from the Japanese iris, lilies, daylilies, and reseeding daisies. So I could replant the foxgloves and sweet Williams each fall, fertilize them with Osmocote (14-14-14) at planting and again early each spring with perennial booster (9-12-12), and have an outstanding spring display. Now, my total planting time is a Saturday morning any time in fall after a killing frost.

In the future when I have more time, I will set out several nursery flats of orange pansies to vary the planting from year to year. Additional all-season color comes from Flower Carpet roses that are carefree except for regular fertilization and winter pruning.

As the garden transitions from spring to summer, the display moves from full-color to a green palette with splashes of color. Summer-flowering Oriental lilies and Queen Anne's lace create focal points, while a white crepe myrtle and butterfly bushes provide additional summer color. If I have time, I'll sow a few seed packs of zinnias for cutting.

As fall approaches, I depend on the Flower Carpet roses and a mass of perennial asters along with some late-flowering crinum bulbs to provide the flower color. There is fall foliage color from the crepe myrtle and October Glory red maples.

While I know that I might like a more refined garden, this is one I can manage with a couple of hours a week in spring and fall plus a few Saturday mornings throughout the year. It gives the avid gardener in me satisfaction and peace. ◇

(For sources turn to pages 250–251.)

As the garden transitions from spring to summer, the display moves from full-color to a green palette with splashes of color.

PHOTOGRAPHS: TINA CORNETT

Rose Campion

Brilliant flowers and fabulous foliage make this biennial a favorite.

The strong stems of rose campion appear silvery-soft with fuzzy foliage. Flowers skip along the tips in brilliant magenta and white.

Silver is a welcome color in a flower border, and the pearl gray foliage of rose campion *(Lychnis coronaria)* is no exception. Quarter-size magenta flowers dance on top of sturdy stems, and the colorful relationship between foliage and flower is dynamic.

This biennial thrives in full sun and will tolerate light shade. In spring, silky white stems emerge from a rosette of leaves close to the soil and grow 1½ to 2½ feet tall. The tip of each stem yields several flowerbuds, and the vibrant blooms begin in May, continuing through June.

There is also a white-flowering selection: Alba. It provides an arresting foil to the magenta flowers of other selections. This combination of fuzzy silver leaves and white blooms is as stunning as its bright pink companion. With both colors, a mass planting provides the most effective display. There are other selections that introduce soft pink to the color palette. Angel Blush and Oculata are gentle hues that soften strong contrasts.

This plant thrives on less than perfect conditions. It flourishes in average, dry soil and requires little fertilizer. Planted in rich, well-irrigated soil, it will struggle and ultimately fail.

After blossoms fade, this biennial will produce seeds and die. To maintain a healthy spread of flowers from year to year, allow the seeds to mature and drop into the garden. They will germinate wherever they land.

For more control, collect the seeds and drop them where you want them to grow. To prevent plants from wandering, deadhead spent blossoms before seeds are produced.

Allowed to mix and mingle, color variations may ensue. To maintain color integrity, separate magenta and white seeds. Otherwise, seedlings may appear with assorted pinks and drab white. While these shaded cousins may be interesting, the impact of bold color and silver foliage will be diluted.

Few plants have such a lovely combination of blooms and foliage. This prolific biennial can easily become a welcome member of your garden family.   *Ellen Riley*

ROSE CAMPION
At a Glance

Type: spring-flowering biennial
Light: full sun to light shade
Soil: prefers average, dry soil
Flowers: magenta, white, or pink in May and June
Nice to Know: It's a rampant re-seeder. For control, collect seeds, and plant them in chosen places.

Virginia Sweetspire

Fragrant spring flowers and vivid fall color make this shrub a winner.

Henry's Garnet turns scarlet to reddish purple in the fall.

Decorated with tiny white fragrant flowers, this Virginia sweetspire is right at home on the creek bank.

Lining Southern creeks and riverbanks like old fishermen on a hot summer day, Virginia sweetspire has long, arching canes that sometimes dip right into the water. Because of its good looks, this wild, sprawling, woodland shrub is being tamed and is making its way into residential landscapes.

Virginia sweetspire *(Itea virginica)* does best in moist soil and will even take soggy to wet conditions. It grows 4 to 5 feet high and is considered a small to medium-size shrub. It can spread 8 to 10 feet in width and will form colonies if left untended. Underground roots reach out and send up little shoots or suckers around the parent plant. These small shrubs can be easily dug and relocated to other areas.

It may not be the best plant for tight spaces, but if you have some room or need a shrub that will take wet feet, try this carefree plant. The tips of the stems are decorated with 3- to 6-inch tiny, white, sweetly scented blooms around May and June. The individual flowers may not be large, but clustered together on the stem, they make quite a show.

Once flowers fade, Virginia sweetspire becomes rather inconspicuous until fall. That's when the green leaves begin to turn deep red. One popular improved selection named Henry's Garnet sports reddish to purple autumn leaves and its flowers are superior. Little Henry is a recently introduced selection that is making its way into the trade. It has a more compact, mounding form, growing only 18 to 24 inches tall and spreading 3 feet in width. Like Henry's Garnet, it also has spectacular fall color.

Virginia sweetspire grows fine in sun or shade. A sunny site usually produces a full, more uniform plant. Ones grown in deep shade are more sparse and loosely shaped. It is the perfect shrub for natural areas and can be planted by a stream or lake or close to a downspout. Some landscape architects are using Virginia sweetspire to help prevent erosion. When planted along the water's edge, it helps stabilize banks and prevent washouts.

Even if you don't have a damp spot in your yard, you can grow this shrub as long as you keep it watered during summer droughts. This Southern native will delight you with its aromatic clusters of flowers in the spring, and in the fall you can watch its foliage magically change from green to red.

Charlie Thigpen
(For sources turn to pages 250–251.)

VIRGINIA SWEETSPIRE
At a Glance

Flowers: small but numerous and extremely fragrant in late spring and early summer
Foliage: Leaves turn deep red in fall.
Location: sun or shade; prefers a moist site and tolerates wet feet

BEFORE

The hot, hard parking area Jacque Bell remembers from her youth has become a garden spot and the focus of her family's outdoor life.

From Garage to Garden

Asphalt has given way to a stone terrace and soft, fertile beds of flowers.

A father's regret becomes a daughter's pride. That's how Jacque Bell sees the entry to the home she watched her father build—the one she now shares with husband, Randy, and their children.

It is a gracious home with lots of windows and a view of a lake on the family's 26-acre property in Greenville, South Carolina. But everyone parked in the driveway facing the garage and walked in the kitchen door. "I remember him saying that he regretted positioning the garage entrance so near the kitchen door where most guests entered," Jacque says. "There was no parking for the front door. And when the garage door is open . . . you know how the garage gets. So we said, 'Let's just change it.'"

With the help of residential designer Jack Thacker and builder J. W. Roberts, Jacque and Randy closed the front of

the garage and knocked out the back. French doors replaced garage doors, and a wall was built inside to create a narrow sunroom. The family now drives around back and enters the garage on the other side. Guests would never know it had been any different.

Jacque called landscape architect J. Dabney Peeples of J. Dabney Peeples Design Associates in Easley, South Carolina, to give the sunroom a garden setting. He enclosed the area with a white picket fence that made the approach to the door more interesting. "The little fence gives you a sense of arrival, and then you actually go through a gate, into the garden, and to the door or sunroom," says Dabney. "The white woodwork is casual, but a little bit dressy. We didn't want to lose the flavor of a nice country place."

An arbor draped with silver lace vine continues the woodwork inside the

The view from the Bells' kitchen door is an inviting one, which explains why they enjoy so many meals outdoors when the weather is mild.

garden for a sense of unity. The stone terrace repeats the Tennessee crab orchard stone that Jacque's father used on the steps and in the facade when he built the house.

When it comes to the garden, Jacque has picked up where her mother left off. Dabney understood this and was sensitive not to change it too much and destroy the connection between the generations. Because the large dogwoods and hollies were established, the garden appeared to have been there a long time, even when it was new.

"Mother was a grand gardener," Jacque says. "When I was young, I didn't give her credit. She's been gone more than 20 years now. Even before I got involved, there was always something to pick and bring in the house year-round."

In the midst of all those acres, Jacque finds relief in the small enclosed garden. "I've found out over the years that clients need to have some sort of intimate area to do trowel work," Dabney says. "With those acres, you can put in 700 of this and 300 of that, and they just disappear down a hole. But this way, when she gets the urge to garden, Jacque can zip up to the nursery, get a few things on a sunny afternoon, and she's done something."

Jacque agrees, "I'm not a perfectionist, but sometimes I wished I had one little area that I could keep looking good. I've really enjoyed this garden, and I have both sun and shade."

The terrace is a few steps from the kitchen. In good weather, the family eats breakfast, lunch, and dinner outdoors. "It's just another room of the house," Jacque says. "And it's especially nice to sit in the sunroom when it's raining."

The single swing that hangs from the arbor signifies the success of the design for Dabney. "Whoever gets home first gets dibs on the swing," he says. It's good to have a garden where the gardener actually rests, where the family gathers, and where the generations, separated by time, feel a connection nevertheless.   *Linda C. Askey*

Blanketed with silver lace vine, the arbor in front of the old garage and new sunroom is just wide enough for a single swing.

Variegated spider plant, corn plant, and rubber plant deal with toxins from new furniture.

Green Air, Clean Air

Ah, the lush green complexity of jungles and rain forests, source of so much of our planetary fresh air. Wouldn't it be splendid to have your own little rain forest to refresh you while you sleep, work, or watch TV? And wouldn't it be delicious to forget about irritated eyes, sinus congestion, raw throat, headache, fatigue, and all the other symptoms brought on by exposure to indoor toxins?

It turns out you really can get fresh air, without even opening your windows. In fact, if you grow any houseplants at all, you've made a start. As Dr. Bill Wolverton, a retired NASA research scientist and president of Wolverton Environmental Services, puts it, "Why did it take us so long to recognize that plants could clean the air indoors, when we know we could not live on this planet without plants to purify and revitalize the outdoor air?"

I decided to test Bill's advice recently, when I purchased some new furniture and soon began to suffer for it. My bedroom suite included materials made of particle board and plywood, plus varnishes, stains, and adhesives. All of these emit formaldehyde and other toxins, and I was waking up in misery until I surrounded myself with houseplants. The atmosphere had noticeably improved within 24 hours.

"In our carefully sealed and insulated dwellings, houseplants are no longer luxuries, but essential to health," says Bill. "They are nature's living air purifiers, with years of documented scientific evidence to prove it." So have as many plants as you can because it's a jungle out there, all right. Treat yourself to a jungle indoors as well. *Liz Druitt*

HOUSE CLEANERS

lady palm (*Rhapis excelsa*)

rubber plant (*Ficus elastica*)

English ivy (*Hedera helix*)

peace lily (*Spathiphyllum* sp.)

corn plant (*Dracaena fragrans*)

pothos (*Epipremnum* sp.)

Warneckii dracaena (*Dracaena deremensis* Warneckii)

schefflera (*Brassaia actinophylla*)

mother-in-law's tongue (*Sansevieria trifasciata*)

spider plant (*Chlorophytum comosum*)

Container Success

A pot of flowers is like a pot of gold. It might not make you wealthy, but it sure will make you smile. A colorful display in containers placed close to your house, deck, or patio adds warmth and charm. If you have minimal time or space, potting up a few planters is the perfect way to garden.

Containers are available in every size, shape, and color. Select a planter that complements your house. For instance, an orange terra-cotta pot might clash with a redbrick house, whereas a gray concrete container may be better suited. Also make sure your pot is the right scale for where you intend to use it. A 6-inch pot on a large front porch will go unnoticed and won't make an impact.

Once you find the right container, keep the same principles in mind when choosing plants. White blooms in front of a white house won't show up. Use dark foliage and bright flowers against a light-colored house, and use light foliage and pastel flowers against a dark house for maximum impact.

Before you plant, make sure your containers have unobstructed drainage holes in the bottom. If they don't, use a drill to make new holes or expand existing or clogged ones. If the potting soil you are using is light and likely to sift through the drain holes, place a coffee filter, pot chards, or window screen over them. This will keep the soil in the pot, yet allow the water to drain.

There are many potting soils available, so select a premium mix. Some contain lime to balance the pH, controlled-release fertilizer, and water-retaining polymers. Read the labels and ask for recommendations at the garden center. Avoid buying cheap soils that don't list their contents. You may have to try a few brands to find the one that's right for your plants.

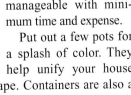

Finally, choose the correct-size plant for your pot. There should be enough room for plants to continue to grow and fill out. Small trees and shrubs add height and nice lines to a large container. Ornamental grasses can also provide bright color with interesting form. Don't forget to use foliage plants. They might not have showy flowers, but they can supply lots of color.

Think about where to place your planters for the most impact. Use plants in pots as design elements. Next to steps, they may signal a grade change or mark entryways. Or use them as focal points to draw you into a garden or onto a deck. A cluster of pots can create a small garden that is manageable with minimum time and expense.

Put out a few pots for a splash of color. They help unify your house with the landscape. Containers are also a good way to introduce yourself to plants if you're not a seasoned gardener. They will decorate your home's exterior and add your own special signature style. *Charlie Thigpen*

Small shrubs such as this standard peegee hydrangea, underplanted with blue browallia, petunias, and ivy, look handsome in large containers.

CONTAINER TIPS

■ Make sure your containers are located no farther than the length of a hose for convenient watering.

■ Shredded bark, pine straw, gravel, or small pinecones make attractive mulches for topping planters. They also help reduce moisture loss.

■ Change soil every couple of plantings. Reach down in the pot, and loosen soil with your hands between each planting.

■ When selecting several different types of plants for one pot, make sure they all share the same sun and water requirements.

RIGHT: *Though there are plenty of flowers in the garden, its overall theme is green. A rich brocade of foliage edges a velvet panel of fescue lawn.* BELOW: *A bevel trim keeps boxwood hedges narrower at the top than the bottom, allowing sunlight to reach the underside of plants for allover lush foliage.*

Tapestry Of Blooms

Hidden behind a tidy Atlanta home, a garden grows, squaring off beside a woodland of towering Georgia natives. The plants in this garden are woven together in such expert fashion that it is impossible to single out a particular specimen for admiration; but it doesn't hurt to try. It is the scene that captivates.

In spring, dogwoods standing in the corners of the yard unfurl head-turning bracts when leaves are just pointy green promises clinging to wintry stems. White Triumphator

tulips balance their snowy cups on towering green stems. Bedded down each fall, the tulips steal the show in early spring. Next, stalky foxgloves take center stage.

New Dawn roses climb up and spill over a trellis, antique pink blossoms clamoring coyly for attention. By the time those blooms have faded, the chartreuse flower heads on Annabelle hydrangeas change to cream. Even August, any garden's nemesis, finds fragrant trumpets of Royal Standard hostas and pink sprays of hardy begonias embroidering the scene.

Garden designer Ryan Gainey tailored the garden to the seasons. He also trimmed it neatly with a low boxwood hedge for greenery year-round. Winter Gem Korean boxwood was chosen for its vigorous growth and fresh color that doesn't fade in cold weather. Only about 6 inches tall when they were planted, the shrubs quickly grew together. Pruning three or four times a year keeps the hedge low and neat.

A bed of airy flowers, hemmed in by the Winter Gem boxwood hedge, is buttoned down with clipped balls of American boxwood. Matched pairs of conical boxwoods anchor the ends of planting beds. "We planted the shaped boxwood pretty large to start with, for the effect," says Ryan. "The Americans grow slower than the Korean ones, so they need to be sheared only once or twice a year to maintain their shape."

Though pruning is important, the garden doesn't demand endless hours of effort from the homeowners. Annuals growing in containers are easy accents that can be changed at whim. Permanent plants in the garden dutifully add seasonal interest year after year.

Ryan kept maintenance in mind when he planned the intricate design. "Because the garden changes seasonally, there are certain things to do each season. But it isn't overwhelming," he says. "There's just enough to do to keep from depriving you of the pleasure of work." *Jo Kellum*

TOP AND ABOVE: *New Dawn roses festoon the garden with pink blooms in spring. Their showy flowers and dependable nature make them a favorite for arbors and trellises.*

Raised beds for drainage and gravel mulch promise success for lavenders.

heavy rain. And I thought the white granite looked artificial. But I did like the gravel," she says. She now spreads a 2- to 3-inch layer of pea gravel over the soil after lavenders are planted.

Madalene also suggests these tips. Be sure you give lavenders plenty of space for air circulation when you plant. If you add them to an existing flower border, pull back the wood or pine straw mulch, and add a pea gravel mulch under them. Water deeply once a week with a soaker hose. If you water by hand, do it around the base of the plant, not on the leaves. Madalene also recommends fall planting so lavenders can develop a good root system before summer. "If spring planting is done, grow them in a 12-inch container so watering can be controlled. You're guaranteed to lose them in a smaller pot. They must have full sun and light watering daily in that size pot. Regular feeding and light pruning after blooming should carry them to fall when they can go into the ground," she says.   *Liz Druitt*

(For sources turn to pages 250–251.)

A Silver Lining

Why grow lavender? The silvery-gray foliage and blue, white, or purple blossoms blend deliciously with other herbs and flowers. Lavender's scent—dry and sweet and clean—is the essence of grandmother, of cool healing hands on a hot forehead. The very name of it is redolent of nostalgia. But, boy, is it tough to keep alive in the humid gardens of the South.

Many a Southern gardener has had the experience of planting lavender and being encouraged as it seems to thrive. One night it's beautiful, the next morning the pewter foliage is dead, dark gray—a rain cloud with no silver lining. Fortunately, pre-eminent Southern herbalist Madalene Hill has perfected a growing technique that will allow anyone to enjoy this historic herb.

It took her almost 20 years of determination and wrestling with the details to grow lavender successfully. Madalene's method is the result of trial and error, sharing information with fellow herb gardeners, and personal taste.

Lavenders like moist, but not wet, soil around their roots, so the first necessity for success is good drainage. They can be grown very nicely in containers, but if you're planting them in the ground, make a raised bed. Madalene has even added a slight slope to her lavender bed to be certain there's never any standing water.

The second critical factor is mulch. Lavenders are extremely sensitive to dampness on their foliage, and this is what makes them so tricky in the South. The perfect mulch is one that not only will dry out quickly after rain (or a humid morning), but also will reflect heat upward to help keep stems and leaves dry. Madalene tested builder's sand, white granite chips, and pea gravel. All three worked well for the lavender, but not for Madalene's artistic eye. "I didn't like the sand, which always had a hot, arid look and got splashed around if we had a

PHOTOGRAPHS: VAN CHAPLIN

TIPS FROM MADALENE

■ "The secret to growing lavender in the South involves two things: Number one is drainage; number two is a dry, heat-reflective mulch."

■ "I always tell people to go ahead and try any lavenders they like—stretch the limits. After all, we do have these fluctuating winters in the South, and it's always a surprise what will grow. And if something dies, just try it again! Next year may be different."

Tucked into a corner of the yard, a garden grows in quiet splendor.

A Quiet Corner

Every time she looks out the window, Betsy Trow thinks of her mother. A lovely garden flourishes in her memory. Though Betsy was always a gardener, this corner of her Richmond yard was nothing but grass for years. Overgrown azaleas grew along the back edge and a sweet olive hedge lined one side.

But when Betsy received Turtle Baby, her mother's beloved bronze fountain, she knew she had to create a setting worthy of her inheritance. Betsy turned to landscape designer Carrington Brown for help. Carrington drew a plan for a brick patio centered in a perennial garden. Beside it, a precast concrete basin forms an elegant little pool, Turtle Baby's new home. A low brick wall turns the corner behind the flower border and the fountain, giving the garden a sense of seclusion.

The patio is about 15 feet square. Carrington suggested a 10-inch-wide planting strip in its design to provide a green frame within the brickwork. Dwarf mondo does the job beautifully and doesn't mind getting stepped on occasionally. Betsy included a circle of handmade hexagonal brick in the center of the patio to echo a pattern found in older parts of the garden. Though the six-sided bricks are new, all of the traditional bricks in the walls and patio are old. The combination of aged brick and mature background plants makes the garden appear as if it has been there a very long time, but it's actually just a few years old. "The garden is very near to a glassed-in room, so you see the details close-up," explains Carrington.

She helped Betsy with suggestions for the perennial border. Betsy also studied books, visited nurseries, and chose many plants herself. The resulting

White balloon flower protrudes from a patch of New Hampshire Purple cranesbill geraniums. Dark-leaved Purple Palace alum root provides rich contrast.

flower and foliage combinations are delightful. Light-colored blossoms such as white bleeding heart, dianthus, and balloon flower show off against clusters of foliage with contrasting textures. "The first house we lived in, we had no sun," says Betsy. "So I could only deal with the foliage plants. And I began to love the leaves. Flowers are so brief; the foliage is the most important part of the plant to me."

Though the corner garden where Turtle Baby now stands is small enough to devour in a glance, the richness of colors and details begs for continued admiration. It is a place painted with happiness and memories as the legacy of a daughter's love grows with each passing season. *Jo Kellum*

Simply Smashing, Y'all

Born in England, Exbury azaleas became world famous. But getting them to weather our hot summers meant giving them a Southern accent.

Most barons I know have time on their hands. They don't mow the lawn, scrub mildew from the shower, or take the Bentley in for a brake job. In short, the best things in life pass them by. Which may explain why, during the 1920s and 30s, Baron Lionel de Rothschild of Southhampton, England, decided to busy himself by creating a new class of azaleas on his Exbury estate.

Having reportedly wearied of running the hounds each morning, the baron (known simply as "Larry" to his friends) took a fancy to deciduous azaleas. In an effort to produce plants with larger, showier flowers and brilliant new colors, he crossed existing hybrids with species from North America, China, and Japan.

The resulting Exbury azaleas, of which there were hundreds, proved to be a big smash. His plants were hardy and vigorous, growing 5 to 10 feet tall. They featured huge,

The showiest of all deciduous azaleas, Exbury hybrids produce huge, fragrant trusses of flowers in midspring. Crossing them with heat-tolerant native species made them better performers in the Deep South.

fragrant flowers of just about every color. Many even displayed colorful fall foliage. They quickly took Europe by storm, then conquered the American Northeast, Northwest, Midwest, and Upper and Middle South.

But when they moved into the Lower and Coastal South, they encountered one teensy problem. The summer heat killed them. Some of their parents, including Japanese azalea *(Rhododendron japonicum),* Chinese azalea *(R. molle),* and Western azalea *(R. occidentale),* didn't like to sweat. About the only Exbury that thrived in the Deep South was an orange selection named Gibraltar.

Fortunately, one enterprising Southerner didn't leave it at that. Thirty years ago, Gene Aromi from Mobile began crossing Exbury hybrids with Southern native azaleas, including Florida azalea *(R. austrinum),* Piedmont azalea *(R. canescens),* Texas

These flowers come in many different colors, including yellow, red, orange, salmon, pink, and white. Many are bicolored.

EXBURY AZALEAS
At a Glance

Size: 5 to 10 feet tall
Light: half sun, half shade
Soil: moist, well drained, acid, lots of organic matter
Range: Upper and Middle South for Exburys; Upper, Middle, Lower, and Coastal South for the new, more heat-tolerant hybrids
Growth rate: moderate
Pests: lacebugs, borers

azalea *(R. oblongifolium),* and swamp azalea *(R. viscosum).* Today, his heat-tolerant Aromi hybrids include Sunstruck (lemon yellow), High Tide (white and pale pink with a gold flare), and Tipsy Tangerine (orange blend with yellow blotch).

"My azaleas don't look a bit better than the Exburys," admits Gene. "The important difference is—mine live."

Gene wasn't alone in his efforts to Southernize Exburys. In nearby Semmes, Alabama, Tom Dodd III crossed Exburys with Florida azaleas to produce superior plants, including Colonel Mosby (salmon-pink with yellow flare) and J.E.B. Stuart (deep pink with a yellow blotch). And at Pushepetappa Gardens in Franklinton, Louisiana, John Thornton and Loyd Cotton are growing heat-tolerant hybrids created from similar parents.

Unlike the pure Exburys, these new hybrids grow well from the Midwest and Upper South down to the Gulf Coast. Both prefer moist, well-drained, acid soil containing lots of organic matter. They tolerate light shade, but the more sun you give them, the more blooms you'll get. Plant them on the edge of woods, in foundation plantings or shrub borders, or in the understory beneath tall shade trees.

You can find Exbury azaleas at most garden centers and home-center stores. However, the new, heat-tolerant hybrids can be hard to find. Whatever you do, don't call Larry. Having lost interest in breeding more azaleas, he's devoting himself to better things, like cleaning out his gutters.

Steve Bender

(For sources turn to pages 250–251.)

Shucks, It's Good

Fresh sweet corn is a little like love. You crave it every day.

My wife once asked me if I could have any food in the world, what would it be? I pondered her question for exactly two seconds, then answered, "Silver Queen corn, right out of the garden."

Put simply, ripe Silver Queen corn is nature's most nearly perfect food—so sweet, so tender, so delectable. To this date, no known human has ever gotten his fill. Trouble is, Silver Queen maintains peak flavor for about as long as Charlie Sheen stays out of trouble. So unless you beam the ears directly from the field into a pot of boiling water, they turn starchy. At that point, you can do as my aunts and mother always did—cut the kernels from the ears and make stewed corn, which is delicious too.

Some folks, though, weren't satisfied with this. They wanted white, yellow, and bicolored corn that stayed sweet longer. So they fiddled around with genetics and eventually created two classes of improved sweet corn. The first, called "sugary enhanced" corn, is about as sweet or slightly sweeter than regular corn. But the "se" gene slows the conversion of sugar to starch to as many as 14 days. Among the top "se" selections is bright-yellow Breeder's Choice. Maturing in 73 days, it bears 8-inch ears inside tight husks that discourage earworms and birds.

The second class, "super sweet" corn, contains twice as much sugar as regular sweet corn. You sometimes see it designated as shrunken or "sh2" corn, because the gene responsible for the added sweetness also causes dry kernels to look shrunken. Super sweet corn stays sweet for days after picking, as long as you refrigerate it promptly. Recommended selections include How Sweet It Is (white, 80 days), Honey N' Pearl (bicolor, 76 days), and Early Xtra-Sweet (yellow, 71 days). And if you thought Indian

corn was just for decorating, try the 2000 All-America Selections winner: Indian Summer. Its red, yellow, white, and purple kernels are exceptionally sweet.

KERNELS OF WISDOM

Sweet corn is a warm-weather crop, so don't rush planting in spring. Seed planted in soil cooler than 65 degrees will sit there and can rot. The soil should be warm, loose, crumbly, and easily workable. About a month after the last frost is a good time to plant. Work 1 cup of 10-10-10 or 10-14-10 fertilizer per 10 feet of row into the soil before planting. Plant seeds 1 inch deep (¾ inch deep for super sweets) in rows spaced 2 to 3 feet apart. Then water well. Thin seedlings to a foot apart when they're 6 inches tall.

Don't plant just a few long, skinny rows or you won't get much corn. For kernels to form on the ears, pollen must drop from the tassels atop the plants to the silks below. One pollen grain falling onto one silk produces one kernel. But a stiff wind can send the pollen from one or two rows flying in a useless direction. So always plant in blocks of at least five rows deep to ensure pollination.

Never let super sweet corn cross-pollinate with other sweet corn or the kernels of both will be tough and starchy. Isolate super sweets from other types either by distance (at least 200 feet away) or by time (staggering plantings so that different types don't form tassels at the same time). However, it's okay to plant sugary enhanced types near regular sweet corn.

Corn has a hefty appetite. Fertilize plants when they're 8 inches tall and again when they're 18 inches. Apply a half cup of slow-release 10-14-10 fertilizer per 10 feet of row each time. Regular watering is critical, too, especially during tasseling. Drought-stressed plants produce puny ears with missing kernels that look a lot like the teeth of Alfred E. Neuman.

How much sweet corn should you plant? Some books say 15 feet of row for each person is enough. My estimation is a little different. I say, go out in the garden and start planting. I'll yell when it's time to stop.

Steve Bender

(For sources turn to pages 250–251.)

Tassels atop the corn stalks produce wind-borne pollen. Regular watering is crucial during tasseling to produce a good crop.

Each silk that is pollinated produces a kernel. To foil corn earworms, place about a teaspoon of mineral oil on the tips of each ear when the silks appear.

FLOWERS
tell the story

Margaret Moseley's life is chronicled in her garden. Caring for her living history helps keep her young.

Some people capture memories in photos. Others preserve them on video. Margaret Moseley grows her memories in a garden filled with plants handed down by generous gardeners. From a comfortable chair in her sunroom, she says, "I think I can name every friend I have just by looking out there."

But this energetic octogenarian seldom sits inside for long. Every day she faithfully makes the rounds of her spacious garden, watering, weeding, planting, fertilizing, and deadheading. Her only concession to age is letting someone else cut the grass.

It was 35 years ago that Margaret and Lamar Moseley built their house in the country in Decatur, Georgia. Formerly an old cotton plantation, the land was choked with weeds. "There was nothing but pine trees, honeysuckle, and blackberry vines," she recalls. "You couldn't even walk outside."

BY STEVE BENDER
PHOTOGRAPHY VAN CHAPLIN

Then, as the last of her four daughters departed for college, Margaret found herself saddled with time. "I started to study piano, but I couldn't sit still and stay inside," she says. "I wanted outside. So I started gardening and it just grew." She was 52 at the time.

Today, her backyard garden consists of multitudinous island beds connected by wandering grass paths. She gathered many of the rocks that edge the beds during walks through the country. "And if I were going someplace in the car and saw a pile of rocks, I'd stop and pick them up," she adds. A veritable plethora of flowering shrubs, trees, perennials, and bulbs erupts from the beds, showering every season with color. She gets her planting ideas from leafing through gardening magazines and visiting nurseries. "I have every plant I can find," she declares unabashedly. "I have it all."

That's certainly true when it comes to hydrangeas, which bloom here in colors of white, pink, rose, blue, lavender, and deep purple. Her favorite is a lovely white one growing at the foot of the toolshed. "I bought that one many years ago. All the plant tag said was, 'White Hydrangea,' " she remembers. "It's a really good one because it always blooms whether you trim it or not."

As you walk with Margaret through her garden, the memories come with each passing plant. A stunning clump of scarlet Saint Joseph's lilies *(Hippeastrum* x *johnsonii)* dominates one island bed. "The man who gave me that is dying of cancer," she says sadly. "He brought it to me on the top of a garbage can lid 20 years ago." At the rear of the garden, a 50- x 60-foot bed of red poppies originated from a single seedpod. "When I was 12 years old, my next-door neighbor sold bunches of poppies for 35 cents," says Margaret. "After we moved to this house, I brought her out here. She was so happy I was going to have a garden. She must have been 90 then. And I got one poppy plant out of her garden. Now there are millions."

But of all her plants, one stands out in her mind—the gardenia. She has at least a half-dozen kinds, including August Beauty and First Love. Her prize, though, is an unnamed plant she discovered in a cemetery. "About

Thousands of red poppies, started from a single seedpod received decades ago, bloom with larkspur each year. Margaret lets the pods ripen and drop seeds in place into an unmulched bed.

Her ³/₄-acre garden consists of island beds connected by grass paths.

30 years ago, I went to a funeral in the country and this gardenia was blooming in the graveyard," she recalls. "I thought it was so beautiful and fragrant, I picked a twig and rooted it in water." Never damaged since by winter cold, her "cemetery gardenia," now 7 feet high, blooms off-and-on from June through September.

When you're talking with Margaret, it becomes clear Ponce de Leon had it all wrong when he searched for the Fountain of Youth in Florida. He should have looked in a backyard in Decatur. "Some of my friends wonder why I don't give my garden up," she says. "But I couldn't stand living in an apartment or condominium. Gardening is so *exciting*—watching over plants and waiting for them to bloom. That's what gets you outside. There isn't anything like it. I'm 84, and I can't wait to get out there." Coffee cup in hand, she heads out for the morning inspection. ◇

Pink azaleas, strawberry geraniums, and the fading blooms of Lenten roses mark the entry to Margaret's garden in midspring.

Bright pink loos
against a backdr

...and pale pink common rose mallow ...repe myrtles (See page 138.)

June

Checklist for June

EDITOR'S NOTEBOOK

Nothing is more humiliating than writing about gardening for *Southern Living* and having the weediest lawn in the neighborhood. It isn't as if I don't try. I aerate the lawn every spring to reduce compaction and provide oxygen to soil microorganisms. I apply slow-release fertilizer. I put down lime and gypsum to add calcium and adjust the soil pH to optimum levels. I also use a mulching mower to return nitrogen and other essential nutrients to the soil. I apply weed preventers and weed annihilators, and even call the Psychic Network every Friday—all in vain. The ground ivy just laughs at me. The dandelions make rude comments about my mother. But I think I've finally hit upon the answer—radioactive weedkiller. Now my lawn's so thick and green, it positively glows. You should see it at night.

Steve Bender

◀**Birdhouses**—Keep a close watch to make sure that fire ants do not invade nests. Apply a 1-inch-wide band of sticky substance, such as Tree Tanglefoot Pest Barrier, to a post holding a birdhouse to deter ants. Fire ant baits and controls may also be placed at the base of the post.

☐ **Lawns**—It is a good time to patch warm-season lawns such as Zoysia, St. Augustine, improved Bermuda, and centipede with sod of the same type grass. You can also sow seeds of turf-type fescues or cool-season blends to thicken bare or thin areas of a similar type lawn.

☐ **Shade**—Protect new transplants from direct sun for about a week until the roots get settled in their new location. A light layer of pine needles or hay will help, or you can construct a small shelter from a mesh plant tray supported by sticks or dowels. ▶

☐ **Sundials**—To accurately set the time, place the sundial in your garden on the summer solstice, June 21st.

☐ **Vegetables**—String biodegradable twine between two posts, and let vining types of cucumbers, squash, and gourds grow upward. The fruit will be cleaner and more uniform because it does not touch the ground.

☐ **Water**—As the weather gets hot, remember that new additions to your garden will need watering more often than established plants.

PLANT

☐ **Annuals**—Summer flowers such as gomphrena, celosia, zinnias, marigolds, and tithonia set out now will provide you with months of cut flowers and garden color.

☐ **Caladiums**—When buying tubers, select large or jumbo-size ones, and plant now for summer color. Choose a site that is shady or at least protected from afternoon sun. Place the tops of the tubers about an inch below ground, and space them 1 foot apart. Water thoroughly after planting.

◀**Ginger**—One good way to have fresh ginger is to grow your own. It's also a great project for kids. Buy a gingerroot (actually a rhizome) at the grocery store, and barely cover it with soil in a partially shaded location. It will produce a big, very tropical-looking plant within weeks. Then in October you can dig your own gingerroot for cooking.

☐ **Pineapples**—In the Coastal and Tropical South, grocery store pineapples are a good source of plants for the garden. Twist the leafy top off a ripe fruit. Allow it to sit out in the air for several days to dry off the wound at the base. Then plant the top in a sunny location in soil that has been improved with compost. The plant will grow to be 2 to 3 feet tall and wide and will bear fruit in about two years.

PRUNE

☐ **Blueberries**—Southern highbush blueberries *(Vaccinium corymbosum)* ripen in late May and early June, and rabbiteye types *(V. ashei)* ripen later in the month. Prune the old bushes after harvest to remove old, weak, and twiggy canes, leaving the strong, firm ones for next year's growth.

☐ **Caladiums**—When caladiums produce their white, calla-like flowers, it's wise to remove them to encourage the plant to make more leaves. Cut the blooms at the base of the stalk. ▶

☐ **Petunias**—Pinch back plants several inches to prevent long, stringy stems and to encourage repeated bloom through the summer. You may need to pinch a couple more times during the season. Fertilize with timed-release granules, such as 17-17-17, or water with liquid 20-20-20 every other week.

FERTILIZE

☐ **Iron deficiencies**—If new leaves of trees and shrubs in the Coastal and Tropical South are yellow with greenish veins, apply an acidifying fertilizer containing iron or a chelated form of iron, such as one formulated for azaleas and camellias (Vigoro 15-7-7 or Miracid), to the soil. Foliar sprays of iron often do more harm than good by burning the foliage, so they are not recommended.

☐ **Lawns**—Now is an ideal time to fertilize permanent lawn grasses. Consult your county Extension agent or local nursery for information on soil testing. Timed-release fertilizers such as those containing Polyon last longer but are more costly than conventional types. Water lawn areas well immediately after applying fertilizer.

☐ **Tomatoes**—Watch for signs of drought stress on your tomatoes. Apply several inches of mulch in a 3-foot circle around each plant. Water thoroughly every five to seven days. Rather than sprinkle tomatoes, use soaker hoses or drip irrigation at the base of each plant. Feed with Vigoro Tomato and Vegetable Food (12-10-5) or Osmocote Vegetable & Bedding Plant Food (14-14-14) as directed on the label.

☐ **Water gardens**—Apply balanced aquatic fertilizer to pots of water lilies, sedges, iris, and lotus. Place fertilizer tablets directly into pots, according to label directions. Look for tablets where water garden supplies are sold.

CONTROL

☐ **Slugs**—These pests can be especially damaging to hosta foliage, leaving it marred for the entire growing season. To be sure the problem is slugs, look for the dried slime trail on the leaves. Slugs feed at night, so you rarely see them during the day. Although effective, slug bait pellets can be poisonous to children, pets, and birds. You might find a saucer of beer or a sprinkling of fireplace ashes in the mulch around the plants just as effective, cheaper, and safer than commercial baits.

☐ **St. Augustine lawns**—Weeds in St. Augustine lawns may be the result of overwatering. Allow the grass blades to begin to curl slightly before watering. It won't hurt the lawn, and it will inhibit many weed species. If weeds are present, apply a weed-and-feed product recommended specifically for this type of grass, such as Vigoro 30-3-4 with Atrazine or Miracle-Gro Weed and Feed for St. Augustine grass.

☐ **Weeds**—Pull as many invaders out of your flower and shrub beds as you can before they produce seeds (and therefore more weeds). You'll find that they are easier to pull after a rain. If your forecast is dry, use a sprinkler the day before you plan to work in the garden. If you have a lot of weeds to pull, try using a long-handled scuffle or stirrup hoe to save your back and knees.

June notes:

summer's gems

*Peppers are among the easiest plants to grow,
and now's the right time to get them in the ground.*

BY CHARLIE THIGPEN / PHOTOGRAPHY VAN CHAPLIN

W hether you like them hot or sweet, there's a perfect pepper for you. And it takes little effort to produce basket loads of these colorful summer jewels. They come in nearly every shade of the rainbow, including red, orange, yellow, green, and purple. The waxy-looking, showy fruit dangles from shrublike plants in the heat of summer and into the fall. They can brighten a flower border and even look attractive in containers with herbs or low-growing annuals.

Pepper plants need at least six hours of sun and good soil. When first set out, transplants require thorough waterings, but once established and rooted, they are remarkably drought tolerant. Well-drained soil is a must. Because they will not tolerate damp soil, peppers work great in raised beds.

You can grow them from seeds or transplants. Many of the gourmet pepper plants aren't readily available at garden centers or nurseries, so you might have to start them from seeds. They should be started indoors or in a greenhouse six to eight weeks before you intend to set them out in the garden.

If it's late in your area to start seedlings, look for healthy transplants that are short and stocky and don't have blooms or fruit forming. They should have dark green foliage. Lightly brush the tops of the plants with your hands. If white flying insects appear, the plants are probably infested with whiteflies.

Space peppers 18 to 24 inches apart in rows that are 2 to 3 feet apart. Set bamboo stakes next to young plants. They will come in handy later in the season as the peppers become top-heavy with fruit. Use twine to loosely tie the plants to the stakes. Mulch, spread around the base of plants, will help keep moisture in and weeds out.

Don't set peppers out too early in the season; they are sensitive to cold. Night temperatures should be above 60 degrees. If put out too early, the plants will wait until temperatures rise and the soil warms before they'll stretch out and flush with foliage.

A light application of liquid feed or a sprinkle of slow-release vegetable food will keep them healthy. Don't overfertilize—this can lead to blossom drop. Overwatering and underwatering can have the same effect, so keep plants evenly moist, especially once they begin to flower.

The small white blooms are a signal that the peppers will soon be forming. The fruit can be harvested once it reaches a usable size. Use a sharp pair

RIGHT: *Sweet banana peppers change from light yellow to orange to red. The extremely hot habaneros start out green then turn a pumpkiny-orange.*
BELOW: *When allowed to fully ripen, California Wonder bells turn crimson. This makes them sweeter in flavor and higher in vitamins A and C.*

of clippers or a knife to remove it from the stem. When picking hot peppers, such as jalapeño or habanero, you might want to wear gloves. Never rub your eyes when picking or chopping these fiery fruits.

Some of the sweet peppers, such as bell and banana peppers, will change colors when left on the plants. These mature peppers, much sweeter in flavor, are higher in vitamins A and C. However, if you let peppers mature, the plant will not produce many new fruits. So set out a few extra plants if you want fully ripened fruit.

Peppers have few pests, but tender young plants can be inviting to aphids. Control aphids by spraying plants with SunSpray, an ultralight horticultural oil that smothers the tiny insects.

Sweet peppers sometimes slow down their fruit production during the height of summer when temperatures can climb into the 90s, but they will resume production as soon as the days cool down. Hot peppers are more tolerant of the heat, producing steadily throughout the summer. Peppers can get sun scald, but most healthy plants have lots of foliage to help protect the fruit. In extremely hot climates, you should set the plants in partial shade.

One of the biggest difficulties in growing peppers is trying to decide which ones to grow. Sweet peppers are extremely tasty and can brighten up any summer dish.

If you like the hot ones, be careful where you plant them in your garden. Small children find brightly colored fruit irresistible, and these peppers can easily burn their tender skin.

If you don't like the taste of peppers you may want to grow a few anyway. Their beauty in the garden is unmatched, making them a great choice for ornamental purposes. This summer, don't forget to plant a peck of peppers. ◇

Not Your Mother's Abelia

CHINESE ABELIA
At a Glance

Light: full sun
Soil: well drained
Size: 5 to 7 feet unpruned
Foliage: green, deciduous
Flowers: white, fragrant; June through September; a butterfly favorite

Glossy abelia is a garden staple, enduring for decades. Although this familiar abelia *(Abelia grandiflora)* never stops traffic with its small white flowers, it is rarely without blooms from late spring through fall.

As strange as it may seem, gardeners are rediscovering one of the hybrid's parents, Chinese abelia *(A. chinensis)*. While glossy abelia's flowers are sprinkled along its new growth, Chinese abelia produces big clusters on the tips of its branches. The white petals backed by pink sepals lend the plant a familiar look, but the fist of flowers at the tip of each branch gives this abelia greater impact. Left on its own, it will grow arching stems 5 to 7 feet in height. However, you can shape it into a smaller and more compact shrub.

"You need to prune them pretty hard in March," says Ginny Gregory, head horticulturist at Fearrington Village in Pittsboro, North Carolina. "Cutting them back to 12 to 15 inches in height will remove most of their growth, but they'll sprout again and bloom on their new shoots."

These shrubs need full sun and well-drained soil. Ginny suggests giving them a background to silhouette the blooms, and in marginal climates, putting them on the sunny side of a building or hedge.

Although less hardy than its offspring, Chinese abelia is dependable in the Lower and Coastal South. In colder areas, it will come through mild winters unscathed. After extremely cold ones some gardeners find it will sprout in spring like a perennial, while others have had it killed by long freezes in the teens.

But no matter where you plant it, you are in for a summer surprise. In addition to being fragrant, Chinese abelia is a butterfly magnet. The bonus of these colorful creatures makes this shrub a summer must.

Linda C. Askey

(For sources turn to pages 250–251.)

PHOTOGRAPHS: VAN CHAPLIN

ABOVE: *A hard pruning in March results in a compact shrub full of flowers in summer.* **INSET:** *Unlike the sprinkling of flowers produced by the more familiar glossy abelia, Chinese abelia bears clusters at the tip of every branch.*

Parking Made Easy

When you live on a busy street, getting people to the front door isn't always a matter of convenience. Sometimes it's a matter of survival. And when your home sits on a small corner lot, like this one in Dallas, problems multiply. Guests who would park on either street worried about fast-moving cars ramming them from behind.

Landscape architect Rosa Finsley of King's Creek Landscaping in Cedar Hill, Texas, had the answer. The parking area she designed allows visitors to pull up to the front of the house from both streets. It's also spacious enough that they needn't be concerned about getting blocked by someone pulling in behind.

Many parking areas are purely functional with little thought given to aesthetics. But Rosa employed a couple of simple, straightforward tricks to make this one an asset. First, she stained the concrete gray. This not only complements the color of the house but also reduces glare. Second, she bordered the area with a mixed planting of easy-to-maintain ground cover, shrubs, and flowers. The planting contributes seasonal color and visually softens the paving. Moreover, it incorporates the parking area into the overall design.

Large houses on little lots often make for little privacy. Rosa countered this by planting a screen of yaupons, other hollies, and small trees to the left side of the front steps. Together with the flowers and shrubs on the opposite side, these plants define the entry and voice a silent welcome. And welcome is just how visitors feel as soon as they park their cars.   *Steve Bender*

Cars can enter and exit the parking area from either the front or the side street bordering this corner lot. Wrapping the paving with a lush planting of shrubs, ground cover, and flowers visually softens the concrete while also defining the entrance.

French hollyhocks are framed by white flowering tobacco and purple butterfly bush at the New Orleans Botanical Garden at City Park.

Vive le French Hollyhock

This is the hollyhock with a difference, a petite long-bloomer that adds a debonair touch to any garden. Its flowers of pale lilac striped with dark mauve are tucked in above every leaf, resembling boutonnieres in a row of buttonholes.

French hollyhock (*Malva sylvestris* Zebrina) grows to a modest 2 or 3 feet high and blends charmingly with other annuals and perennials in the garden. This useful little plant reseeds energetically and offers multiseason value. Its bright blossoms present a charming contrast to the broad foliage throughout the summer months. In winter, barring a hard freeze, the distinctive clumps of deeply lobed leaves stay vivid green, giving a look of lushness to otherwise barren months.

French hollyhock is a traditional Southern pass-along plant with a place in both formal borders and casual cottage gardens. It's a particular favorite of Arkansas gardener Nancy Porter, who grows it at her home just outside Little Rock.

"They reseed all over the place; that's why I love them," she says. "I like a natural-looking garden—helter-skelter—I don't like things all lined up. I've grown French hollyhocks probably 20 years. I ordered seeds from a catalog, just because I thought they looked pretty. Once I had them going, they stayed.

"They hop and skip all over the garden, wherever the seeds fall, even in the paths," Nancy explains. "If I notice them before the taproot gets too deep, I can move them where I want. If they get too big, they don't transplant as well, and I have to just pull them up. But I have so many I can easily spare a few. They bloom just about all summer, because different ones come on at different stages, all over the garden. I have a lot better luck with them than I do with regular hollyhocks. They really are beautiful and very easy to grow."

While French hollyhocks don't live very long (only a year or two), as old plants die, new ones come up. They are more resistant to rust, spider mites, and leaf miners than are the taller hollyhocks and are even quite tolerant of alkaline soils. As a result, this versatile and persistent flower is welcomed as a desirable addition to gardens everywhere.

Liz Druitt

(For sources turn to pages 250–251.)

FRENCH HOLLYHOCK
At a Glance

Range: thrives in all but Tropical South

Light: full sun to light afternoon shade

Soil: not choosy—may actually flower best in poor, well-drained soil

Moisture: tolerates drought but flourishes with a weekly watering

Bloom season: late spring through early summer, continuing sporadically into fall

Propagate: by seeds or cuttings

PHOTOGRAPHS: JEAN ALLSOPP

A Family Garden

*Durant Bauersfeld
started a garden
as a way to lessen
stress in her life.
Ten years later, a
beautiful backyard is
an added bonus.*

I have a confession to make. I'm not a garden editor. Granted I write for *Southern Living,* but my specialty is homes not plants, flowers, or recipes. But that's not to say I can't truly appreciate a lovely landscape or a delicious meal—I do.

When photographer Jean Allsopp and I were in Virginia on a homes assignment, she suggested a little detour to visit a garden. Off we headed to Annapolis to check out the collaborative efforts of the Bauersfeld family: Durant, Harry, and their two daughters, Larkin and Ashton.

Jean had spoken to Durant, who said her New Dawn roses were about to bloom. The roses were right on schedule, and we weren't disappointed. In fact, the entire garden proved to be just as impressive as the gracious rose-covered arbor that welcomes visitors.

For a brief moment, I had a fantasy that I could have a garden like Durant's. I already had a little arbor in my backyard that bloomed with wisteria in spring. In my mind, I figured I could go to a local nursery, buy one of these New Dawn roses, and by summer's end have a backyard that would resemble hers.

I told Durant about my plans, and then I asked her to tell me her secret. She ever-so tactfully informed me that this lovely little hobby started more than 10 years ago with four truckloads of dirt and sand and the operation of heavy equipment. I quickly came to my senses.

The rear garden is not large, and there are neighboring houses positioned along both the sides and behind the Bauersfeld home. Landscape designer Stratton Semmes developed a thoughtful landscape plan. Then Durant and Harry set out to turn the small space into an attractive, creative, and comfortable garden.

A picket fence delineates the garden's straightforward layout, which consists of a gently rounded lawn and deep beds lining the perimeter. Harry, an engineer, designs and builds the garden structures and leaves the plants to his wife.

Durant's skillful plant selection creates colorful and lush beds that make the most of the compact space. The level, grassy lawn has a bonus: it makes it easy for their wheelchair-bound daughter, Larkin, to accompany her mother as she works in the garden.

Over the years, Durant has retained the basic bones of the garden while constantly changing and adding new flowers. She has at least 10 different clematis on arbors, fences, and one that's even climbing up into a tree. "And I've just ordered three more," she adds. "That's the fun of a garden."

Lynn Nesmith

Facing the street, the arbor offers a glimpse of wonderful things to come. Durant doesn't play favorites with her flowers, but she does confess a bias to clematis, especially in bold jewel tones.

A SECOND OPINION

Because I don't have a green thumb, I asked a real garden editor and rose expert, Liz Druitt, to offer a few tips on New Dawn. Of course, I agreed to help with color options next time she paints her home.

New Dawn is a lovely, repeat-blooming climbing rose that has been popular in gardens since its introduction in 1930. It will tolerate a wide range of soils and growing conditions, performing well from the Coastal to Upper South.

The long canes can reach up to 20 feet, so plan on training them by fastening them down to a structure, especially if the rose is growing where people will pass nearby. Annual care involves training new canes and pruning out dead wood. Climbing roses shouldn't be cut back, but can be thinned of older canes if they get too bulky. New Dawn is also great for naturalizing at the edge of a meadow or growing into a tree.

Comfortable seating and tall trellises punctuate the garden's lush curving beds.

Carefree Combination

French hydrangeas and daylilies are a simple and showy summer pair.

There's a dynamic duo in the garden and it's not Batman and Robin. This pair makes a strong showing each summer. One is a shrub, and the other is a perennial. I can count on them to save the day when some of my spring-flowering plants are beginning to fade. Try planting French hydrangeas and daylilies together for a great look.

These two plants perform well in a moist, fertile, well-drained site. Daylilies will take full sun but also flourish in filtered light. Hydrangeas do best when protected from the western sun. When planted around large deciduous trees or beneath tall pines where they receive filtered light, both plants thrive.

This combination looks great in a flower border or in a naturalized area. The hydrangeas can be used on the back side of the border. They may grow 4 to 6 feet high in a mounding form, making a bushy backdrop. The daylilies look nice as a mid-range planting in the center of the border. When creating a naturalized area, plant a large grouping of hydrangeas; then set out daylilies in the foreground. Because daylilies multiply rapidly, it doesn't take many to fill up a bed quickly. (They should be divided about every five years to prevent overcrowding.)

Neither of these plants is terribly fussy once established. The hydrangeas perform better if irrigated during dry summer periods. There's no doubt when they need water. Their large leaves wilt as the shallow roots get thirsty. For healthy hydrangeas, keep them evenly moist and don't let them dry out for extended periods.

The large flower clusters of French hydrangeas hold their blue color for several months. The long blooming period allows the daylilies some overlap time, so they will flower in unison with the hydrangeas. There are so many different selections of daylilies, you can choose varieties that bloom early and ones that bloom late for a staggered show. Many new selections are bred to bloom a second time, so you get flowers throughout the summer. Daylilies are readily available at most nurseries, and you can often buy them in bloom from a roadside mom-and-pop grower.

The orange and yellow daylilies in my garden provide a striking contrast to blue hydrangeas, but you can choose the color combination you like for your own yard. Whatever the choice, this duo can't be beat for pleasing summertime blooms. *Charlie Thigpen*

Gazing globes ranging from 3 to 5 inches are interesting additions to a small water garden. Choose colors to complement your water plants.

Bubbles of Color

Set atop a pedestal, a gazing globe will reflect the world around it in its mirrored, spherical surface. Lately these ornaments have reclaimed a place in the hearts of gardeners after being banished for decades as the very essence of tacky. But today they rarely keep a solitary vigil at the center of a garden as they did in times past. They are more likely to work as a multi-colored pack. And with the growing enthusiasm for water gardens across the South, it was only a matter of time before we launched these mirrored orbs upon the glassy water.

One difficulty with floating gazing globes is just that—they float and move around, clustering against each other and a rocky edge with only the slightest push from the breeze. Second only to the sound of a fingernail on a blackboard is the chink of glass upon glass or stone. In addition, handblown globes are not evenly weighted and may even turn stem side up. That would take the mystery out of these colorful bubbles in the garden pool.

Solve the problem by weighing them down. With a few items from the hardware store, you can fashion a watertight remedy (see photo at right).
Linda C. Askey

Prevent your gazing globes from colliding by placing an eyebolt in each open stem where the glass was blown, and sealing it in place with silicone. Then use nylon cord to fasten a brass ring to each bolt. This will slow their drift, but allow enough movement to make the scene interesting.

Playful Potted Garden

Summertime should be casual and fun. Containers overflowing with color fit right in with that laid-back attitude. These potted gardens add that ambience to places where digging is not an option.

We started our collection with galvanized buckets—two round and one oval. When choosing your own containers, remember it's easy to arrange odd numbers and different sizes. We painted the pails strong colors to complement our flower choices. That way, the brightly hued containers became part of the overall scheme instead of invisible vessels.

Who says container gardens have to be stuffy and formal? Get creative with fanciful pots and bold colors.

UP ON FEET

Elevating the pots serves both functional and decorative purposes. A container sitting directly on a flat surface may have drainage problems. Lifting it slightly allows water to escape easily. This also helps air to circulate underneath, keeping the temperature of the container cooler. And metal—even galvanized—can leave behind a rusty ring when set directly on a deck or patio.

From a decorative aspect, pot feet are an opportunity for amusement. We tried wooden drapery finials and copper plumbing floats. The finials were painted to match the containers. The round pots each have three feet placed in a triangle pattern; the oval container requires four supports.

To attach the finials, use a nail and hammer to punch holes in the bucket bottom, and insert the finials' screws through the openings. Inside, thread a small piece of wood onto each

BY ELLEN RILEY / PHOTOGRAPHY VAN CHAPLIN

LEFT: *Hardware stores offer all sorts of materials to create easy and amusing containers.* INSET: *You can bring containers to their feet using drapery finials and copper floats.*

screw to keep the finial firmly attached. The copper floats are fastened in a similar way; punch holes in the container, and insert washers and screws from inside the pot to the outside. The floats easily thread onto the screws.

Make additional holes in the container bottoms for adequate drainage. Fill containers with good-quality, moist potting soil before planting.

FRIENDLY FLOWERS

Our bloom choices work well in both sun and light shade. Red New Guinea impatiens, purple petunias, Marine heliotrope *(Heliotropium arborescens* Marine), and wishbone flower *(Torenia fournieri)* provide rich color. To add sparkle to these vibrant shades, lime-green licorice plant *(Helichrysum petiolare* Limelight), grass-like variegated Japanese sweet flag *(Acorus gramineus* Ogon), green-and-gold Swedish ivy *(Plectranthus coleoides* Marginatus), and chartreuse creeping jenny *(Lysimachia nummularia* Aurea), were added to the arrangement. In the small yellow container, asparagus fern and petunias proved a good mix.

The planters require water on a daily basis if placed in full sun. In light shade, watering every other day should be sufficient. To keep flowers abundant, feed with a water-soluble liquid such as 15-30-15 once a week. Always water the pots with clear water prior to fertilizer application. As blossoms fade, remove the old, so new ones can form. With a little grooming, you'll have fabulous flowers in fun containers throughout the summer. ◇

(For sources turn to pages 250–251.)

Backyard Paradise

It took a windstorm in Lakenheath, England, near London, to jump-start Jan King's gardening instincts, but once she started digging and got that first layer of dirt under her fingernails, she was hooked for life. Jan's backyard in North Little Rock comes to life with the riot of color and blooming abandon of a cottage garden. Her inspiration was the real thing, a genuine English cottage garden.

"My husband, Peter, was an Air Force pilot, and we were stationed in Lakenheath," she recalls. "One day a windstorm blew down the fence around the yard next to ours and revealed a beautiful English garden. I thought to myself, 'I'd like that.' Ten years later, I have it—in Arkansas."

Unfortunately, the soil of Arkansas and England are not only thousands of miles apart, but also of a completely different makeup. "Our soil is extremely rocky," Jan says. Her one wish in life is to have a yard where she can sink a shovel into the ground. If the rocky soil wasn't enough of a challenge, the backyard sloped—not just in one direction, but in two. "We could have overcome the slopes, if they were the only problem, but the rocky soil was impossible. So, we decided to build up."

Jan and Peter created 17 raised beds, which sprout everything from tomatoes to clematis, from joe-pye weed to coreopsis. The beds are 8 feet wide, bordered with pressure-treated 4 x 4s. It took two years and three (10-cubic-foot) dump trucks loaded down with fill dirt to lay the base for the garden's black gold. Today, after nine years of faithful composting and soil amending, Jan's rocky Arkansas backyard boasts soil worthy of Kew Gardens in England.

Rich soil is important in raised-bed gardening. Jan has learned that even though the beds drain well (which is what raised beds are supposed to do), the nutrients tend to wash away too. Her fertilizing strategy lies in her two-bin composter. "I just put down a little compost around the plants in spring, before everything starts popping up," she says.

Once the compost is down and the plants are up, Jan relies on an elaborate labyrinth of soaker hoses to keep the heat of summer from sizzling her season-long show of color. "My first summer I set all of my hoses on timers, and I started killing things," she laughs.

"It was calling for 97 degrees and drought, so I set the timers to come on twice a week. The next thing you know, it rained and turned cool, and I lost plants." Today she turns on her watering system manually, watering once a week for three hours. "With soaker hoses, you need to water for longer periods of time," she says.

ABOVE: *The gates to Jan's corner of Arkansas suburbia open to reveal a cottage garden that's filled with a tangle of textures and colors from spring until frost.*
LEFT: *Jan and Maggie, her terrier, spend most of their time in the backyard garden. Jan chases down weeds; Maggie tracks squirrels.*

Designing plantings for raised beds is like creating color and texture combinations in any other garden, with two exceptions. "In a raised bed, space is limited," Jan stresses, "so you need to be careful when planting things that like to spread." She contains all of her favorite wandering plants—mints and bee balm, for instance—by planting them in plastic pots and burying the pots rim-deep. "It sure beats digging up mint four times in one summer!" she says.

The second thing to consider with raised beds is softening their harsh edges and corners. Jan's collection of plants that tumble over the timbers comes straight from the school of trial and error. "I've planted things that are natural cascaders, and then I've discovered other flowers that trail beautifully," she says. Her favorites include blue phlox, thymes, lamb's-ears, speedwells, soapwort, nierembergia, germanders, yarrow, and goldentuft alyssum (Aurinia saxatilis).

With the edges softened in a tumble of blooming beauty, the rest of Jan's beds flower in a delightful confusion of colors, scents, and textures. Like all gardeners, she has a hard time choosing favorite flowers,

but she will admit to adoring larkspur in spring, blackberry lilies in early summer, and herbs and scented geraniums all season long.

On any given day, you can find a sign tacked on Jan's front door that says, "I'm in the garden." With the charm of an English countryside tucked into her suburban backyard, it's no wonder she prefers the garden to the house. *Julie A. Martens*

TOP: *Raised beds sprout from the sloping yard, taming the incline with 8-foot-wide terraces.* ABOVE: *In this tiny patch of paradise, the stillness of morning is punctuated only by birdsong and the soft buzzing of bumblebees.*

Pulling It All Together

LEFT: *Crepe myrtle and loosestrife color-coordinate with bright pink blooms. Pale pink common rose mallow prevents monotony by interjecting a different shade of pink and a contrasting flower form.* BELOW: *A monochromatic color scheme is pure repetition.*

Using colors repeatedly gives a garden unity, making pretty pictures out of assorted plants and pulling distant beds together in visual harmony. It can mean the difference between "growing flowers" and "having a garden."

Repetition can be accomplished in several ways. First, pick up the dominant color already existing in a garden and repeat it elsewhere. In the photo above we see the use of magenta, pulled from the summer canopy of a crepe myrtle and repeated in the beds. It's much the same as a woman having shoes and handbag that match a portion of the dress she is wearing. The repetition makes her outfit an ensemble.

Another way to use repetition is to repeat the same color periodically in a bed. For example, in the bed backed by a weathered picket fence (shown at right), red flowers of the rose on the fence repeat the red in the foreground from Texas sage *(Salvia coccinea)*. Red was an excellent choice for accent and repetition. Otherwise the visually quiet blue of Indigo Spires salvia and white narrowleaf zinnia would recede into the leafy green background.

A third way to unify a garden through repetition is to choose a color scheme and repeat

it throughout the bed for a monochromatic look. The most common example of this is a white garden where white flowers and silver foliage echo each other for a soothing effect (see top right photo). The same can be accomplished by choosing yellow flowers and golden foliage or blue flowers and blue-gray foliage. You can also celebrate the warm colors (yellow, orange, and red) or the cool colors (blue, purple, and lavender) in color-themed plantings.   *Linda C. Askey*

ABOVE: *The repetition of red—a red rose on the picket fence and the red Texas sage—ignites this otherwise quiet border of blue Indigo Spires salvia and white narrowleaf zinnias.*

Best Bets for Color

Gardeners talk about annuals and perennials as exclusive and separate groups, but some plants can be either, depending on your climate. Cold winters mean some tender perennials must be treated as annuals and replanted each spring, but all of the following give great color whether they have been established for years or are newly planted each spring.

Melampodium, butter daisy

(Melampodium paludosum)

A carefree annual for sunny places, melampodium produces yellow flowers on a 1- to 2-foot plant from summer into fall. It often reseeds in the border and is one of the easiest of all color plants.

Narrowleaf zinnia

(Zinnia angustifolia)

The only annual even easier than melampodium, these little orange, white, or yellow flowers produce throughout the growing season. They are perfect for edging a bed or for planting in containers.

Flamingo Feather celosia

(Celosia spicata Flamingo Feather)

Fun, unusual, and dramatic, this annual celosia is gracefully tall (to 4 feet) and topped with feathery pink flower spikes; Flamingo Purple sports purple spikes. It gives long-lasting garden color from summer to fall and dries well for indoor arrangements. It's easy to grow from seeds sown directly in the ground.

Pincushion flower

(Scabiosa sp.)

Butterfly Blue is the favorite selection for Southern garden climates, and it's one of the best for cut flowers. It produces powder blue flowers from summer through frost if the plant is kept deadheaded. It blooms in sun to half shade. Treat it as a tender perennial.

PHOTOGRAPHS: VAN CHAPLIN

ABOVE: *Goodness Grows veronica sends up spikes of blue.*
LEFT: *The little blooms of narrow-leaf zinnia are easy to grow.*

Mexican heather

(Cuphea hyssopifolia)

Glossy leaves make a bright green backdrop for tiny pink, purple, or white flowers throughout the season. Mexican heather gives any garden a dressy look. Treat it as an annual.

Goodness Grows veronica

(Veronica alpina Goodness Grows)

This classic perennial sends up blue flowers in such profusion that you might think it is an annual. In a border, the blue helps to blend other colors. Remove spent flower stalks to promote blooming from late spring until frost.

Moonbeam coreopsis

(Coreopsis verticillata Moonbeam)

The pale yellow flowers on an 18- to 24-inch mound of lacy foliage may look delicate, but they are reliable for color even with drought and neglect. Moonbeam and the more compact, darker yellow Zagreb are serious bloomers from late spring until autumn. Treat them as tender perennials.

Brazilian sage

(Salvia guaranitica)

This tall sage (3 to 5 feet) will bloom in sun or part shade with spikes of deep blue flowers from summer to fall. A wide range of selections include pale blue Argentina Skies, bicolor Black and Blue, and deep violet Purple Majesty. Plant several colors together for a visual delight and to draw butterflies. Treat Brazilian sage as a tender perennial.

Goldsturm rudbeckia

(Rudbeckia fulgida sullivantii Goldsturm)

The longest-blooming perennial black-eyed Susan for the South, Goldsturm produces rich yellow daisy-like flowers with dark brown centers throughout the entire summer if kept deadheaded. Plant it for a strong statement in the color border and for a great cut flower.

Tall verbena

(Verbena bonariensis)

A tall airy plant with spikes of purple flowers, this verbena makes a great vertical accent and has a long bloom season. Treat it as an annual for the Upper South.

Liz Druitt

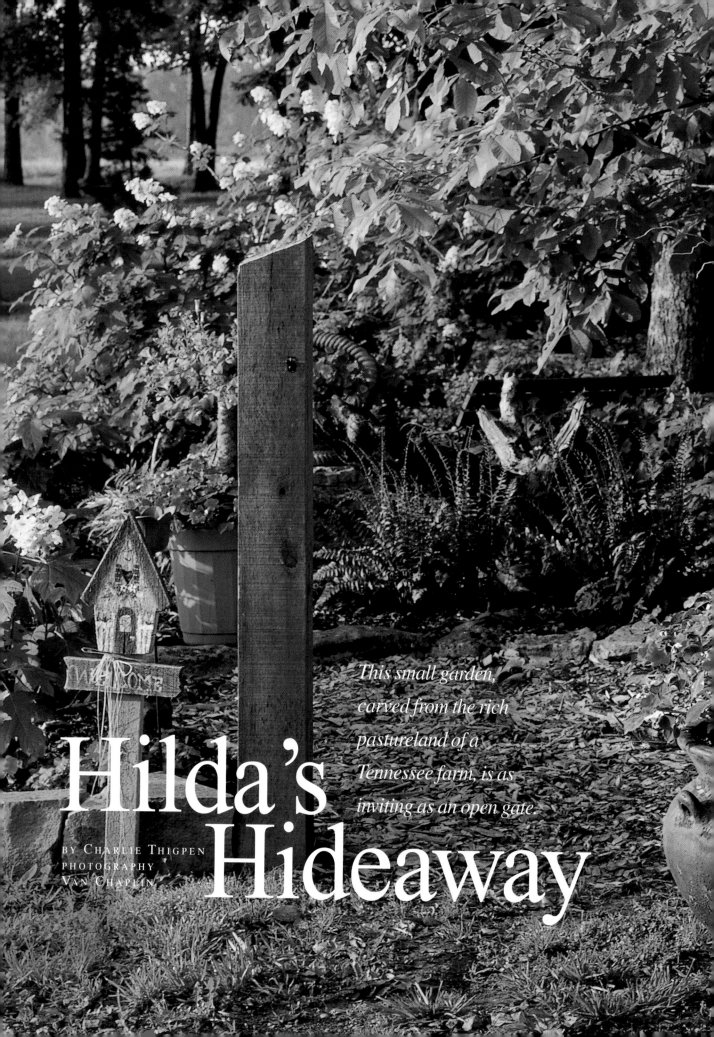

*This small garden,
carved from the rich
pastureland of a
Tennessee farm, is as
inviting as an open gate.*

Hilda's Hideaway

BY CHARLIE THIGPEN
PHOTOGRAPHY
VAN CHAPLIN

WELCOME

Last year a reader wrote to us about an interesting garden near Murphreesboro, Tennessee, she had seen on a tour. She thought we might want to take a look. It didn't hurt that the owner, Hilda Bolin, was said to be a big fan of *Southern Living* magazine. I called Hilda and told her I was going to be in the area soon and asked if I could stop by.

A few days later, I get to the Bolins' property and drive through the gates. All I can see are cows and pastureland. Then I notice a thick cluster of trees on, truly, the back 40. A cabin surrounded by ferns and flowers materializes in a grove of hardwoods. Dappled light filters through a canopy of branches, making the setting look cool on the hot summer day. The rays of light that weave through the numerous limbs are like spotlights shining on the garden floor.

Hilda steps out of the rustic home and into the yard. Her wide smile is definitely that of an accomplished gardener who's getting ready to show off her handiwork. With introductions behind us, we set off along the mulched paths.

Moss-covered logs, carefully placed along the paths, lend a sculptural look to the garden.

Flower arrangements are strategically placed on the gates and tabletops. She says she always puts flowers out when guests are coming—and many guests flock to the garden in the spring and summer. Garden clubs tour the yard, and two of Hilda's children were married in this delightful setting.

I comment on the beautiful arrangements and ask if she's had any formal training in flower arranging. Hilda replies, "I don't arrange flowers. I just cut them, set them in a basket or container, and they arrange themselves." She refuses to let anything become complicated.

Rocks, gathered from around the farm, edge the bark chip paths that weave through the garden. There are also huge boulders set around the front yard. One of her favorites is a massive gray boulder shaped like a whale. She tells me that her husband, Wendell, maneuvered the giant rock into place with a bulldozer. Farm manager Paul Young works on the Bolin farm during the day and occasionally helps Hilda with some of the heavy gardening work in the afternoons. Together they

TOP: *Farm manager Paul Young and owner Hilda Bolin wear the smiles of proud gardeners. Here they stand next to the flowering butterfly garden.* ABOVE: *A galvanized watering pail comes to life with daylilies, hydrangeas, Queen Anne's lace, and the veiny foliage of hardy begonias.*

Hilda and Wendell Bolin have a great cabin on the back side of their farm. Over the past 13 years, Hilda has worked to surround the cabin with beauty. Sweeps of impatiens add bright color to the shade.

have selected interesting-looking logs from the woods behind the house and tucked them along the pathways. Many of these moss-covered pieces of wood are crooked and twisted, creating naturally sculpted forms. Ferns unfurl around the wood and rock, making areas in the front look like a woodsy fern glade.

Hilda likes to plant impatiens around the front yard to add color. Big sweeps of these shade lovers make quite an impact in their dark confines. Various selections of large-leaved hostas look great mixed with ferns. Shrubs such as hydrangea, mahonia, and nandina create a nice backdrop for annuals and perennials.

As I follow Hilda around, her excitement grows as she tells stories about plants and the garden. Many of the plants were dug from her childhood home.

The garden that sweeps around the front of the house is now brimming with plants of all shapes and sizes. It's

> Plants are a lot like people. Some are real fussy, while others are easy and just kind of take care of themselves.
>
> —*Hilda Bolin*

constantly maintained during the growing season, but Hilda is now putting her efforts into a butterfly garden located on the back side of her house.

The back garden is very sunny and quite different from the shady one in front. The sunny site allows Hilda to grow sun lovers, such as butterfly bush, lantana, blue salvia, and loosestrife, that attract butterflies.

Hilda is a natural when it comes to gardening. She doesn't consider it work; it's more of a love. "Plants are a lot like people," she tells me. "Some are real fussy, while others are easy and just kind of take care of themselves." She says at this stage of her life she is more likely to set out plants that take care of themselves so she has more time for being a grandmother to Taylor and Caitlyn.

I'm delighted to have met Hilda, and I'm sure glad one of our readers took the time to tell us about her. Keep those letters coming, please. ◇

Flowers for the Fourth (See page 152.)

July

Checklist for July

EDITOR'S NOTEBOOK

Long a plague in the Upper South, Japanese beetles have now spread into the Middle and Lower South and are destined to affect every Southern state. What's so bad about them? They're gluttonous little slobs, gobbling the flowers and foliage of roses, althaeas, grape vines, Japanese maples, and dozens of other plants. Some people seek to thwart them by putting out Japanese beetle traps. These devices use two scented lures—a "floral lure" for the females (girls love flowers) and a "sex lure" pheromone for the males (guys love girls). Trouble is, people put the traps right next to their flowers. And guy beetles being guys, they decide to stop off for a little dinner before romance. There go all your flowers. So, if you're going to use beetle traps, put them a safe distance from your flowers, and let the party begin.

Steve Bender

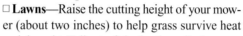

□ **Birdbaths**—Place your birdbath in a shaded spot so the water won't get hot or evaporate as quickly. A large shrub or small tree nearby will encourage use by making a nice shelter for birds before and after their bath.

□ **Butterflies**—A butterfly garden is great for late-summer and fall color. Butterfly weed, blue porterweed, zinnias, pentas, butterfly bush, purple coneflowers, and joe-pye weed are magnets for butterflies. Glossy abelia, althaea, and turk's cap are shrubs also guaranteed to draw them. Many of these plants can still be found in local nurseries and garden centers. ▶

□ **Lawns**—Raise the cutting height of your mower (about two inches) to help grass survive heat and drought. Taller turf shades the soil, slows evaporation, and discourages weeds.

□ **Vegetables**—Continue to pick squash, cucumbers, okra, and pole beans to encourage plants to continue producing. If vegetables are allowed to overmature, the plants will rest. Small, young vegetables are the tastiest anyway. If you are going to be on vacation, ask a friend or neighbor to pick for you.

□ **Water**—Irrigate lawn and garden areas only when they show signs of moisture stress, such as wilting or curling of foliage, or for lawn areas, when footprints remain in the grass. A shallow trench around plants will help capture irrigation and rain and encourage water to soak into the soil. ▶

◀ **Fennel**—Although originally considered an herb, bronze fennel has proved its worth as a perennial. Lacy foliage and tall, long-lasting flowers make it a great addition to the back of the border. Once established, it will yield flowers for arrangements as well as flavorful foliage for cooking.

□ **Flowers**—Narrow-leaf zinnias, purslane, and portulaca can still be set out in the Lower and Coastal South to freshen up the look of hot, dry, hard-to-maintain places, such as between the street and sidewalk.

□ **Flower seeds**—To raise your own transplants of biennials, such as hollyhocks, or perennials, such as purple coneflowers, sow seeds in a pot of seed-starting mix, and then transplant into individual containers when the second set of leaves develop. They'll be ready to place in the garden in October.

□ **Mangoes**—More types of mangoes are ripe this month in the Tropical South than any other time of year. If you're thinking of planting a mango tree, it's a good time to visit roadside stands and taste-test the fruit; then you can purchase your favorite tree at a nursery. Give trees plenty of room, preferably 20 feet in all directions, as they grow very large.

□ **Tomatoes**—Plant now in the Lower, Coastal, and Tropical South for harvest this fall. Purchase new transplants or root cuttings from your favorite selections already in the garden. To start new plants, take 4- to 5-inch tip cuttings, remove the bottom leaves, and bury them up to the base of the top leaves in a container of moist potting soil. Be sure to keep them out of direct sunlight, and water them daily until new growth begins to form. Then plant directly into the garden. New transplants should be partially protected from direct sunlight for the first few weeks.

☐ **Vegetables**—Now is the time to plant okra and Southern peas. Sow seeds in open spaces created by removal of spring crops. Space 2 to 3 inches apart, and thin seedlings to 6 inches apart. Mulch open areas with grass clippings, hay, or similar materials to reduce weed growth, lower soil temperatures, and conserve moisture.

PRUNE

☐ **Annuals**—If your impatiens are getting leggy (too tall with foliage only at the tips of the stems) cut them back by half, and fertilize with a timed-release product such as annual booster 17-17-17. They'll be back in shape in a few weeks, about the time the weather cools down enough to enjoy being in the garden again.

☐ **Crepe myrtles**—Now that crepe myrtles have produced their first big flush of the season, it's a good idea to cut off the faded flower heads so they will bloom again. By diligently dead-heading them, you can have almost continuous bloom until September. For more crepe myrtle pruning tips and information, see page 151. ▶

☐ **Hedges**—This is a good time of year to groom the shrubs in your garden that are pruned into hedges. If it is difficult to keep the hedge line level, use a string stretched between stakes as a guide. Be sure to cut the bottom of the hedge wider than the top so it will get enough light to grow leaves all the way to the ground.

CONTROL

☐ **Citrus**—Dooryard citrus trees are fairly carefree; many people never even spray their trees at all. But one application of light horticultural oil this month will control greasy spot disease (which causes black spots on the leaves and makes them fall prematurely in the winter), aphids, whiteflies, rust mites (which give oranges a dark brown or blackish color in the fall), and sooty mold (which produces a black, powdery coating on the leaves). Spray them either early in the morning or in the evening, being certain to avoid the hottest part of the day.

☐ **Pests**—This time of year, watch annual flowers for problems with aphids (tiny green, gray, or black insects) on the younger leaves. If ladybugs are present, they'll eat the aphids. If not, consider spraying with an insecticidal soap solution.

☐ **Roses**—This is one of the wettest months in much of the Lower and Coastal South. Roses should be sprayed regularly (every 7 to 10 days) with a labeled fungicide, such as Funginex. It's a good idea to stay on top of foliage diseases such as black spot because once they start, they are extremely difficult to control.

July notes:

TIP OF THE MONTH

People in our neighborhood often put out grass clippings in plastic bags to be picked up as trash. We collect these clippings and spread them between our rows of corn, tomatoes, and beans. This keeps the ground moist and also makes it possible to gather produce without making a mess when the ground is muddy.

MRS. ROBERT F. THOMAS
KINGSPORT, TENNESSEE

*Natural stone and
shade-loving plants
tamed this slope into
a welcoming entrance.*

Curbside Character

BEFORE

Several years ago, Editor-At-Large Philip Morris bought an attractive 1920s cottage that needed some improvements. The house looked nice, but it wasn't terribly inviting from the road. No walkway led to the front door, and plants grew sparsely on the shady lot.

After remodeling the interior of the house, Philip added red awnings over the porch and the large front window. He then chose a new blue-green trim color to complement the awning and echo the foliage of the surrounding trees and shrubs.

Before installing any plants, he made plans for a parking strip, steps, and walkway to connect the street to the house. First, he built a small pull off on the edge of the road for on-street parking. A low stacked-stone wall holds the bank where it was cut out for the parking pad.

Stones matching the front wall were set in concrete to edge the walkway and form the steps. Long brick-on-sand landings between the steps afford a smooth transition up the sloped lot. Philip replaced the original concrete steps on the front of the house with brick ones and added a simple iron handrail.

With the house and walks complete, the time came to install a landscape that would enhance the English-style cottage. The thick canopy of a large red

Before, this house was rather discreet, but now it draws attention. The heavy shade and lush plantings make for a cool walk even on a hot summer day.

BY CHARLIE THIGPEN
PHOTOGRAPHY JEAN ALLSOPP

Soft Touch hollies top this pot, and variegated ivy helps soften the rim. The purplish-green, puckered foliage of Catlin's Giant ajuga complements the cool color scheme.

oak, dogwood, and redbud allowed the site to receive only dappled light throughout the day, so Philip selected shade-loving shrubs and perennials to grow underneath the established trees.

Because turf would be hard to maintain under the trees, he chose to eliminate all the grass. Instead, ground covers such as common periwinkle and mondo grass now provide low-growing and low-maintenance sweeps of green year-round. In the spring and summer, hostas and ferns create a tapestry of textured foliage. A mixture of evergreen and deciduous shrubs, such as oakleaf hydrangeas, sasanqua camellias, rhododendrons, and nandinas, adds color with blooms and berries throughout the seasons.

Six strategically placed terra-cotta containers, two flanking each step, signal a grade change. Philip waterproofed the exterior of the pots with Thompson's Water Seal to prevent spalling and cracking that can often occur during winter freezes. He then waterproofed the inside with roofing tar and planted Soft Touch hollies in the center of each pot. As a finishing touch, he tucked variegated ivy around the edges to spill over the rolled rim.

Today, a large annual bed sweeps across the middle of the yard. Philip selects white-blooming plants to stand out against the green shrubs. Impatiens provide billowy mounds of color in the summer. In early autumn, he sets out pansies for fall, winter, and spring blooms. A window box repeats the annual color.

For nighttime visitors, a 92-inch-tall lamppost provides a nice, inviting glow. The large lamp is in scale with the house, and a photo cell automatically turns the three 15-watt lights on at dusk and off at dawn.

The new on-street parking, walkways, and plantings make this house accessible and attractive. All these improvements have taken time, but the landscaping gives this 1920s cottage new life and a new look. ◇

ADDED FOR STYLE AND FUNCTION

■ Use landings to break up a slope and provide a smooth path to the front door. Place seasonal containers to indicate grade changes.

■ For evening visitors, install either low-voltage lighting near your steps or a yard lamp in proportion to the house.

■ Awnings soften a facade and can transform a hot terrace into a made-in-the-shade retreat.

■ Window boxes add a cottage feel. Remember to add drainage holes to your box and to hang the box slightly away from the house facade to avoid rotting.

■ Don't struggle with turf grasses in shady locations. Plant large masses of ground covers and shrubs that require little sun such as mondo grass, vinca, hostas, hydrangeas, and nandina.

■ Use pine straw as mulch on a sloped lot. Bark mulch floats and washes away during heavy rains.

Crepe Myrtle Pruning Tips

Summer in the South would not be complete without the clusters of lacy blooms that top our beloved crepe myrtles. These carefree trees load up with flowers and rain their ruffled petals like an afternoon shower. Once the flowers are gone, small seedpods form on the tips of the limber branches.

These seedpods are heavier than the flowers, and the added weight causes the limbs to sag. The drooping canopy of the once vase-shaped trees, gives them a weeping characteristic. Clip off the seedpods to help take the heavy burden off the arching stems.

Always use sharp clippers for pruning. If your trees are tall, use pole pruners. Most models come with a saw and a clipping mechanism; a rope activates a cutting blade, which is perfect for pruning hard-to-reach branches. When using pole pruners, avoid power lines. Lopping shears work well cutting intermediate-length limbs.

Make cuts right below the green seedpods, removing only the very tips of the branches. Usually the limbs spring back to their normal upright position once the pods are removed. Many gardeners leave these round seed capsules on the trees thinking they are flowerbuds. The seedpods are bigger than the bloom buds and are also hard and woody.

The removal of seedpods not only raises sagging limbs, but it also encourages more flowers. All the energies used to produce seeds can be directed toward flower production. Trees loaded with seeds can also get too heavy during hard rains; the added weight of water may even break branches.

Give your crepe myrtles a lift this summer by removing the seed clusters. It makes trees look cleaner and flower more, and it will save you from dodging low limbs that droop across the landscape. ◇

LEFT: *The green seedpods cluster on the tips of the crepe myrtles, making their limbs sag from the added weight.* ABOVE: *Clip directly behind the seed clusters and new blooms will quickly appear.*

Fourth of July Flowers

Independence Day stirs the heart with red, white, and blue. While you're planning for the holiday, include a pot of patriotic posies for your table or set one by your front door. Better yet, jazz up your window boxes with stars-and-stripes colors. There are numerous flower combinations to consider, whether you have sun or shade.

FOR SUN

Red geraniums are a nostalgic favorite. Their classic flowers and sturdy foliage provide a substantial starting point for a combination planter. Other sunny choices for this vibrant primary color are Red Hot Sally salvia, with crimson spikes topping out around 12 inches tall, and trumpetlike petunias with a shorter, bushy attitude. Sun-loving red coleus, too, offer vivid foliage and strong texture.

White flower choices abound. White Madness petunias fairly glow in tandem with red and blue companions. White Star zinnia and verbena blooms swell gently over the pot's edges. The frothy flowers of sweet alyssum add a bit of fluff.

Majestic blue is not as plentiful, but these plants prove to be dependable bloomers. Blue Wonder scaevola is a tough perennial that loves the heat. Place it along the edge to cascade with fan-shaped flowers. Blue Victoria salvia will stand tall and salute with spikes of deep blue blossoms. Place it as the tallest flower in your container.

These choices appreciate full sun to light afternoon shade. Place tall selections, such as the salvias or geranium, to provide height in the center or back of the container. Fill in with shorter plants, such as petunias, and then head for the edge with cascading flowers. Purchase plants in full bloom for a last-minute project.

FOR SHADE

If your garden is shady, you can still stick with the red-white-and-blue theme. Plant White Christmas caladium, red and white impatiens, and Blue Bells browallia for a fabulous-looking Fourth of July container. The caladium and browallia provide the tall elements, and the impatiens fill in below. Add green-and-white variegated ivy to drip over the sides of the container.

Flowers always add a festive spark to any occasion, and these summer blossoms are guaranteed to produce a flag-waving display. With these plants you can keep your patriotism growing even after the all-American holiday.
Ellen Riley

PHOTOGRAPHS: JEAN ALLSOPP

ABOVE: *This old bike is a trip down memory lane, decked out in Fourth of July finery. For patriotic fun, we filled the basket with red geraniums, White Star zinnia, and Blue Wonder scaevola.* INSET: *Add a few small flags and your all-American planter is complete.*

WHEN THE FIREWORKS HAVE FADED

If red, white, and blue don't suit your summer color scheme, add yellow or purple and pink flowers to the mix—once the Fourth is over—for a vibrant seasonal collection.

A Honey of a Shrub

PHOTOGRAPHS: VAN CHAPLIN / DESIGN: JEREMY SMEARMAN, PLANTERS NURSERY, ATLANTA

LEFT: *Tucked in among large boulders, boxleaf honeysuckle works as a graceful foil to this massive outcropping.*
ABOVE: *The dense foliage gleams.*

The selection called Baggesen's Gold has a spreading habit, with tiny lime-green leaves cloaking dense, graceful branches. It matures at about 4 feet tall and may be easily contained and kept neat with just a bit of seasonal pruning.

Boxleaf honeysuckle grows well in full sun, and this selection also adapts to a little shade. As light diminishes, though, so will the golden color. Once established, it is fairly drought tolerant. In winter, this shrub is semi-deciduous—losing only a portion of its foliage. The leaves that remain will sport a stunning bronze or plum-colored hue. Be warned: In the Upper South, it's not reliably cold hardy.

Plant boxleaf honeysuckle where a gentle surprise is needed. Placed along a walkway, it will drip over hard edges. In front of dark green shrubs, such as boxwood, it provides a fluffy spray of light. To show off its graceful growth pattern, leave plenty of room for it to spread out and shine. Its growing requirements are refreshingly simple, and it takes only a few shrubs to bring a light, airy quality to your yard.

Look for boxleaf honeysuckle at your local nursery. Your search will be worth the effort. Its grace, texture, and color make this one honey of a shrub. *Ellen Riley*

BOXLEAF HONEYSUCKLE
At a Glance

Light: full sun to light shade
Soil: well drained
Size: Baggesen's Gold matures to 4 feet tall and wide.
Nice To Know: Will tolerate shade, but color may fade.

Boxleaf honeysuckle *(Lonicera nitida)* is one bright beauty. This shrub can bring gentle radiance and soft foliage to otherwise dark and hard places in the landscape.

If you keep up with botanical names, the word *Lonicera* conjures the image of rampantly twining Japanese honeysuckle vines, the ones blessed with small trumpets of fragrant flowers. It's hard to imagine that this graceful shrub—valued for its golden foliage—bears the same name. But in spring, boxleaf honeysuckle's fragrant, tiny, white, tubular blossoms will remind you of its showy cousin's.

Savvy Ways With Succulents

Plants—like fashion and food trends—come in cycles. Back in favor once again, succulents have become plentiful and easy to find. This broad category includes old favorites such as hen and chickens *(Sempervivum* sp.), sedum, and ghost plant *(Graptopetalum* sp.).

Succulents willingly adapt to containers, and their colors and textures provide a springboard for the imagination. Fleshy leaves range in shade from deep black-green to blue-silver to chartreuse. Collect them in a pot that enhances their color and complements the display. Their sculptural qualities will be appreciated up close, so put them in a prominent place.

A well-designed container should have plants with wide, large leaves as well as a combination of round and pointed ones. Succulent foliage may be as small as a pinhead or as large as your hand. Many selections, such as hen

A wide, shallow metal basket allows succulents to creep among themselves and cascade gently over the edge. In summer's hottest months, even these tough plants appreciate some shade from the midday sun.

PHOTOGRAPHS: JEAN ALLSOPP

ABOVE: *A long, narrow cedar box made from fencing is a perfect centerpiece. The succulents stay low, with trailing sedums to soften sides and spill onto the table. Drainage holes in the container bottom assist in the long-term health of the plants.* BELOW, RIGHT: *These succulents were chosen to play off the blue-green glaze on the strawberry pot. Together, they make a dynamic, harmonious display of color and texture.*

and chickens, grow in a tight rosette like a flower. Use all different types of succulents to create beautifully textured containers.

PLANT YOUR POT

Succulents are choosy about one thing—wet feet. Heavy, damp dirt is the kiss of death for this crowd's root system. Start with quality potting soil, and add perlite and sand to the mix. These two amendments will help keep the soil aerated and prevent roots from becoming boggy. A drainage hole in the container is also a must.

Fleshy leaves are tough and require good sunlight to flourish. But even the sturdiest leaves appreciate some protection from summer's searing afternoon rays. Provide succulents a minimum of four hours of direct sunlight. If you live in the Lower South, make sure they get a little light shade in midday.

Water is not a daily requirement for succulents, making them the perfect choice for weekend and vacation homes. In all but the most extreme conditions, they may be content to have a drink about once a week. These plants also have no need for excessive feeding. A light application of water-soluble fertilizer (20-20-20) once a month should be sufficient.

Succulents don't mind crowds, so pack them tightly together. Your container will look well established and lush immediately and will require only maintenance trimming during the growing season. *Ellen Riley*

On a quiet tree-lined street in Georgetown, Texas, a cluster of freestanding structures frames a backyard garden and provides spaces for artistic endeavors, reflection, and just plain relaxing.

A Place To Grow

Ann and Farley Snell have some pretty definite ideas about the future. Farley is appropriately philosophical, musing that "we are going to take time to enjoy each other and our garden." He served as campus chaplain and professor of religion at Southwestern University for more than 25 years, and his prospects for the next stage of life are befitting of the way he's conducted his affairs.

Always the pragmatist, Ann has more ambitious plans. She is leaving a dynamic full-time law practice and admits to being ready for a new challenge. "Right now, I'm not sure what it will be. It might be painting; it might be photography; it might be pottery," she says. "Whatever it is, I know I'll be intense. That's my personality."

You wouldn't expect two such thoughtful individuals to take on a major life change without exploring their options. The Snells had lived in their cozy bungalow near the college since they moved to Georgetown in 1972, and they had no desire to live anywhere else.

LEFT: *The gazebo is the perfect place for Ann and Farley Snell to entertain and enjoy one another's company.*
TOP: *The water sculpture by Austin artist Beverly Penn provides a focal point that complements the garden structures.*

BY LYNN NESMITH / PHOTOGRAPHY SYLVIA MARTIN

ABOVE: *The artist studio, the largest of the three new structures, was positioned to highlight an existing stand of crepe myrtles.* RIGHT: *Using iron furniture designed for outdoors helps blur the distinction between inside and out.*

But Ann and Farley also knew they needed their own spaces when they retired. "Virginia Woolf's *A Room of One's Own* made an impression on both of us years ago," says Farley. "Rather than expand our house, we wanted to encompass the whole property in a renovation." Austin architect Lou Kimball agreed it was a great idea and proposed a series of outbuildings to frame a rear garden.

Lots of clients bring some kind of requirements to the first meeting with their architect. The Snells' list wasn't like any Lou had ever seen. "Every architect dreams of clients like Ann and Farley," says Lou. "They talked about what they enjoyed doing in the yard—

lying on chaise longues and looking at the stars at night, watching the birds, sitting on the deck with a cup of coffee on weekend mornings, entertaining friends outdoors." That's not the typical impetus of a major renovation. But there's nothing typical about Ann and Farley.

The most ambitious structure of the compound is Ann's new artist studio. Tall ceilings, abundant natural light, white walls, scored concrete floors, and open timber trusses enliven the 600-square-foot structure and make it feel much larger than its actual dimensions. Ann keeps the space bright, spartan, and meticulously clean—features that showcase the play of light and throw architectural details into strong relief.

Early 20th-century poet Douglas Malloch wrote, "He who makes a garden works hand-in-hand with God." He could have had Ann and Farley Snell in mind.

ingenious ways. "The proportions of each structure are in keeping with the main house, but each is original in its form," says Lou.

The materials and forms of the buildings are simple—wood framing, concrete floors, asphalt shingles. The French doors, fixed sidelights, and transoms are standard items. The large square window that punctuates the studio's gable end is a fixed tempered pane of glass simply framed with carpenter trim. "These details are more economical than custom windows and doors," says Lou. "When the scale and proportion are right ordinary materials transcend the commonplace."

Although Ann admits she never had time to garden before leaving the full-time practice of law, she knows it has always been in her blood. "My mother had nine siblings, and they all loved the woods, plants, and flowers," says Ann. "I remember an aunt who always kept a shovel in the trunk of her car and would dig up plants and trees along the side of the road."

Now Ann finally has her own garden. The Snells worked with Austin landscape architect Eleanor McKinney to establish a garden that would make the most of the relatively small backyard and also complement the buildings. A combination of paths and landscaped borders defines the garden; perennials, native grasses, and hearty shrubs ensure it looks good year-round. Ann adds annuals for splashes of color. Farley readily admits she's the creative force in the landscape. "I just do the mundane things like mulching, mowing, raking, and digging the holes," he explains.

Don't let Farley's modesty about the menial labors fool you. His status as the garden's philosopher-in-residence is secure. Although he no longer has office hours at the college, he often can be found sitting under the shade of a large oak with a professor or a former student.

Recently, I was lucky enough to spend time with Farley in the garden. Our conversation touched on everything from architecture to love to career to ginger ale to the kinds of clouds Jesus ascended on. It's an afternoon I cherish. ◇

(For sources turn to pages 250–251.)

Farley's private retreat is a study in contrasts. His claim is to a pair of small spaces attached to the garage—a workshop with tools and garden supplies and a smoking/reading room. "They are basically two little caves," says Farley, "but I love my space."

There also needed to be some common ground in the garden to enjoy each other. The octagonal-shaped gazebo happily fills that requirement. Measuring 14 x 14 feet, the structure is crowned with a steeply pitched ceiling that rises to 18 feet. Lou incorporated standard 2 x 4 framing and simple carpenter trim for the screened panels and ceiling details.

There's an appealing sense of elegance to all the new structures in the garden. Lou achieved this refinement, not through expensive custom fixtures, but by using stock elements in the most

medicine
for the soul

Yard artists don't need your approval, but they'd like it.
Purveyors of artwork both weird and wonderful, they put
joy and themselves into their creations.

Benjamin Franklin once wrote, "Beauty and folly are old companions." Being nearly sautéed by lightning while flying a kite may have inspired this particular thought. Yet it aptly applies to a form of garden decoration called "yard art." Is yard art silly or is it sublime? That depends on which side of the fence you happen to be sitting.

The artists in the story may seem way out at first. But listen to their words. You'll realize that in some ways, they're a lot like you—folks who grasp life's joy by expressing themselves in their work. And, boy, do they express.

Contrary to what you might think, whirligigs, pink flamingos, tire planters, and concrete chickens are not the sole province of the rural and working-class South. Actually, they reflect attitudes toward gardening that originated in upper-crust Europe. "Back in the 1800s, every proper Englishman's garden had a folly—some whimsical thing you put there to show your neighbors that you weren't completely buttoned-down," explains garden writer Felder Rushing.

"Buttoned-down" is not a term anyone applies to Felder. His front yard

BY STEVE BENDER
PHOTOGRAPHY
VAN CHAPLIN

ABOVE: *Greg Duke uses salvaged materials and architectural fragments to fashion a variety of birdhouses, like those shown here and on pages 160–161.*

RIGHT: *An old bathtub adorned with glass doorknobs, bottles, and mirror shards; a pink flamingo; and a concrete chicken greet visitors to Felder Rushing's home.*

in Jackson, Mississippi, is a horticultural amusement park, replete with bottle trees, bathtub sculpture, painted tires, steel girder gongs, copper toilet floats drifting lazily across a fishpond, and a model train chugging through zinnias. Some neighbors love his garden. Others move away. But Felder staunchly defends his art. "Anyone with a recycled whiskey barrel planter can't say anything about a person with a recycled tire planter," he asserts. "And anyone who hangs gaudy earrings from holes punched in their ears can't say squat about those of us who hang bottles in our trees."

Greg Duke of Andalusia, Alabama, is more mainstream. He builds birdhouses. But not dime-store-quality birdhouses. No, his handcrafted creations are eagerly sought by high society and plain folks alike. He sells them through garden shops. He also ships from his home. (Check out his Web site www.duke birdhouse.com.) Prices range from $150 to $750 plus shipping. Though his houses do accommodate birds, Greg designs them primarily for display. "I don't build for the birds," he states. "I build for the customer."

Lest you think Greg is too conventional, guess where he secures his raw materials. "I recently bought a 77-year-old school. I've been tearing it down for a year and a half," he says. "That's where I'm getting 90% of my materials. I use the tongue-in-groove lumber for ceilings and walls and old tin for roofs. I take doors apart and build birdhouses out of the panels. This school is so big, I'll probably get 1,000 birdhouses out of it, Lord willing."

You can't help but smile when you arrive at the home of L.V. Hull in Kosciusko, Mississippi. L.V. owns more shoes than Imelda Marcos. Only hers are painted and mounted on stakes.

Displayed among such heirloom plants as golden glow, four-o'clocks, tiger lilies, and old purple phlox are all sorts of gaudily painted articles—tires, TV sets, clocks, hats, plastic flowers, bottles. Colorful wooden signs reveal the rules she lives by: "Be true." "Mind your business." "Jesus is coming to Kosciusko." "If you don't know where you're going, any road will take you there."

L.V. utilizes found and discarded objects. Though you might dismiss her raw materials as junk, she claims other primitive artists in the area compete fiercely for them. "Some folks are like dogs on a haystack," she proclaims. "They can't eat it, but they don't want anybody else to have it."

It doesn't matter what you do, your neighbor is going to talk about you anyway.
Felder Rushing, yard artist, philosopher

ABOVE: *Painted shoes by the hundreds mark the home of L.V. Hull. "Most artists I know went to school," she says. "But you don't go to school for this."*

Her ideas, she believes, are gifts from God. "If they weren't, I couldn't do this," she contends. "I have lots of imagination." Yet she doesn't really care if the population at large understands her work. "In my line of art, people don't know what I'm thinking, and thank God they don't," she declares. "It's good to create something that somebody loves that they don't know what it's about."

Visitors may leave L.V.'s yard scratching their heads, but few leave empty-handed. Plunking down cash for a fanciful shoe, bottle, or whirligig, they rediscover aspects of themselves long suppressed—a childlike innocence, sense of humor, and longing for fun.

"It makes you feel good when you make something that somebody else likes," L.V. explains. "That's some good medicine. You don't need to go to the drugstore to get that."

Yard art may not suit everyone's taste, but who would want that anyway? No one ever established a beachhead by being like everyone else. So tonight, when it's dark and no one is looking, give in to the urge. Stick a bottle tree in your yard. I promise that as soon as the sun rises, no neighbors will ever see you or your garden in quite the same light again. ◇

A Louisiana garden filled with period charm
(See pages 180–183.)

August

Checklist for August

EDITOR'S NOTEBOOK

Admit it—your garden doesn't look that great in August. Don't feel bad. Mine looks worse. Where I live in Alabama, it has already been hot for two solid months. And it's going to stay hot for two months more. I'm burned out, and my plants are burned up. There is one plant to recommend for August, a Southern native called turtlehead. Growing 2 to 3 feet tall with rich green foliage, turtlehead thrives in light shade. It likes fertile, acid soil that's either wet or well drained. Few pests bother it, and it's easy to propagate by seed, division, or cuttings. But what makes it really valuable is that it's one of a few shade perennials that bloom in August and September. Three species offer different flower colors. There's white turtlehead *(Chelone glabra)*, pink *(C. lyonii)*, and rose *(C. obliqua)*. When people see it in my garden, they take notice. Why? Because aside from my plastic flowers, it's about the only thing blooming.   *Steve Bender*

☐ **Amaryllis**—If you want your bulb to bloom again for the holidays, it's time to force it to rest. Place your potted bulb in a cool, dark place, such as a basement, and let it dry completely. Remove withered leaves when they turn brown. After two to three months, check the bulb every week or so for signs of growth. When you see a green bud peaking out, bring the pot back into the light, and resume watering.

☐ **Daylilies and iris**—Now's the time to divide overgrown plants in the Lower South. Cut the foliage back to about 3 to 6 inches, removing any damaged portions. Reset the divisions into well-prepared garden soil. Space about 1 foot apart in loose groups of five or more. The new plants should have plenty of time to grow prior to blooming next spring.

☐ **Mulch**—Be sure to provide several inches of mulch around the roots of coleus, wax begonias, impatiens, and caladiums, as well as other summer annuals. Water regularly to keep them in full color into the fall months. ▶

☐ **Pots**—This is the time of greatest stress for container plants, so move them to areas that are partially shaded by house walls, trees, fences, or other structures to protect them from the dryness and overheating caused by too much sunlight. Pots should be watered daily. You know you've done a thorough job when water flows from the drain holes.

◀ **Roses**—Now is the time to get your roses ready for their fall revival, even though it is still hot and flowering has reduced. Water well once each rainless week, fertilize monthly with a product specially formulated for roses as recommended on the label, and prune out weak or misshapen growth up to one-third of the plant.

☐ **Watering**—Remember that roots grow where the moisture is. If you give your garden a light sprinkling each evening, your plant roots will grow mainly in the top inch of soil, making them even more susceptible to drying. So water your garden only once or twice each week, and do it thoroughly. That way the roots will be deep and drought-resistant.

☐ **Bulbs**—In case you think bulbs are only for spring, check your garden center. Fall-blooming crocus, colchicum, and spider lilies are available now and offer immediate results. They will bloom almost as soon as you put them in the ground.

☐ **Fragrance**—Consider planting cape jasmine, star jasmine, night-blooming cestrum, or a stephanotis vine to perfume the air around your home in the Coastal and Tropical South. But don't make the mistake of planting too many different types close together—if they happen to flower at the same time, their fragrances may be overwhelming.

◀ **Hardy plants**—Select hardy, heat-tolerant plants such as Autumn Joy sedum and soft leaf yuccas for use in containers. These species will tolerate extremes of heat and cold while requiring only occasional watering and care.

□ **Vegetables**—Gardeners in the Upper South should plant the fall garden this month. In the Middle and Lower South, take stock of supplies to prepare for planting later this month and next. Vegetables you can plant from seed sown directly in the garden include radishes, carrots, lettuce, spinach, kale, mustard, turnips, and peas. Set out vegetable transplants for fall crops of collards, squash, cucumbers, cabbage, and broccoli. Transplants will get a better start if shaded from the afternoon sun and watered every day or two for the first few weeks. ▶

PRUNE

□ **Crepe myrtles**—If your tree is small enough that you can reach the tips of the branches where the seedpods are forming, use loppers or a pole pruner to snip off these clusters. Your tree will rebloom. In addition, removing the weight may help lift low-hanging branches that are in the way. If not, remove the entire branch (without leaving a stub) to raise the canopy.

□ **Perennials**—Lightly trim fall-blooming perennials such as Mexican mint marigold, Mexican bush sage, autumn sage *(Salvia greggii),* and chrysanthemums so that they will be more compact and less likely to need staking when they bloom.

FERTILIZE

◀ **Bananas**—Because they need a constant supply of water and nutrients for good growth and production in the Tropical South, continue to feed banana trees monthly with a 4-8-8 or 5-10-10 granular fertilizer at the rate of 5 pounds per month for a mature clump. Then water at least twice a week, year-round, unless heavy rains occur.

□ **Fruit trees**—Citrus, mango, and avocado trees should receive their last fertilizer application of the season. This will give the trees time to finish their growth for the year before they go dormant for the winter.

□ **Lawns**—This is the time to apply a pre-emergence herbicide if annual bluegrass was a problem in your lawn last spring. It will germinate again in late summer and early fall from the seeds that fell a few months ago, so now is the time to treat.

CONTROL

□ **Chinch bugs**—Now is the time to be on the lookout for chinch bugs in St. Augustine grass. Visible damage usually shows up as a spot of yellowing, drying grass near the street or driveway. The spot tends to get larger as the chinch bugs spread, and the grass inside the spot gets browner and drier as the insects feed. Apply Dursban around the infested area to control the insects.

□ **Lacebugs**—These ⅛-inch insects are known to attack azaleas, sycamores, and avocado trees this month and next, causing the leaves to look dusty, turn yellow, and fall from the plant. Spray with a product labeled for those plants, such as acephate (Orthene), dimethoate, cygon, or diazinon.

This Fern Won't Burn

Not all ferns cry for shade. Southern shield fern is one for the sun.

DESIGN: NAUD BURNETT, DALLAS

Welcome to another fascinating installment of *Everything You Thought You Knew About Ferns Is Wrong.* Today's episode features Southern shield fern—a plant that's the perfect choice for people who kill ferns faster than halitosis kills romance.

Southern shield fern *(Thelypteris kunthii)* contradicts conventional wisdom about ferns in two significant ways. First, it doesn't need shade. In fact, although it grows fine in light shade, it grows even better in full sun. Second, it's not a water hog. While it prefers moist soil, it also tolerates considerable drought. This comes in handy if you're like me and think watering is only slightly more amusing than driving cross-country with a colicky baby.

This fern has one more thing to recommend it. As opposed to many other ferns that form clumps, this one steadily spreads. The richer and looser the soil, the faster it goes. If you dig up and divide clumps in early spring, the two clumps you started out with can form a luxuriant border in just a few years.

Its only apparent fault is that it's deciduous. In winter, it dies down to the ground and then returns the next spring. If you consider deciduousness a grievous character flaw, you'll be glad to hear about another shield fern: Florida shield fern *(Dryopteris ludoviciana).* "Although we grow both, we actually prefer Florida shield fern," says Bob McCartney of Woodlanders Nursery in Aiken, South Carolina. "It's cold-hardier, so it's better for the Upper South. It's also evergreen."

You'll find many ways to use Southern shield fern (also known as wood fern). Its light green fronds contrast splendidly with the darker greens of holly, laurel, yew, and boxwood. You can also use it to edge a lawn or pathway or combine its feathery foliage with perennials. About the only maintenance it requires is using hedge clippers to cut back the old, brown fronds in winter.

Join us next week on *Everything You Thought You Knew About Ferns Is Wrong,* when we'll debunk the myth about ferns transported by ancient spacecraft. ◇

(For sources turn to pages 250–251.)

SOUTHERN SHIELD FERN
At a Glance

Size: 2 to 3 feet
Light: sun or light shade
Soil: moist, well drained, lots of organic matter
Range: Middle, Lower, Coastal, and Tropical South

BY STEVE BENDER / PHOTOGRAPHY VAN CHAPLIN

PHOTOGRAPHS: VAN CHAPLIN

A handsome gazebo provides a respite from the sun for those not in the water. The wrought iron fence keeps out unattended children, while permitting views of the St. Johns River beyond.

Cool by the Pool

When you live in Florida and want to sit by the pool without getting roasted like a chicken, what do you do? Jacksonville landscape architect Bob Hartwig supplies the answer.

This attractive pool he designed serves dual purposes. The owners' grandchildren can splash in the shallow end, while adults can use the deeper part to swim laps for exercise.

But as anyone who's experienced a Florida summer knows, when you're not in the pool, you're in the oven. So Bob added a gazebo, then placed a long, L-shaped arbor next to it. The angled slats in the gazebo's roof permit the free flow of air, yet block most sunlight during the hottest part of the day. The arbor also de-emphasizes the height of the privacy wall and gives a sense of shelter. Two other features deserve mention. The arbor's posts—pressure-treated pine 6 x 6s—rest on short stone piers that repeat the stone used in the columns of the wall. The piers keep the posts from making ground contact.

To satisfy ordinances requiring pools to be enclosed for safety, Bob chose a 4-foot-high wrought iron fence with self-closing, latching gates. Each gate is 4 feet wide. Two pairs of these gates can be swung open to permit access to the pool for parties. Notes Bob, "Opening the gates turns the pool deck, gazebo, and brick patio into one cohesive space." It also makes it easier to escape the Florida furnace. *Steve Bender*

Gates swing wide to permit easy access from the patio. The arbor tones down the height of the privacy wall behind it.

Long-Blooming Gaura

Like a swarm of delicate white moths, the blooms of gaura continue through the hottest summer. This may be our region's longest flowering perennial.

Given the option, many Southerners would awaken with the summer sun, rest through the heat of the day, and then revive in the cool of the evening. That is precisely the schedule that gaura keeps. This native Southern perennial knows how to survive in the hottest season of the year, blooming nonstop from early summer into October.

Found growing wild in Louisiana and Texas, gaura *(Gaura lindheimeri)* can take all the abuse our climate can dish out. Each 1-inch white flower is as delicate as a moth. Although fresh in the morning, the blooms will wither under the onslaught of the sun. Then as the day cools, new ones open.

Flowers held atop wiry stems 3 feet and taller make foliage near the base hardly noticeable. You might think the plant sounds too thin and leggy to make a show, but blooms are produced in sufficient numbers to do for a flower border what baby's-breath can do for an arrangement. Planted with other perennials, gaura weaves its stems in and out of more round and regular plants, loosening the overall appearance.

The delicate spur on the back of each flower is tinged with pink. There's also a totally pink-flowered selection called Siskiyou Pink. Corrie's Gold sports white flowers with variegated foliage.

The root of gaura is carrot-like, growing deep into the ground in search of moisture. This perennial will thrive in dry, sandy conditions but not in soil that is slow to drain. Rich, moist soil will encourage rampant, floppy growth. Here's a plant that looks better when kept on a diet.

Gaura is easy to grow from seed and will bloom the first year if the weather is warm. In fact, some gardeners report self-sown seedlings appearing in the area of an established plant, although these are never a problem.

Linda C. Askey

GAURA
At a Glance

Light: full sun to partial shade
Soil: well drained
Season: late spring into fall
Hardiness: Upper, Middle, Lower, and Coastal South
Expect to pay: $5 to $8 for a blooming plant

PHOTOGRAPHS: VAN CHAPLIN / STYLING: ELLEN RILEY

Benjamin spends time growing his own dinner in a small vegetable garden in the backyard.

Kids and Vegetables Do Mix

As head gardener, he has the opportunity to share vegetables with his dog, Spanky.

Like most children, Benjamin McGarity likes to play in the dirt. But his mom doesn't mind, because when Benjamin gets muddy, a fresh harvest of vegetables is soon to follow.

With some help and encouragement from his mother, Celia, 7-year-old Benjamin has developed quite a green thumb. After deciding what to grow, he helps dig planting holes and sow seeds. He even pulls weeds—when he has to. "I like to water, but not weed. When I'm hot, I run the water on my face," he says.

His chosen vegetables are warm-weather plants that thrive in the spring and summer. When school breaks, Benjamin has months of potential boredom looming ahead, so caring for pole beans, bell peppers, cherry tomatoes, squash, and cucumbers keeps him occupied and continually learning.

Benjamin and Celia plant a selection of basic vegetables, concentrating on quick and easy growers. Compact bush cucumbers are great for limited garden space. Summer squash comes in all shapes and sizes. The best for eating are yellow straightneck and crookneck and green zucchini, also available in bush varieties. Help ensure a long tomato harvest by setting out early, midseason, and late selections. Not many plants are needed; two of each selection should suffice for a family of four. For wilt-proof success, choose plants resistant to common diseases.

Celia has cleverly kept Benjamin's interest piqued with various garden projects. He had a great time when she suggested he spell his name in the garden with carrot seeds. After planting pole beans, they made a bean tepee with sticks tied together at the top. Scarlett runner beans also work well this way and provide summer color.

He has discovered many gardening tricks, such as building a scarecrow to protect his hard-earned harvest. "It keeps away the birds," he says. "I had another one with a cowboy hat, but it broke down." To make the scarecrow, they gathered old clothes from around the house. "Do you know what that thing is that we used for his head?" asks Benjamin, proudly pointing to the nose peeking out from under the scarecrow's hat. "It's one of those garden gourd things. We bought it at the store."

He has also learned that half-eaten leaves usually mean insects have discovered his tasty garden. "Sometimes caterpillars get on the plants, but we just kill them," he says nonchalantly, poking a stick in the dirt. Other times, he gets upset at the squirrels that try to invade his little garden. "If squirrels come near my plants, I chase them," he says, quietly surveying the trees for signs of the intruders.

Benjamin is still busy harvesting this year's crop, so he hasn't had much time to think about what he might plant next summer. But he does have plans to enlist more help. "Next time, I'll let my dog, Spanky, dig all the holes."

Linda Smith and Zophia Rendon

ABOVE: *A whimsical scarecrow sets just the right tone for a child's vegetable garden.* RIGHT: *Kid-size cherry tomatoes are easy to grow and reward gardeners with a good harvest.*

If squirrels come near my plants, I chase them.

Benjamin McGarity

THE ABC'S: A CHILD'S GARDEN PRIMER

A is for attention span. Choose vegetables that come to harvest quickly for short attention spans. Radishes are especially quick, with good results in usually a few weeks. Frequently harvesting vegetables stimulates the plants to keep producing. To keep kids interested during the growing season, make daily trips to the garden to water plants and check for insects.

B is for bugs, lots and lots of bugs. Ladybugs are great kid-friendly garden helpers. They eat aphids, mealybugs, leafhoppers, and other pests in the egg and larval stages, reducing the need for other pest controls. Ladybugs and other beneficial insects can be bought through mail-order retailers such as the Bug Store at www.bugstore.com or 1-800-455-2847.

C is for chemical free. Remember that garden insecticides and other chemicals can be very harmful to

children who eat everything they see. Organic fertilizers, such as compost, and natural pest controls are the only choice for safety. Yellow sticky traps snare bugs and let young gardeners

get a glimpse of what lives in the landscape.

D is for definition. Define your child's garden with a boundary. A fence, planting bed, or rock wall will certainly help the young gardener feel a sense of propriety, while keeping pets and other critters from damaging your child's hard work.

E is for an easy start. Setting out transplants provides instant gratification for children, while sowing seeds for the future teaches them important lessons for life. Seed tape (seeds that come inside biodegradable tape, which is then planted) can be a simple and easy way to make sure that plants get the correct spacing.

For more information about gardening with children, visit the National Gardening Association's Web site: www.kidsgardening.com.

This garden art form requires frequent, but easy, maintenance.

Patterns in the Air

I wanted to create an illusion veil, a see-through net instead of a solid screen." That's how Phillip Watson, of Phillip Watson Designs in Fredericksburg, Virginia, explains the unusual espalier fence he created at the home of Jacques and Valerie Riviere. Then he gets down to the practical side. "I also needed air circulation because of the nearby black asphalt driveway. If I'd put a solid hedge there it would have held in the heat and baked everything."

Phillip chose blue Atlantic cedar *(Cedrus atlantica* Glauca) for the espalier to balance the unusual color of a large Colorado blue spruce in the front of the Rivieres' house. The front garden also features a boxwood grid parterre, so the espaliered cedar repeats the parterre's pattern in a sort of vertical echo.

"To be honest," Phillip admits, "the main reason I decided on a freestanding espalier is because I love a pattern in the garden. I think your eye goes to patterns. As a gardener or garden visitor, you may appreciate all the color mixed together, but you can't really focus on it.

A pattern, such as the loose grid of this espalier, is like a key for unlocking what you're seeing."

For gardeners who want to try this unique and handsome method of creating an airy, living fence, Phillip offers his secrets.

Step 1: Look for trees with branches spaced where you'll want to train them. Either request semi-trained espaliered trees from your nursery, or prepare them yourself by removing the central leader and any superfluous branches. Three to four pairs of branches are ideal.

Step 2: Set posts (pressure-treated pine) at the width you expect the lateral branches to reach, so that no empty wire will be visible when the espalier matures. Phillip suggests 8-foot spacing as a maximum for keeping wires taut, even with the help of a turnbuckle. Attach galvanized wire to hooks or eyebolts at the correct spacing for the branches of your trees.

Step 3: Plant each tree in the exact center of the space it is to fill, at the same depth it formerly occupied in its container. Secure the branches firmly to the training wires with jute, wrapping the twine in a figure eight pattern so that it crosses between the wire and the branch for protection. Check these ties regularly and adjust them as the tree grows, so they don't cut into the bark.

Step 4: Expect to prune two to three times a year (depending on the growth habit of your chosen tree). Remove at the base any sprouts that project up or out, and leave any sprouts that drape downward from the main branches. The branches will get thicker and thicker, and eventually heavy laterals will just droop naturally in a waterfall effect.

Be patient! Espaliers take several years to mature; the exact number depends on your choice of tree.

Liz Druitt

GOOD TREES FOR TRAINING

Espaliered trees need to be weeping or have wide-spreading limbs, so they'll naturally follow horizontal lines and not keep putting up vertical leaders. Good selections, according to Phillip, include blue Atlantic cedar (great color), weeping yaupon (for hot climates and acid or alkaline soils), pyracantha (quick-growing, so needs more maintenance), crabapple or semi-dwarf apple (good fall color plus spring bloom), and Little Gem magnolia (for a larger grid, with the branches farther apart).

Gardening With Your Dog

Does your beloved pet tear up your backyard? Dig holes? Trash plants? Jump fences? Try seeing things from his point of view, and you can learn to enjoy your pet and your garden.

It's very difficult for us dog lovers, but we sometimes need to recognize that our dogs really are dogs, not humans in furry suits. Canines have certain needs, such as exercise, entertainment, and quality time spent with their pack (you). And they do certain things, including running the fence line and digging up the pansies. Can you make them stop? Probably not. But you can solve a lot of problems if you consider their needs when designing your garden, and you can redirect their outdoor activities in positive ways.

Your dog is a territorial animal and will use certain pathways through the yard on a regular basis, especially around the perimeter. Patrolling is part of his job. Instead of yelling at him, use those paths to define your garden spaces. Don't put your rose bed along the back fence and expect him to keep out of it, because he can't. Instead, consider planting roses at intervals in large tubs (he can go around these), and put the rest in a bed outside of his working area.

If your dog is bred to be a world-class digger, think about providing him with a personal sandbox. Sand is easy to brush out of fur and blends nicely with most heavy clay soils should Fido get wild and messy. Put the sandbox in a shady area, so he'll have a cool spot for lying in his nice holes. You can even landscape around it with rock or bricks to blend with the rest of your garden.

Water-loving canines are in much the same category as diggers. If swimming is in his genes, what about adding a water feature just for him? It can be as simple as a kiddie wading pool or as pricey as you can afford. Dogs have no preference, thank heavens—they just want to get wet. Be very clear in explaining which pool is Fido's and which is yours. Throw in some heavy rubber toys to ensure he leaves your expensive koi alone.

Some dogs run right through flowerbeds, and then seem confused about your anger. Make sure your garden areas are clearly defined, with visible edging or even low border fencing, and try to use a different mulch in the beds than on pathways. This will make it much easier for your pet to learn what you want him to do. Upside-down mousetraps can sometimes speed the learning process by startling Fido without harming him.

Pets that cause a lot of destruction are frequently bored and under-exercised. Long walks, dog sports (such as agility), and training classes can be a big help, especially when combined with quality toys for daily entertainment. Another option for plant protection is a fully fenced run as a garden feature.

The truth is, as much as he loves you and wants to please you, he's always going to be a dog. The more you provide for his needs in your landscape, the happier the two of you will be in the garden together.

Remember, a tired dog is a good dog! Make sure he gets plenty of aerobic exercise and an interesting walk every day, and you might find yourself living with a canine angel.   *Liz Druitt*

Clearly marked flowerbeds and a relaxed, well-exercised pet are a perfect combination for happy gardening with your dog.

Located between the driveway and house, the raised lawn looks lush and serene in the waning afternoon light.

Room for Quiet, Room To Party

Modular trelliswork customized on-site provides a sense of enclosure. It's made of African iroko, a weather-resistant wood similar to teak.

To most people, the primary function of grass is to cover the ground and keep your feet from getting muddy. But as this yard in Easton, Maryland, demonstrates, a lawn can do much more.

Designed by Jan Kirsh of Bozman, Maryland, this raised lawn rests between the driveway and house and satisfies both psychological and practical needs. "It's a quiet, reflective place when viewed from inside the house, either from the living room on the first floor or the master bedroom on the second floor," says Jan. "At one time, we talked about putting a water feature in the center and flower borders around the edges. But we never did it, because we liked the sense of calm and quiet."

The lawn's practical side comes into play when the homeowners entertain. "When they're having a party, guests simply spill out into that space," she explains.

Modular trelliswork, made in England and imported by Country Casual in Gaithersburg, Maryland, provides a comforting sense of enclosure. Modules come in different sizes and include gates, finials, and convex and concave arches. "You can play with this stuff to your heart's content," says Jan. "But you need carpentry help to do it right." A local carpenter customized the trelliswork to her specifications.

The wood is African iroko, a rot-resistant material that weathers like teak. "My client wanted to paint it white," recalls Jan, "but I said, 'No, no, no, you want it to weather and go natural. You don't want to paint it every year.'" During the last eight years, the trelliswork has changed from a honey brown to a silvery gray.

Even though iroko resists rot, Jan didn't want it touching the ground. So she set the posts in concrete, then enclosed them within a brick footing wall at the base of the trelliswork. The footing wall adds definition to the lawn, creating visual impact in every season.

Steve Bender

(For sources turn to pages 250–251.)

Late-Summer Arrangements

BELOW: *You don't need a lot of any one flower to make a stunning arrangement. In this casual basket, bold colors stand out, and the pink knotweed adds lacy softness.*

ABOVE: *Warm pink cosmos, globe amaranth, wheat celosia, and spirea are gathered from the garden, with a few store-bought mums added for impact. The flowers, held in place with a pin holder frog, appear at ease in the glazed green container, which complements the color of stems and foliage.*

Even though summer's dog days are panting through the garden, there are plenty of flowers to cut and enjoy indoors. Our simple arrangements, by floral designer and author Libbey Oliver of Williamsburg, Virginia, illustrate the rich colors and textures found this time of year. "Colors begin to regain a boldness in late summer," Libbey says. "Outdoors, the light is a little different and colors seem to improve."

WHAT TO CUT?

Some heat-loving flowers are just hitting their stride when August arrives. The round heads of globe amaranth are becoming fat and full, and wheat celosia is filling out. Cosmos, zinnias, and roses, cut back in July, are flush with new blooms. Coleus foliage and coneflower seedheads add a nice late-summer look to arrangements. Japanese anemone, spider lilies, and patrinia are just beginning their bloom cycles.

If the garden can't provide everything you need for an arrangement, add a few store-bought additions. An orange lily or a few purple mums may be all it takes to give a finishing touch.

PERFECT PLACE AND PERFECT VASE

A great arrangement is a marriage between vessel, flowers, and location. "Vases and containers are accessories, just like anything else in your home," Libbey says. "They should suit your style. I've chosen containers to go in certain locations in my house. They stay there as ornaments all the time, and when I bring flowers indoors, the fresh blooms simply add to the setting. The flowers reflect the style of the container, and it all works together."

When choosing a container, consider how it lends itself to a cut arrangement. "My favorite containers are the ones I don't have to do a lot of work with, or think about how to arrange the flowers," Libbey says. "I look for vases that require only simple mechanics, like a pin holder frog, or don't require anything to hold flowers in place." *Ellen Riley*

(For sources turn to pages 250–251.)

TIMING AND TIPS

The way flowers are cut and conditioned determines how long they last indoors. Always harvest your blooms early, before the sun becomes hot. Take a water container into the garden and place freshly cut stems in it immediately. Indoors, allow the flowers to rest in a cool, dark place for several hours before arranging.
■ Prior to arranging, remove all foliage that may be under water.
■ To keep the arrangement fresh, change the water daily.
■ Keep fresh flowers out of direct sunlight.

Libbey's latest book, *Flowers Are Almost Forever,* provides step-by-step instructions for handling fresh blooms. Every gardener who loves to cut should have this helpful book.

Native materials and garden art tie together three rooms in this Louisville backyard retreat.

Outdoor Oasis

A gardener knows it's as important to furnish the outdoor rooms of a house as it is those indoors. Ellen Collier was thinking about her new house from this perspective. When she and her husband, Norman, found their Louisville garden home, she knew the backyard needed a total overhaul.

"With our children grown, Norman and I were ready for a smaller house and lot," says Ellen, "but we didn't want to give up the joy of a wonderful terrace and outdoor space." They called landscape designers Mary Webb and Barbie Tafel Thomas for help with transforming the backyard.

"The house was in a very desirable neighborhood," says Barbie, "but the backyard was long and narrow and completely exposed to a road."

As a plus, the house had separate views into the backyard from the kitchen, living room, and master bedroom, offering inspiration for this design.

"We simply divided the backyard into three areas that lined up with the interior room views," says Barbie. "We used low boxwood hedges to outline each area. A brick terrace and walk are the hardscape common elements that tie the design together."

Here's how Barbie and Mary organized the outdoor rooms.

Dining area terrace: French doors from the kitchen lead to a brick terrace with an outdoor dining area and grill. Barbie and Mary planted the space with a side border of arborvitae and a background of white Cherokee Princess dogwoods.

Formal area with birdbath: Opening off the living room and in full view of the front door, this part of the garden needed to look green year-round. Boxwoods frame the area, and ivy adds to the lush look. Norman and Ellen selected white crepe myrtles to anchor the spot. Hostas and Delaware Valley white azaleas accentuate the birdbath made by metal artist Tom Torrens.

Koi pond: This outdoor area is visible from the master bedroom. The couple wanted a water feature here to show off their prized koi. A distinctive copper weather vane placed behind a shell-shaped fountain adds personality to the pond and provides a focal point for the axial view from the terrace.

The Colliers also wanted a private backyard retreat, but their property looked directly into their neighbor's yard. Mary and Barbie created a living screen of saucer magnolias and white pine. For privacy at the rear of their property, the Colliers interspersed white pines with river birch for texture and year-round color.

"I enjoy decorating, and I was lucky to have a hand in the finishing touches on this property," says Ellen. "I've always felt that a house isn't a home unless the outdoor areas work as one with the indoor rooms." *Eleanor Griffin*

DESIGNING YOUR OUTDOOR ROOM

Barbie and Mary recommend these tips.

- Repeat common hardscape materials, such as brick or stone, that are used on the house for a seamless look.
- Plan outdoor rooms based on the views seen from indoors.
- Use native plants whenever possible.
- Personalize your space with unique elements such as sculptures, benches, and architectural fragments. In outdoor scale, bigger is better for impact in the landscape.

The showy foliage and interesting burlike fruit of castor bean mix well with red ornamental grasses in this border.

PHOTOGRAPHS: VAN CHAPLIN

Castor Bean, An Age-old Beauty

BEAN BIZ

■ Market bulletins put out by state Departments of Agriculture are a great place to locate castor bean seeds, along with those of other old-fashioned plants.

■ Be warned: The attractive red fruit contains seeds that are poisonous. This plant should never be grown near children's play areas.

This old-fashioned pass-along plant has deep and long rural roots. Popular in the Victorian era, castor bean flanked many a walkway leading up to the front door. And even today, while rumbling down a country road, you often see its distinct form towering over flowers such as zinnias or cosmos.

The vigorous annual might be at home in the country, but plenty of the South's more urban gardeners like the exotic look and tropical feel it lends their yards. The striking, long, palmate leaves resemble an oversize hand that waves with even the slightest breeze that stirs on a hot summer day.

Castor bean can reach 10 feet high and 6 feet wide during a Southern summer. (Shorter selections, such as Dwarf Red Spire, grow only 6 feet tall.) This height makes it a great choice for the back side of a deep border. When planted in a row, it can form a thick hedge. Castor bean also makes a fine specimen in a formal courtyard.

No matter the use, this plant is so eye-catching it's sure to become a conversation piece. The leaves come in a variety of colors, depending upon the selection. Some are green while others have a deep burgundy hue.

Big, spiny, bright red fruit forms on the plants in late summer and early autumn. Brown, bean-size seeds grow inside the prickly fruit. These seeds produce medicinal castor oil and they contain a poison—ricin—that's not present in the oil. As a precautionary measure, remove the seeds before they ripen. This plant should never be grown around children's play areas. In fact, even adult gardeners with sensitive skin should wear gloves and a long-sleeved shirt when working around castor bean because contact with the leaves or seedpods can cause an allergic rash.

Still, don't let these negatives scare you away. Castor bean is a prolific grower, and its huge, 1- to 3-foot-wide leaves are an impressive addition to any garden. Plus, if you decide this plant is not for you, the spiky form is up and gone in a single season.

Charlie Thigpen

(For sources turn to pages 250–251.)

Period charm is enhanced by using flame as the primary lighting. The fountain, acquired in France, is a reproduction of ancient street corner watering places in Provence.

CREOLE COURTYARD

*The richness of Louisiana history permeates
this charming outdoor room.*

Majestic live oaks provide the classic Southern frame for this picturesque garden. Courtyard walls of softly faded brick enclose paved and planted spaces with a European flair. Bananas, palms, and gingers spill over in tropical luxuriance. American and old-world influences come together for perfection in Herb and Nan Boydstun's Baton Rouge backyard.

Their property already boasted live oaks deserving of historic markers. These trees are so grand that they have been a favorite backdrop for local weddings. The Boydstun's house is Louisiana Creole in style, designed by architect Al Jones and built by Larry Normand. It's what Herb and Nan happily describe as "an American house with a lot of French influence."

Descendants from the original French settlers of Louisiana, Creoles were known for their strong interest in the colonies where they settled. Ditto for the Boydstuns. They're originally from Mississippi but have lived in Louisiana all their married life. "We're hoping to stay permanently in Baton Rouge," says Nan. "This is a really friendly town, and it fits perfectly with all our interests."

BY LIZ DRUITT / PHOTOGRAPHY VAN CHAPLIN

It all goes with the Cajun meaning for the word "lagniappe," a little something extra. *landscape designer Michael Hopping*

The Boydstuns adore both European antiques and tropical plants, so the warm, multicultural atmosphere of Baton Rouge offered them a perfect opportunity to combine the two. When their house was almost finished, they consulted landscape designer Michael Hopping to ensure that the French flair continued in their back garden.

"For this large a home, it's not a very deep yard," says Nan, "but we don't have anybody who needs to play football in the backyard anymore. We wanted some way to use the fountains we'd purchased on a trip to France, and we knew we wanted a lot of banana trees." Because they also needed privacy and a place to entertain, Michael's inspiration was to create a walled courtyard containing several charming spaces that flow into each other. His attention to historic detail has kept the Creole feeling woven throughout the garden.

"We do have an earned right, from the 18th century, to be a little more European here in South Louisiana," Michael explains. "I think of it as not unlike a recipe for gumbo—a hodgepodge of ingredients—blending textures and flavors of what it's like living in this historic place and the hot, wet climate that we love to create a marvelous result."

For Michael's garden gumbo, bananas, elephant's-ears, and a short allée of crepe myrtles are surrounded by angled courtyard walls that match the Old New Orleans Red brick of the house. The sunny fountain on the terrace is splashed with bright annual flowers in pots. Trills of birdsong compete with the gurgling water. Several brick-edged planting beds support shady Drake elms.

Michael compiled a dramatic palette of contrasting tropical and semitropical vegetation to create the effect he sought here. "What's really important is using plants that work in the landscape of South Louisiana. That's what's valid for a garden like this, not creating a horticultural wonderland." It's clear that instant gratification is something that does work here, because the lush garden is just a few years old. "Exuberance is from the choice of plant materials, not from the size of specimens. Except for the crepe myrtles and Drake elms, it was all little stuff," says Michael.

Taking the Boydstuns' pleasure in entertaining into account, Michael added the pavilion and its outdoor fireplace to make it possible to be in the garden even in cool weather. Then he filled in beautifully around the courtyard's central features with flat, quarried rock similar to the old ballast stones used to pave French Quarter courtyards.

He also helped set a more primitive atmosphere with flame. Gas lanterns around the courtyard walls enhance the old-world feel, with electric lighting used sparsely and indirectly. Finally, Michael chose genuine French olive jars as accents. Used to store perishables on long sea voyages from Europe, they are another tie with the history of this port city. "It all goes with the Cajun meaning for the word 'lagniappe,' " Michael says, "a little something extra."

The delicious outcome is a garden courtyard that elegantly mixes old and new, French and American, in the best Creole style. In addition, it provides plenty of comfort for both the Boydstuns and their guests.

"Anything we do in this garden, we just do for the pleasure of it," Nan says, leaning back comfortably. "Herb and I often come out here before dinner in the early evening. That's when the angel's trumpets open their blooms, and their fragrance fills the air. We give lots of parties, but we enjoy this wonderful space the most with our family and close friends. Our courtyard is such a good place to visit and talk." ◇

An open gate and softly glowing gaslights heighten the mystery and romantic invitation of the courtyard entry.

*Autumn sage in Pink Perfection and an
aromatic aster (See page 197.)*

September

Checklist for September

EDITOR'S NOTEBOOK

If there's one thing I've learned while writing for this magazine, it's that you can poke fun at people, government, and institutions, but if you don't want to change your name, you better not say anything bad about dogs. So when asked how to keep rambunctious canines from annihilating gardens, do I suggest restraint and discipline? No way. Do I intimate that dogs and beautiful gardens are mutually exclusive? Are you quite mad? Instead, I point out the benefits of boisterous play. For example, those bus-size holes Fido digs in your rose bed improve drainage. And those prized blossoms he eats before the flower show keep you humble. So the next time your dog confuses your flowerbed with a sofa, don't look to me for answers. When it comes to being candid about canines, I've learned to let sleeping dogs lie. (If you want more practical info, see "Gardening With Your Dog" on page 175.)   *Steve Bender*

"Gardening With Your Dog" on page 175.

TIPS

☐ **Azaleas and camellias**—Fall watering is particularly important as buds are forming at this time. Hollies, pyracantha, and other berry-bearing plants also benefit from such extra attention.

☐ **Bulbs**—Arriving in garden centers this month, spring-flowering bulbs, such as daffodils, tulips, and hyacinths, are some of the most rewarding flowers to grow. Buy early for the best selection. To protect from heat as well as freezing, store them in a ventilated bag in your refrigerator or vegetable bin until you are ready to plant, which is best done from mid-October until year's end. ▶

☐ **Dried flowers**—Many flowers in bloom now can be picked and dried for use in arrangements. Some of the best include celosia, gomphrena, Mexican bush sage, and goldenrod. To dry, bundle the flowers together with a rubberband; then hang them upside down in a dry, sheltered area.

☐ **Garden cleanup**—Wake up a tired garden by pulling out the dead and dying, cutting back and staking the leggy and leaning, and filling in the gaps. Marigolds and chrysanthemums make excellent fillers now when it's still too early to set out winter annuals. Otherwise, use mulch to groom bare areas.

☐ **Irrigation**—This is often the wettest month in the Tropical South. If your sprinkler system is on a timer that doesn't include an automatic rain cut-off, consider installing one. Otherwise, monitor rainfall and adjust the timer to water less often when rains are heavy and frequent.

☐ **Mulch**—Rake pine needles that begin falling, and stockpile them. Then use the needles as a clean covering for beds after the leaves have fallen.

☐ **Seeds**—Collect seeds of garden flowers such as zinnias, cosmos, nicotiana, hollyhocks, and spider flower (cleome), particularly old-fashioned types that may be difficult to find if yours fail to reseed. (See "Keeping Cleome" on page 193.)

☐ **Tropical foliage**—When temperatures dip below 55 degrees, remember to bring in foliage plants that have spent the summer outdoors. Plan ahead and treat plants before bringing them in with SunSpray Ultra-fine Oil to kill mealybugs, aphids, and scale.

(See "Keeping Cleome" on page 193.)

PLANT

☐ **Annuals**—In the Lower, Coastal, and Tropical South, plant cosmos, nasturtiums, and marigolds now from transplants or from seeds, and they will mature and perform beautifully until frost. In late October and early November, plant violas, pansies, stock, sweet alyssum, and ornamental cabbages that will usually last through the spring. ▶

☐ **Chrysanthemums**—Choose budded plants in pots, and arrange them in drifts of at least five to seven plants of a single color. Locations having at least a half-day's direct sunlight work best. Chrysanthemums prefer well-drained soil and fairly moist conditions.

◀ **Color**—Sow seeds of cool-weather flowers such as petunias, pansies, and snapdragons in pots or flats early this month (Coastal South) or later in the month (Tropical South). They'll be ready to set out in the garden next month to provide fall and winter color.

☐ **Cuttings**—Take cuttings or divisions of your favorite coleus, tender salvias such as pineapple sage, lemongrass *(Cymbopogon citratus)*, Aztec sweet herb *(Stevia rebaudiana)*, lemon verbena, and Joseph's Coat *(Alternanthera* sp.) to preserve hard-to-get types through the winter. Dust 4- to 6-inch tip cuttings lightly with rooting powder, and place in pots of prepared potting mix. Water well, and put in a bright window or greenhouse until next spring. ▶

☐ **Herbs**—While it is time to harvest most herbs, it is planting time for chervil, cilantro, and parsley. Sow seeds in a well-prepared garden bed. Chervil enjoys partial shade; cilantro needs sun; parsley likes either.

☐ **Vegetables**—Although it may still be warm outside, it is time to plant the fall garden. Set out transplants of cabbage, broccoli, brussels sprouts, collards, and leaf and head lettuce. Sow seeds of mustard, kale, radishes, turnips, and carrots. You can also sow lettuce from seeds, but germination improves if you lightly shade the soil or sow seeds after soil temperatures cool down.

☐ **Wildflower seeds**—When starting wildflowers from seed be sure to choose a mix adapted to your area. Till the soil to loosen the top layer. After scattering the seeds, firm the soil by rolling or tamping with the back of a steel-tined rake. Wildflower plantings make an excellent transition between wild and cultivated areas of your property. Once established, they should reappear each year with little maintenance or supplemental irrigation.

PRUNE

☐ **Hedges**—This is a good time to give your sheared hedges one last clip. They still have time to grow a bit and harden off before growth stops for the winter.

CONTROL

☐ **Exotic weeds**—This is a good time in the Coastal and Tropical South to remove plants and seedlings of Brazilian pepper tree, cajeput *(Melaleuca* sp.), bischofia, Chinese tallow tree, and Australian pine *(Casuarina equisetifolia)* from the garden. These plants were all introduced to the area as carefree landscape plants, but they have escaped and are becoming noxious weeds in many areas.

☐ **Red-banded thrips**—If a bush has a dusty gray look to the foliage, turn a leaf over and look for thrips. Thrips are tiny ($\frac{1}{16}$-inch) brown, yellow, or black insects that attack plants. Most kinds feed on flower petals, but red-banded thrips live on the undersides of leaves, rasping away the outer layers. In Florida, they seem to be a problem this month, especially on roses. If thrips are present, spray as directed with a labeled insecticide such as acephate (Orthene) or dimethoate (Cygon).

September notes:

TIP OF THE MONTH

When you're working in the garden and get stung by a bee or wasp, rub raw onion on the sting. It takes the swelling out right away, and soon you'll never know you were stung.

ESTHER DASCENZO
HARTWELL, GEORGIA

Royal Oak Leaf and Black-seeded Simpson lettuces, along with Purple Vienna kohlrabi, guarantee cool-weather flavor.

Salad Days

Libbie Winston could no more spend a season without gardening than live without breathing. Gardening weaves through her thoughts in a way that's integral to her existence. Flowering shrubs, historic plants, rare natives, and great sweeps of bulbs are all part of her landscape. And, for at least 35 years, she's been planting vegetables in the fall and the spring.

"One reason I keep the garden going year-round is the extraordinary beauty of cold-weather vegetables," says Libbie. "Fall vegetables take the place of spring and summer bedding plants in a flower border. Think of the various cabbages and the beauty of arugula when it blooms in the early spring. This is all quite apart from the incredibly delicious heirloom selections, especially lettuces, that have been reintroduced in recent years."

As a Lower South/Central Texas gardener, Libbie grows seven or eight different lettuces

By planning now, Libbie Winston keeps fresh vegetables on her table year-round.

every fall, plus a huge selection of complementary leaf vegetables. "My favorite cool-weather green is corn salad [mache]," she says, picking the leaves to add to the salad fixings in her basket. "It has this extremely nutty flavor and buttery texture. Corn salad only likes cold weather, and it makes a lovely border of little clumps. I start direct seeding it in October and do repeat sowings of seed into December; then I can often harvest it all the way through spring."

Cool-weather gardening is not just about greens, Libbie points out, but includes the best root vegetables. "Beets, carrots, and turnips are very cold hardy," she says, "and can also be very attractive. Beets, in particular, have come back into fashion with chefs these days. Golden beets are very mild flavored without the earthiness of red beets. I like beet greens too. After all, chard is basically just a prettier beet green with no beet underneath."

BY LIZ DRUITT / PHOTOGRAPHY SYLVIA MARTIN

Top: *Tatsoi, a Chinese vegetable, is tasty, elegant, and cold hardy.* Above: *Red Giant mustard greens grow tall in autumn.*

TO MIX THINGS UP

Libbie suggests trying a broadcast bed, just for fun, with seeds of spinach, lettuce, beets, carrots, radishes, and turnips—or whatever strikes your fancy.

"Mix the seed up," she says, "and broadcast it over a small prepared plot. Rake it lightly, and then tamp it down a little. As you pull out the early radishes, you make some room for the other vegetables to grow. And you have the joy of eating the most tender little seedlings of all, while making room for the others to get bigger!"

Libbie is used to dealing with the Lone Star State's blistering heat at inconvenient times. She grows most vegetables from seed and protects the seeds she starts in late summer under a shade cloth or in a greenhouse. This is not necessary if you start your garden a little later in the fall with the transplants available from nurseries and feed stores. Both seedlings and transplants can be set out by mid-September in her area, and she expects to start harvesting by October.

Whether growing your own seedlings or using transplants, Libbie recommends setting them out at staggered intervals of a week or more (succession planting) from September into December. The cut-off date depends on the individual vegetable and on how cold the winter gets in your area. "If I've guessed wrong on the weather," Libbie says, "I protect against frosts with floating row cover cloth or with a loose covering of hay." She adds that it's extremely important to remove the protection as soon as the weather warms a little, or your seedlings may get boiled in their beds.

Fall gardening can be easier than any other time of year.

Other than second-guessing the weather, fall gardening can be easier than any other time of year. Most pests and diseases vanish as the days cool down. "The exception," says Libbie, "is cabbageworms. You have to tackle those when they appear, even when they're infinitesimal. I dust immediately with DE (diatomaceous earth) if the weather's dry, and then follow up in a few days with a spray or dust of one of the Bt *(Bacillus thuringiensis)* products that are so easy to get at nurseries and feed stores now. You can use Bt alone, if you like. The important thing is to act fast, before the cabbageworms do much damage.

"Otherwise," Libbie adds, looking out over her flourishing garden, "if you have good healthy soil with plenty of organic material, the plants should be resistant to everything else. They just grow, look beautiful, and taste great. I get meals out of my garden every day, sometimes twice a day, all through the cool season." ◇

(For sources turn to pages 250–251.)

LIBBIE'S FAVORITE COOL-WEATHER VEGETABLES

Golden beet
Color: golden round roots, green leaves
Plant from seed: 45-90 days before first freeze

Romanesco broccoli
Color: chartreuse heads, green leaves
Plant from seed: 75-100 days before first freeze
Plant transplants: 15-65 days before first freeze

Vulcan Swiss chard
Color: red, green
Plant from seed: 15-100 days before first freeze
Plant transplants: from 60 days prior, up to first freeze

Purple Vienna kohlrabi
Color: dark lilac globes with purple-green leaves
Plant from seed: 40-75 days before first freeze
Plant transplants: from 40 days prior, up to first freeze

Vit corn salad (mache)
Color: soft green
Plant from seed: 45 days before to 30 days after first freeze

Red Giant mustard
Color: purple-red leaves with green reverse
Plant from seed: 15-105 days before first freeze
Plant transplants: from 60 days prior, up to first freeze

Tatsoi
Color: dark glossy green rosette with white veins
Plant from seed: 45-90 days before first freeze

PHOTOGRAPH: TINA CORNETT

PHOTOGRAPH: JEAN ALLSOPP

PHOTOGRAPH: LINDA C. ASKEY

ABOVE: *In full sun and well-drained soil, Jindai aster grows 2- to 4-foot spikes that are self-supporting and showy.*
FAR LEFT: *Buttery marigolds make a worthy underplanting for rusty-red Autumn Joy sedum.*
LEFT: *Hardy begonia returns year after year with its angel-wing leaves and sprays of bright pink blossoms that endure from midsummer until frost.*

Fall for Flowers

It's easy to have a spring garden. Even a summer one comes naturally. But fall is another story. The plants are easy to grow, but we seem to forget about the season's gardening opportunities.

Look around at your neighbors' yards, botanical gardens, and nurseries for inspiration. Take note of the mature size of plants. Some grow quite large because they have all season to do so. Keep this in mind when you set out the 1-gallon pot that appears so tame.

FALL FAVORITES
Asters are the first flower most people name when asked about fall perennials. However, most New England asters bloom in late summer and early autumn, and that's no help for the flower drought of October. Tartarian aster *(Aster tataricus)* is the stretch limo of late asters, reaching heights of up to 10 feet. Fortunately, there is a short form called Jindai, which sports purple-pink flowers in flat clusters. Growing only 2 to 4 feet tall, it is also less likely to spread all over your flower border than its cousin. Give it full sun and well-drained soil, and you'll both be happy.

Hardy begonia *(Begonia grandis)* is not exclusive to the fall garden, it begins to bloom in midsummer. But its shower of pink flowers on tall pink stems endures until frost cuts the whole plant down. Both flowers and foliage are delightful for arrangements. Fortunately for gardeners with shade, this choice perennial likes the shelter of tall trees, where it grows about 2½ to 3 feet tall.

For garden suspense, Autumn Joy sedum *(Sedum telephium* Autumn Joy) cannot be equaled. The tawny flowers are the culmination of a season-long show that begins with a rosette of succulent gray-green leaves. Soon buds emerge, like pale green broccoli, growing steadily larger and taller as the season progresses. Then the color starts, passing from rosy-pink to sunset shades, ending in a rust. Plant in full sun and well-drained soil.

There are more perennials for fall. This is a season too often overlooked. Now that the days have cooled, it's nice to have something to see when we come home to the garden.   *Linda C. Askey*

(For sources turn to pages 250–251.)

Wedded Bliss

Why stand for a crowded stoop when you can have a gracious front entry to meet and greet guests?

As any good preacher, marriage counselor, or talk show host can tell you, the key to a good relationship is communication. When it came to revamping the front entrance to Sally and Earle Russell's residence in an older neighborhood of Greenville, South Carolina, landscape architect J. Dabney Peeples and residential designer Jack Thacker worked to create a design that marries the house with the landscape.

TOP: *With only 10 feet between the front door and the new driveway, a new lawn would seem inadequate. Instead, a spacious terrace welcomes guests. Brick matched to the house weaves a common thread throughout the project.*

The Russells began the makeover process by effectively communicating their problems. Although they loved the location of their home, they weren't thrilled with its rather unfriendly, two-dimensional streetside appearance. There was nowhere for guests to park and nothing to lead them to the front door.

The home's location on the side of a steep slope also offered a challenge to Dabney and Jack. "The new design gives the illusion the house is not in a hole like it seemed before," Jack says. "We did some grading to create the level area for the terrace and the guest parking. Our goal was to make it gracious and simple."

Jack began by adding the portico over the front door and two walk-through bay windows. That gave the front a three-dimensional look and also improved traffic flow through the house. Brick piers and iron gates help separate the driveway and guest parking area from the more intimate terrace. French doors connecting the terrace with the other living areas of the house make it convenient to slip out for a quiet meal or just to relax.

The designers made room for tight plantings that effectively soften the hardscape and join it with the lush surroundings.

Because the home faces northeast, Dabney selected shade-tolerant plants to complement and link the house and terrace with the existing woodland landscape. "We basically used a traditional design to match the Georgian style of the house," Dabney explains. Relying on favorite Southern evergreens created an entry garden that maintains its welcoming appearance all year long. Basic structure comes from banana shrubs, American and English boxwoods, and tree-form wax myrtles, while Lenten roses, cast-iron plants, hostas, pachysandra, and liriope carpet the ground.

With the addition of a brick retaining wall, Dabney and Jack established an area large enough for guest parking opposite the front door. "We created three spaces at a 45-degree angle and used the brick stripes to guide the parking," Dabney says. "There's adequate parking for the family in the rear, so this is truly for guests."

The completed design demonstrates how a little teamwork between designers and homeowners can work wonders when it comes to developing a lasting relationship between the home and landscape. What is properly joined together, let no one put asunder.   *Glenn R. DiNella*

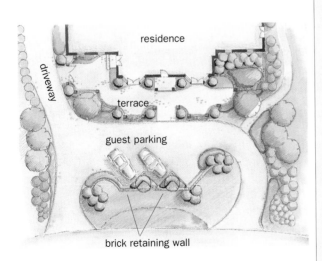

Cleome blooms from early summer to frost if kept in good condition. The seedpods that develop give it the name "spider flower."

Keeping Cleome

The very idea of doing anything to cleome besides enjoying its long-lasting display will raise the eyebrows of gardeners who have grown it. But experience with this Southern stalwart also will reveal the too-tall character of the plant in late summer. Still, all you need is a few minutes and a pair of clippers to solve any height problem.

Hold the stem carefully below the flowers where thorns are few, and then snip off the flower, seedpods, and a portion of the leaves as needed to reduce the height. The key is to cut above a leaf where a new shoot is already growing. The plant will produce new flowers in a couple of weeks, and there probably will be several flowers in place of the one you lost.

Saving seeds from cleome hardly seems necessary in light of the plant's abundant reseeding. But if you mulch heavily, want to spread them to other areas of your garden, or would like to share seeds, cut a few seedpods as they begin to turn brown and split open.

Place the pods in a paper bag where they can dry and drop seeds. Keep seeds in medicine bottles or plastic 35mm film containers. Be sure to label and date them. (Five years from now, they may not be worth sowing.) For maximum viability, store seeds in a cool, dry place until ready to plant. ◇

Waste Not

ABOVE: *Here is the dark, rich finished product.*
BELOW: *This is a gardener's fortune in fallen leaves.*
RIGHT: *More scraps are added to the pile.*

Fall is the perfect name for this time of year, when the sky fills with the downward drift of dying leaves. Fall is about cleaning up the fallen, too, a season of rakes and leaf blowers, heaping the swirling color into huge mounds in the yard.

Instead of throwing away those leaves, how about keeping them? You can build a compost pile with these gifts of autumn.

Compost piles are simple to build, whether you use a bin or not. If you don't have a bin, the perfect location is a bare, shady spot near a water source.

YOU WILL NEED
a) dry, dead stuff (all the leaves you can get your hands on, plus shredded twigs and branches, and even dead grass)
b) moist nitrogen-containing stuff (wilted flowers, frost-damaged plants, vegetable kitchen scraps, and manures)
c) water
d) a few handfuls of fresh soil or old fertilizer (not weed and feed) as a starter

Step 1: Place the coarsest material on the bottom to provide aeration and drainage. (Use a chipper-shredder to grind down branches and twigs a little.) As a rule of thumb, make the bottom layer about 3 inches deep.

Step 2: Add approximately 3 inches of dry material on top of the twigs. Moisten this layer and use your pitchfork to stir until it's evenly damp.

Step 3: Add about 1 inch of moist material. Scatter a few handfuls of old fertilizer or fresh soil on top. Moisten and stir everything again, so it's damp but not wet.

Step 4: Keep adding and moistening layers at the ratio of about 3 inches of dry material to 1 inch of moist material, plus a sprinkling of soil, until the pile measures roughly 4 feet long x 4 feet wide x 3 feet high (or fills the bin). Then it's time to stop and let the living microorganisms break it all down.

You can leave your pile alone, wait a year, and have compost. Or turn the pile once a week for five or six weeks, and the compost will be done that fast. At every turning, the pile heats with new microbial action (95-125 degrees is optimum). Turn it again when the pile starts to cool. When it no longer heats up, the compost is ready.

Your compost pile gradually will break down, and the leaves no longer will be identifiable. Instead, you'll have finished compost, rich and dark and as beautiful—to a gardener—as the colored swirls of autumn leaves.

Liz Druitt

(For sources turn to pages 250–251.)

Make an Entrance

In the state of Kentucky, you can call Churchill Downs for information on horse racing, but if you're looking for landscaping advice, Mary Webb of Louisville is a champion in her own right.

A native Kentuckian who grew up gardening, Mary works with a partner, Barbie Tafel Thomas. Their signature is creating understated landscapes for the traditional Colonial houses typical of Kentucky and the Upper South.

Mary's Louisville home is an example of the classic landscaping she employs. When she and her husband, Sonny, purchased their garden home, she wanted to "age" it and add warmth. Although she and Barbie design some of the loveliest gardens in Louisville, Mary's own landscape revolves around a simple green palette. Here are design tips she used.

First things first. "Screen out the bad views with fences, walls, hedges, or trees. With lots getting smaller, sometimes it takes all four to get the privacy you need," Mary says. "Even with the brick wall we built in our backyard, I still had to add a lattice cap."

Soften the rough edges. Mary trained China Girl holly *(Ilex meserveae)* to climb the walls surrounding her front door and side kitchen entrance. The leafy carpet immediately softens large expanses of brick. China Girl holly is cold hardy and a good choice for Upper South landscapes. A low border of thyme spills over into the pea gravel drive.

Get the steps right. "I'm adamant that outside steps be as wide as possible to welcome guests," says Mary. "Outside risers should never be more than 5 inches high." She had her mason lay the walkway bricks in a herringbone pattern for interest. Rather than trying to train ivy to grow across the path, Mary designed small planting beds across the walkway so it can be grown in place. Occasional trimmings keep it groomed.

Add a personal touch at entrances. Sonny is a graduate of the U.S. Naval Academy. Mary had a naval compass rose recessed into the walk as a tribute to her husband's naval service.

"I was born with a love of gardening and had wonderful training under [the late] Anne Bruce Haldeman," says Mary. "I am a firm believer in keeping things natural. If you start with native plants, the ground will tell you what to do. I've been in this business approximately 40 years, and I'm still learning."

Relaxed and down to earth, Mary is a champion of comfortable designs that add a graceful note to the Kentucky landscapes she shapes. *Eleanor Griffin*

ABOVE: *Mary Webb enjoys her garden.* TOP: *Twin topiaries frame the side door to the kitchen.* LEFT: *English ivy and China Girl holly soften the angles and guide guests to the front entrance.*

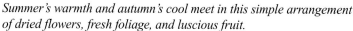

Summer's warmth and autumn's cool meet in this simple arrangement of dried flowers, fresh foliage, and luscious fruit.

A Harvest Display

MATERIALS

FLORIST FOAM

VASE OR OTHER CONTAINER

CHICKEN WIRE

CLIPPERS

FLOWERS AND GREENERY

GRANNY SMITH APPLES (ABOUT 12)

FLORIST WIRE, TAPE, AND STICKS

As the air slowly cools, bringing relief from sweltering temperatures, summer's dramatic colors give way to the earthy tones of fall. This flower arrangement reflects the transition of seasons by combining dried summer flowers, fresh greenery, and autumn apples.

We used dried yarrow along with Japanese andromeda *(Pieris japonica)* for this arrangement, but feel free to experiment with the plants you have at your disposal. Or use fresh flowers purchased from a florist or dried flowers from a crafts store.

To Make the Arrangement

Step 1: Collect fresh greenery, and condition the stems by gently crushing them and soaking them in water overnight.

Step 2: Measure and cut enough florist foam to fit snugly in the vase. Completely soak the foam in water and insert in the vase.

Step 3: Cut a length of chicken wire to mold over the florist foam to give the stems extra support. Tape the wire to the container and reinforce it by placing a second strip of tape horizontally over the first.

Step 4: Gently strip the dried yarrow stems of all leaves. Cut the stems on a slant and place them into the florist foam, arranging the yarrow in the uppermost areas. Add fresh greenery underneath the yarrow, filling in any blank areas as you go.

Step 5: Prepare the apples by inserting a stick into the base of each one; then thread florist wire through the fruit on both sides, twisting the ends of the wire around the stick. This will hold the fruit as it ripens, keeping it in place and stable.

Step 6: Arrange the fruit among the greenery, and fill the container with water.

With daily watering, the arrangement should last between a week and 10 days.

Carole Sullivan and Emily Sollie

A Sage Choice

Birds do it, bees do it. There's no *real* data on whether educated fleas do it, but butterflies eagerly fall in love with autumn sage, and gardeners all over the South do too—with good reason. It's one of the most colorful and cooperative perennials in the garden.

This low-maintenance salvia is not just an attractive, reliable draw for pretty winged creatures. It's also a solid performer either as an individual plant or as a team player in a flowering border. The tiny blossoms, held aloft on airy stems, are deceptively delicate. From a few steps back, the sheer number of those little flowers massed together turns autumn sage into a mound of color. The palette ranges from red to pink and coral to crimson, which explains the alternate name "cherry sage." White forms of *Salvia greggii* are fairly common, as well, and even yellow selections are available.

In the Upper South, cooler temperatures dictate growing autumn sage as an annual. Gardeners there will bless it for its rapid growth and quick onset of bloom. The bushy, slightly sprawling form with tidy little leaves also lends itself beautifully to containers. If you prefer the look of a groomed rather than a casual garden, occasional clipping back will stimulate autumn sage to thicker growth and even more bloom.

Make sure to give your plants good drainage and at least a half-day of direct sun. They cheerfully will earn the affections of butterflies, bees, hummingbirds, and, of course, gardeners.   *Liz Druitt*

(For sources turn to pages 250–251.)

In the Central, Lower, and Coastal South, autumn sage is a nearly evergreen perennial that forms a small, woody shrub. Despite its name, this salvia actually blooms from May through November. The autumn flowers are the most plentiful and richly hued of the year, however, which easily accounts for the common name's focus on fall. As a perennial, autumn sage gets more impressive every year. Replace plants every four or five years to keep them from getting too woody.

ABOVE: *White forms add a clean, bright look to the garden through November.*
RIGHT: *Pink Perfection is a knockout next to an aromatic aster just coming into bloom.*

AUTUMN SAGE
At a Glance

Height: 2 to 3 feet tall and wide
Bloom: May to November
Light: full sun to partial shade
Soil: any well drained
Water: once a week; drought tolerant when established
Pests: none serious
Propagation: cuttings
Range: hardy to 25° as a perennial; throughout the South as an annual

PHOTOGRAPHS: VAN CHAPLIN

BEFORE

The Look Of Age

Disproportionate and unwelcoming. Those adjectives described Arthur and Ellen Powell's courtyard before its amazing transformation.

After the Powells purchased their home, they made immediate plans with Birmingham garden designer Mary Zahl. They wanted an older, established feel for the garden. They dreamed of a courtyard like those found in Charleston and New Orleans—worn brick walkways and perennial flowers. They also wanted it to be easy to care for and comfortable.

Now, from the moment you step off the brick walkway onto the garden path, you know you are entering an intimate, otherworldly space. The main courtyard is divided into two terraces; a stacked bluestone wall and substantial stone coping define the upper terrace.

PHOTOGRAPHS: SYLVIA MARTIN

ABOVE: *The expanded lower terrace embraces a table for entertaining in the midst of lush foliage and cooling shade.*

When Mary began the project, the terraces were the first areas to be renovated. "There was an unusable alley-like space in the lower terrace," she recalls, "and the upper terrace was too big. We changed the proportions by pushing the upper terrace back to make both areas functional."

While designing more functional space, Mary wanted the new garden to respond to the architecture of the house. The previous design featured one set of oversize stairs to the upper terrace. In the new plan, Mary designed two sets of steps aligned with French doors at the back of the house that encourage the flow of guests around the garden.

"Opening up space and views was a driving factor in the Powell renovation," says

Birmingham architect John Carraway, who aided in the project. Before, a deep vine-covered arbor over the French doors prohibited natural light from entering the house, and its supports intruded into the lower terrace. "After removing the arbor, we placed shallow overhangs over the French doors, which are held up by salvaged Victorian brackets," says John. The doors and overhangs, painted an unobtrusive black, allow natural light to enter the living room without overwhelming the courtyard.

Stately Doric columns, found at an architectural salvage shop, and a demure knee wall replaced painted lattice covering the garden's entrance. Parts of the garden wall were raised to give a sense of unity. Ocher-stained stucco applied to the wall has aged quickly, lending to the authentic, old-time feel of the courtyard.

LEFT: *Salvaged architectural columns and a low knee wall frame an open breezeway from the garage to the garden.*

BEFORE

RIGHT: *A fountain serves as a focal point for the courtyard, while the redesigned upper terrace extends a green greeting to visitors.*

Old Carolina brick, made with a soft finish wood mold, paves the courtyard. "Mary chose it because she said it would be weathered in a matter of months," says Ellen. "She was right. The brick looks wonderfully seasoned."

A covered walkway from the house to garage is set in mortar, the bricks lining up like obedient soldiers. In contrast, the courtyard bricks, laid in a diagonal herringbone pattern, all rest snugly in a bed of sand, with bits of moss struggling for elbowroom between them.

Narrow planting beds on both sides define the walkway. These areas receive different exposures that demand different plantings. Lilies, hostas, and strawberry begonias delight in the shade of one side, while white coneflowers, coleus, and Sasanqua camellias bask in the sun of the other. Hydrangeas and hardy begonias thrive on both sides, linking the beds together.

On the upper terrace, perennial planting beds with pockets of annual color enclose a sitting area. Stone planters, bursting with seasonal annuals, stand guard on the steps and upper walls.

A fountain in a curved pool works as the garden focal point. Recessed brick edging behind the fountain creates the illusion of an alcove. "I wanted something different for that area," says Ellen, "but still tasteful and classic.

"It is a very soothing place to be now," she adds. "As we sit out on the terrace and listen to the sound of the water splashing, we feel like our garden is part of the whole house."   *Linda Smith*

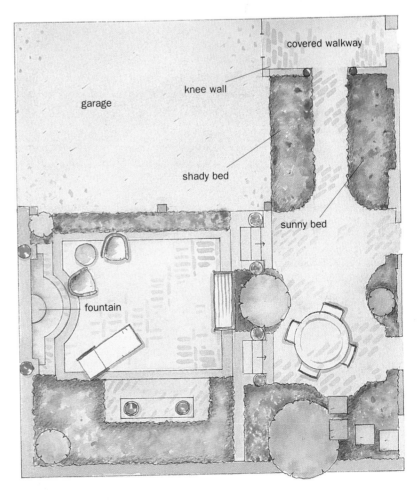

A public garden in Fort Worth (See pages 214–215.)

October

Checklist for October

EDITOR'S NOTEBOOK

Some insects have no sense at all. With millions of plants around to eat that nobody gives a flip about, why pick on one that people will defend with their lives? It's like insulting the Queen Mother when you could just as easily have taken a shot at Camilla. The brainless bug involved in this case is the azalea caterpillar. Scads of these mannerless villains, distinguished by red heads and legs and white stripes, hatch from summer to fall and proceed to wolf down azalea leaves. They can strip an entire shrub in a day or two. While the plant won't die, it will suffer extreme humiliation. What to do? First, get mad. Remember, they're attacking a Southern icon. Then spray according to label directions with *Bacillus thuringiensis kurstaki* (DiPel, Thuricide), rotenone, malathion, or carbaryl. Maybe as a result of your savage defense, a new, more enlightened caterpillar will appear that consumes only crabgrass, golden euonymus, poison ivy, and redtips. Naaaaaah.

Steve Bender

☐ **Birds**—Clean out birdhouses, and fill your feeders to attract migrating birds as well as winter residents. Keep feeders filled, and you'll bring life to your garden all winter long.

☐ **Fruit trees**—Rake up fallen fruit and foliage around your peach, pear, and apple trees. The debris will harbor fungal and bacterial infections through the winter and create problems next season. Also avoid feeding them through the fall and winter. This will help them go dormant for the winter months. You should not water mango and lychee trees for the next 3 months because they need a dry season to promote a good spring bloom.

☐ **Leftovers**—Pesticides that remain after the gardening season winds down should be stored in their original containers in a cool, dry, dark location where kids or pets

will not find them. Never pour pesticides down the drain, onto the ground, or into a storm sewer. If you have pesticide left in your sprayer, apply it to other plants listed on the label.

☐ **Perennials**—This is the prime time to divide large clumps of hostas, Shasta daisies, yarrow, dianthus, or other fibrous-rooted perennials. Set divisions at the same depth they were previously growing, making sure to have both roots and shoots on each piece. Plants currently in bloom can be divided later this fall or in early spring. In the Upper South, make divisions at least a month before any hard freezes.

◄ **Saving summer**—Harvest stems of globe amaranth (bachelor's buttons), cockscomb, and zinnias for winter bouquets. Arrange in loose bunches, and hang them upside down in a well-ventilated, dry area for several weeks.

☐ **Snowflakes**—The best snowflake for the South is *Leucojum aestivum*. Its bell-shaped flowers somewhat resemble those of lilies of the valley with a dot of green decorating each petal.

☐ **Vegetables**—Clean out unplanted areas, and turn under any winter weeds that have sprouted or debris that is not infested or diseased. Then sow a cover crop, such as crimson clover, or mulch with ground leaves or straw to keep down weeds, minimize erosion, and nourish the soil. ►

☐ **Annuals**—Sow seeds of larkspur, poppies, sweet peas, and money plant now for flowers next spring and summer. Prepare the bed by loosening the soil and adding organic matter such as compost. Rake smooth, and sow the seeds. Be certain not to mulch, or you will smother your seeds along with the weeds. ►

☐ **Flower seeds**—In the Upper South, plant bluebonnet seeds now along with other wildflowers. Cultivate the soil 2 or 3 inches deep; scatter the seeds, and then rake lightly. Also sow

larkspur, cornflowers, and Oriental poppies now.

□ **Lawns**—Overseed warm-season grasses in the Middle and Lower South with annual or perennial ryegrass for green turf during the winter months. This is particularly feasible if your lawn is small, easy to maintain, and significant in the design of your garden.

◄ **Spring bulbs**—Begin planting your spring-flowering bulbs such as hyacinths, narcissus, and tulips. Buy large bulbs that are firm to the touch, choosing as you would when selecting onions or potatoes. A well-drained location and six hours of sunlight are essential. Most tulips and hyacinths are treated as annuals in the South, requiring about six weeks of cold treatment in your refrigerator before planting. Many narcissus will naturalize in Southern gardens, increasing in numbers slowly each year. Good narcissus for naturalizing are those in the tazetta class, such as Grand Primo, Silver Chimes, and Golden Dawn.

□ **Vegetables**—Set out plants of cool weather vegetables such as cabbage, collards, and broccoli; sow seeds of carrots, beets, radishes, turnips, and green peas. In the Coastal and Tropical South, it is still not too late to set out tomatoes and peppers and to plant seeds of other warm-weather crops, such as corn, beans, and cucumbers.

PRUNE

□ **Roses**—With cooler nights on the way, roses will produce some of their best flowers. Encourage them now by cutting spent blooms back to the first full-size leaf. Apply 1 cup of 16-4-8 or similar rose food per plant, making sure the fertilizer doesn't touch the canes. Keep the plants well watered. ▶

FERTILIZE

□ **Lawns**—The change in weather will bring out annual winter weeds, so now is a good time to apply a weed-and-feed fertilizer to the lawn. Be sure you buy a brand labeled for use on your particular grass species (St. Augustine, Bahia, Bermuda, Zoysia, etc.), and follow the directions on the bag carefully.

CONTROL

□ **Lace bugs**—Watch for dusty tan spots on leaves of azalea, sycamore, and avocado trees caused by lace bugs. The bugs are tiny (⅛-inch) gray-to-black insects on the undersides of the leaves. Spray with insecticidal soap, diazinon, or malathion to control them.

□ **Poinsettias**—In the Coastal and Tropical South, plants in your landscape will be setting their flowerbuds this month. Avoid shining lights on them at night, if possible, or they may not bloom in time for Christmas. Those under a streetlight may not flower at all, because they need long nights to encourage blooms. Watch out for poinsettia hornworm—a large, green caterpillar that can defoliate the plant quickly. The best way to get rid of pests is to remove them by hand and dispose of them.

October notes:

TIPS OF THE MONTH

I never put discarded tomato vines in my compost pile, as tomato vines usually harbor some sort of disease that could be transferred to a future garden.
CHARLOTTE BRYANT
GREENSBURG, KENTUCKY

When you harvest a cabbage from your garden, don't cut the stalk to the ground or pull it up. Instead, leave as much stalk as you can when you cut the cabbage. Soon you will have a crop of miniature cabbages growing all along the old stalk. They are just as tasty as brussels sprouts.
LORRAINE HANKINS
HOLLY SPRINGS, MISSISSIPPI

Nature's *artistry*

Turn your home into fall's canvas as you embrace the powerful colors of the season.

F all wraps itself around the South like a fragrant wisp of smoke from a distant hickory fire. It sneaks up softly and, when we're not looking, slowly surrounds us with fading ember shades of autumn. Occasional bursts of brilliant foliage illuminate the landscape, and the entire process seems to catch us by surprise. This seasonal celebration goes far beyond colorful leaves. It appears, too, in summer's last vibrant flowers, freshly harvested apples and persimmons, and nandina berries ripening into rubies. Bring the season indoors by using these materials to create festive fall arrangements.

A few carefully selected branches on a windowsill can become a mosaic masterpiece. Maple trees are a fall color icon, but plenty of others offer dazzling shades of red, orange, and yellow. Take

BY ELLEN RILEY
PHOTOGRAPHY JEAN ALLSOPP
STYLING BUFFY HARGETT

LEFT: *Look beyond the traditional for other options on fall color. Crepe myrtle foliage flames bright with shades of crimson and orange.* FAR LEFT: *Preserved celosia, orange safflower, and yarrow are perfect candidates for colorful wreaths.* ABOVE: *Persimmons and pomegranates piled high show how elegant simplicity can be. Each becomes a study of shape and color when used in a large mass.*

another look at crepe myrtle, smooth sumac *(Rhus glabra),* dogwood, and red oak. Their leaves are every bit the essence of autumn. Sourwood, beech, black gum, and Chinese tallow also stage an attention-getting show. In the Coastal and Lower South, many croton selections don the primary palette of this season. While they are not translucent like the others, they still embrace autumn's attitude.

Indoors, these lovely branches last only a short time. To help the delicate leaves remain fresh for several days, take sharp pruners and a bucket of warm water into the garden. Cut each branch at an angle, and immediately place it in water. Once indoors, cut the stem again, underwater, to prevent sap from clogging the water passages.

Place the branches in a west-facing window and the long, golden rays of the

Late-afternoon sun lights up this simple celebration of fall. Branches of red oak and dogwood glow with unexpected color, and goldenrod's frilly flowers fill out a vase. Nandina berries and lady apples show off their best sides.

waning sun will fire the leaves in glowing color. You don't need many—the simplicity of less allows each leaf to shine.

Choose a vase with texture for a natural style. Reed-covered bottles can be found at flea markets and antiques shops, or you can put a water-filled jelly jar inside a rustic basket to hold stems. For a different look, try containers that add unexpected color to the arrangement. Place a number of small green or blue bottles on the window ledge, with one small stem in each. The light will shine through the bottles as well, adding another brilliant tone to the grouping.

FALL FLOWERS

Fluffy yellow goldenrod flaunts itself on the roadside, taunting those with clippers in hand. Despite its reputation, this flower is not a sneezy villain for most folks. As a cut flower it will easily stay fresh in water for a week, and it also dries beautifully. Put the stems in only a half-inch of water, and the blooms will gradually dehydrate, lending themselves to timeless arrangements.

Cockscomb celosia is at its finest in fall and will dry within a few days when hung upside down in a cool, dark place. If you haven't planted any, check local farmers markets for these heady cut flowers. The jewel-tone blooms retain their vibrant color beautifully after being preserved.

Yarrow adds a wonderful touch to an autumn arrangement, although by fall it has already finished blooming. If you haven't been drying flowers throughout the summer, crafts stores and florists have a ready supply this time of year. The shaggy heads of orange safflower also make an excellent addition to the preserved flower palette.

CELEBRATE COLOR

The word that bears repeating is simplicity. Take time to visit a farm stand, and look at the harvest with an artist's eye. A bowl of red lady apples, each kissed with a blush of sunlight, is as elegant and easygoing as an arrangement can be. Persimmons are a vivid reminder that orange is not exclusive to pumpkins. A basket of nandina berries creates a seasonally appropriate centerpiece or accent on a coffee table. Choose any of these elements that sing with fall color, and use them in a mass for simple beauty.

For a final, fitting touch, set the table with assorted sizes and colors of flickering hand-rolled beeswax candles. The slightly honeyed scent and radiant glow guarantee to chase the chill from a crisp autumn evening. ◇

Take Shelter From the Cold

PHOTOGRAPH: VAN CHAPLIN

PHOTOGRAPHS: JEAN ALLSOPP

As October nights turn crisp, the chilling reality of an impending freeze takes root. It's decision time: What will you save from the summer garden to nurture over winter? And the question that looms even larger: Where will these treasures stay warm and out of the way? Will it be another winter of hibiscus in the kitchen, geraniums in the bay window, and ferns in the guestroom?

There are a number of methods to store your garden holdovers without sharing personal space. The easiest, most inexpensive method is with grow lights and a wooden bench or table. The garage makes a good place for this system as it stays cool but rarely reaches freezing. Plug the lights into a timer to automatically turn on each day for eight to ten hours. On warm winter afternoons, leave the garage doors open so your plants can enjoy a bit of natural light and fresh air. Occasionally, put them out on the driveway for a shower and thorough soaking. This no-fuss system also works in a basement.

ABOVE: *A simple system consists of grow lights and a few wooden benches.* TOP, LEFT: *A collapsible greenhouse is handy for winter and can be stored out of the way for summer. Cold winter nights, though, call for supplemental heat.* BOTTOM, LEFT: *Use the space under a porch or deck to make a greenhouse. This permanent addition uses old windows and doors.*

GREENHOUSES

Turn the space under a deck or porch into a greenhouse. If the area above is open to weather, create a rain-free space underneath with rigid plastic sheets. Fasten them to the deck joists, angled so water drains away from the area. Enclose the sides with heavy, clear plastic. Cut lengths long so the bottom can be secured with concrete blocks to close out cold winter winds.

Another option is a portable greenhouse. The aluminum frame is lightweight and not recommended for parts of the South where heavy snowfall may occur. It is best suited to more temperate regions, where night temperatures stay above 20 degrees. Look for a unit with built-in vents or zippered windows to allow fresh air circulation.

SUPPLEMENTAL HEAT

Plants stored in free-standing structures may require heat during cold periods. Generally, a small electric heater will provide enough warmth to keep things toasty. Look for a sturdy, utility-type unit with a built-in thermostat and fan that automatically shuts down if tipped over. Set the heater away from plants and the sides of the structure. Always unplug the unit before watering.

Remember that winter is a time of rest for summer plants. Water occasionally, but not excessively. Grooming is important. Remove leaves that turn brown or fall off as insurance against disease and fungal problems. Come spring, these old friends will be ready for another season in your garden. *Ellen Riley*

(For sources turn to pages 250–251.)

Pirate Playground

Ahoy, mates! Buried booty, secret maps, and treasure troves of high times lie ahead.

When we moved into our new house last year, I promised my son I would build him a playground and fort better than the one we left behind. Jacob has a good memory and wasn't about to let me forget my promise. After settling into our house, he reminded me it was time for his play area.

We agreed on a pirate theme, so I was off to the home center for a few ideas. There are all kinds of kits available that allow you to mix and match pieces of equipment, such as sliding boards, forts, monkey bars, and swings. I wanted to put together a basic kit, and then add a few extra features to make it colorful and fun.

After deciding on a design, I calculated the dimensions of the structure to help me choose the perfect site in the backyard. The area needed to be level for stability, and a little shade would help keep Jacob from baking on hot summer days. I also wanted it to be close to the house so he could be seen easily while playing.

Most home centers that sell the kits will print out a list of supplies needed, including

This playground cost around $500. It has become a great outdoor room for Jacob and his friends.

all the lumber, nails, and bolts. It's helpful to check the list when making your purchases.

The directions with the kit were pretty easy to understand, except for the part that states you can build a play area in a couple of days. It took me about a week to complete the project, but I was able to put in only a

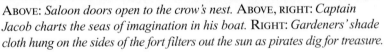

ABOVE: *Saloon doors open to the crow's nest.* ABOVE, RIGHT: *Captain Jacob charts the seas of imagination in his boat.* RIGHT: *Gardeners' shade cloth hung on the sides of the fort filters out the sun as pirates dig for treasure.*

couple of hours a day. The tools needed to assemble one of the kits are minimal. A good hammer, electric drill, circular saw, tape measure, and level will get you started. A socket set also comes in handy for securing some of the long bolts.

Once I assembled the play equipment, I decided to build a boat big enough for two or three children. The boat was made with two 2 x 10 boards, and I chose PVC pipe to hold up the large sail. The sail itself was made from shade cloth. Oars and a rudder made with scrap lumber let children pretend they are steering or rowing the boat.

I purchased a yard of sand for the sandbox, intentionally buying extra so I could fill the box completely. I spread the excess sand under the monkey bars and at the end of the slide to help cushion any falls. Pine straw makes a nice mulch. It was a little sticky at first, but took only a few days to break down and soften up under little feet. (Shredded bark is also a good playing surface.)

To make the area more colorful, we added a couple of hand-painted signs. One reads "Good Pirates Only," and the other, "Crow's Nest." I hung a Jolly Roger flag with the skull and crossbones from the crow's nest to announce that pirates had arrived. Inside the fort, a periscope lets Jacob keep a watchful eye for scoundrels and scalawags.

I know in a few years Jacob will outgrow the playground, but right now I enjoy seeing him wiggling his toes and fingers in the cool sand and watching his growing body stretch as he swings across the monkey bars. Jacob will strengthen his muscles and develop coordination on this playground, and hopefully— with all the fun extras—he'll develop a healthy imagination too.   *Charlie Thigpen*

JACOB'S WISH LIST

■ curved sliding board
■ swings
■ fort
■ hand rings
■ monkey bars
■ periscope

Vine Times of Fall

Spanish flag puts on a stunning show in the fall. The multicolored orange to creamy yellow blooms drape this picket fence.

It's the last hurrah. Vines have twisted, turned, and wiggled their way up and over trellises, walls, and fences, reaching great heights all summer long. The marathon journey has left the plants weary, and now that it's autumn they can climb no more. These vines have produced flowers throughout the summer, but now they are beginning to load up with blooms. With the cooler temperatures, it's almost as if they realize that a killing frost could be right around the corner.

Now is the time to enjoy their swan song of flowers. It's also the time to collect seeds for the following year. Three heavy-blooming vines you can count on to shine in the fall are Spanish flag *(Mina lobata),* cypress vine *(Ipomoea quamoclit),* and black-eyed Susan vine *(Thunbergia alata).* All of them look great in a fall border, on a mailbox, or anywhere you have a sunny spot and need a climber. Here's a brief description of these fast growers that reach for the sky.

SPANISH FLAG

This vine is not found in local nurseries or in garden centers often, but many mail-order catalogs carry its seeds. Spanish flag is easy to grow and has such an unusual look. Under ideal growing conditions it can reach 15 to 20 feet in a single season. Native to Mexico and Central and South America, it's a perennial in zones 8 through 10, but north of zone 8 it may be grown as an annual.

Exotic flowers appear from summer until frost. Several small buds form on

forked stems. At first they are a striking red, but as they grow they turn a vibrant orange. Then the tubular flowers open and change from orange to creamy yellow. The blooms on each stem change at different times, creating a multicolored effect.

CYPRESS VINE
Some gardeners call this vine cardinal climber, but it should be called hummingbird climber because of the strong attraction the little long-billed birds have to the scarlet blooms. It's common to see several hummers duel for the right to enjoy these starlike flowers. But fall flowers aren't the only nice feature of this vigorous vine. Its fine, feathery foliage looks like green lace draped around the garden, creating a graceful form. Each airy leaf resembles a cluster of green threads.

Ipomoea x *multifida* is a cross between *I. quamoclit* and *I. coccinea*. It's identical to cypress vine, sporting the same small red flowers, but its leaves are a little broader.

In the Lower South, cypress vine is considered a weed, but it rarely damages plants because of its wispy nature. The problem is that the numerous seeds dropped by the parent plant sprout everywhere, and these fast growers can consume a tidy garden quickly. Because it has naturalized in much of the Southeast, many seed companies no longer carry it. It's not a problem plant in the Middle and Upper South and has been blooming in gardens there for years. In fact, Thomas Jefferson reportedly planted it at Monticello in 1790.

BLACK-EYED SUSAN VINE
This African vine is damaged by even the slightest frost, but it blooms heavily till the very end. Orange, yellow, or white flowers are usually dotted in the center with black eyes, hence the name.

The arrowhead-shaped foliage has slightly serrated edges. The leaves, supported by winged leaf stalks, are susceptible to spider mite damage

ABOVE: *This bird feeder and post are engulfed by black-eyed Susan vine. The orange flowers look great with a cluster of pumpkins and fall foliage* ABOVE, LEFT: *The scarlet blooms of cypress vine really attract hummingbirds, creating a garden show.*

(sometimes they become speckled or yellow), but this can easily be controlled by spraying plants with insecticidal soap or SunSpray horticultural oil late in the evening as the sun sets.

The vines always twine clockwise and reach 5 to 10 feet in a growing season. Black-eyed Susan vine is often sold in hanging baskets; if it has no support to grow on, it drapes nicely over the edge of containers.

Try growing one or all of these fall-blooming nimble climbers next spring. They will spend their summer on the upward climb, and then the flowers will eventually appear. Be patient; the late-season blooms are definitely worth the wait.   *Charlie Thigpen*

(For sources turn to pages 250–251.)

Pumpkins Stacked With Style

Make a simple vase to celebrate the season.

The abundance of the harvest and warm, toasty colors come together in this easy adornment that will bring the glow of autumn into your home. Perfect for a centerpiece or to spruce up a sparse corner, our pumpkin vase is so simple to make—even children can help. When you choose that perfect pumpkin to carve your Halloween jack-o'-lantern, pick up some mini ones, too, and create a unique arrangement.

To Create the Arrangement

Step 1: Spray a glass, cylinder-shaped container or vase with spray adhesive, one section at a time, and cover with sheet moss. It is important to wear gloves to protect your hands, and make sure the area is well-ventilated (see photo below, left).

Step 2: When the vase is completely covered with sheet moss, begin adding mini-pumpkins. Apply melted skillet glue to pumpkins with a small paintbrush (see photo below, right). Wait a few minutes, and then attach the pumpkins to the cylinder, starting at the base and working up. Arrange leftover pumpkins around the base; tuck in bright autumn leaves for embellishment.

Step 3: Pour water into the vase, and prepare lilies and croton leaves. Using the clippers, cut the flower stems on the diagonal, and strip away leaves from the stems so that no greenery is submerged in the water. Arrange the flower stems in a crisscross pattern for a fuller look (see photo at top).

As a variation, try using a different-size container, such as a coffee can, flowerpot, or paint bucket with florist foam inside.

Easy-to-find materials, such as minipumpkins and sheet moss, adorn a plain container.

Experiment with various seasonal flowers, grasses, leaves, berries, or fruits to create a personalized look. We have continued the harvest theme with a few ears of Indian corn and an inviting bowl of candy corn, but you can add any finishing touches you like to enhance your display.

Carole Sullivan and Emily Sollie

MATERIALS

small glass cylinder

spray adhesive

sheet moss

gloves

36 miniature pumpkins

skillet glue, melted in skillet
(available at crafts
and florist-supply stores)

small paintbrush

lilies or other flowers

croton plant

clippers

PHOTOGRAPHS: JEAN ALLSOPP

This beautiful blend illustrates how good color can be. Imperial Antiques Shades is the dominant color, with Crystal Bowl Rose and True Blue added for depth.

Mix-and-Match Pansies

Pansies are true garden friends. They face winter head-on, and they hang with us from autumn through spring. But the sweetest side of these faithful flowers is the colors they offer through dreary winter months.

With so many choices, it's difficult not to want some of each. The challenge is to choose the best shades for your landscape. Make your own mix with the flowers on this page before you visit the nursery. Follow our tips to achieve the perfect look for your home.

Tip 1: Choose one dominant color. Take your cues from the surrounding structures and landscape. Whether it matches your house or trim paint or contrasts completely, that color is the beginning of the relationship with all other additions. When incorporating other colors, use more of this principal shade. In a brick home, choose pansies that brings out the best of its base tone. Some bricks are red-orange, some can be pink, and others gray.

Tip 2: A one-tone planting presents a formal appearance. To keep things simple but less dressy, add different shades of the same color for softness. For example, a bed of bright yellow pansies can be blinding. Add soft yellow to the mix and the look is still cohesive, but easier on the eyes.

Tip 3: For a casual, mixed-color collection, add one or two different pansies to the dominant choice. More than three colors become visually confusing.

Tip 4: Blue and purple are the graceful bridge between all other colors. Used solo, they recede and become lost in the landscape. But they have the ability to pull other unrelated colors together. Place a soft yellow pansy next to a rosy one. The colors don't clash but are also not exciting. Add a purple blossom, and watch how the trio comes alive.

Tip 5: Consider pansies with the dark blotch, such as Maxim and Majestic Giant, as two-tone blooms. A bed of Majestic Giant yellow flowers is a mass of yellow and black. With the addition of one other blotched blossom, perhaps Majestic Giant blue or purple, the combination presents itself as three colors. The yellow and blue are the primary and secondary colors, with the dark blotch as the third. *Ellen Riley*

Crystal Bowl, Maxim, and Imperial pansies are widely available and offer many shades for a varied color palette.

Beauty Revealed in
FORT WORTH

*An inspiring public garden speaks eloquently
of Eastern philosophy and nature's grand design.*

Sometimes less is more. That lesson never hit home more forcefully than during a visit last November to the Japanese Garden at the Fort Worth Botanic Garden.

I arrived at what I thought would be the peak of fall color in the garden, when scarlet Japanese maples parade themselves in the pond's mirrored water. But a merciless thunderstorm two nights before had stripped away almost every leaf. Its fury revealed a tranquil refuge, sparse and yet rich, defined by line, form, texture, and shadow. That storm opened my eyes to what this garden is all about.

Everything you see here, from plants to rocks to pathways to water, expresses principles of Eastern thought. For example, the garden's labyrinthine pathways create ever-changing perspectives, encouraging peaceful contemplation. "This aspect is fundamental to Zen philosophy," explains garden curator Scott Brooks. "The contemplation of garden elements is intended to bring about sudden flashes of spiritual insight."

Among those insights is the realization that man does not dominate nature, but rather exists within it. Massive trunks and stone outcroppings emphasize nature's ascendance. Except for brief periods in spring and fall, gaudy reds, yellows, pinks, and oranges are absent. "Such colors inhibit introspection," says Scott. Their fleeting presence reflects the Buddhist belief that all material things are transient and pass like leaves on the autumn wind.

BY STEVE BENDER / PHOTOGRAPHY VAN CHAPLIN

LEFT: *Trunks, branches, and leaves mirrored on still water evoke a sense of serenity.* FAR LEFT AND ABOVE: *Viewpoints constantly change along the meandering paths, encouraging contemplation of the overall design.*

What you take away from a visit here depends upon what you bring. "I think of the garden as an unfinished picture within which each visitor's personal experience is developed," says Scott. "That experience is partly stimulated by the external elements of the garden, such as contrasting textures of leaves, stone, and wood. But, ultimately, any emotional or spiritual impact depends on the internal state of the person involved."

The impact on me is telling. For autumn is a favorite season. It's a time for repose, celebration, and renewed wonder at beauty so often looked at, but seldom really seen. In the glint of sunlight bathing naked twigs and in the rustle of leaves scattered upon the ground, I reacquaint myself with my own place in nature's grand design.

The Fort Worth Botanic Garden is located at 3220 Botanic Garden Boulevard off University Drive. Admission is charged. For more information call (817) 871-7686. ◇

Oriental persimmons
(See page 222.)

November

Checklist for November

EDITOR'S NOTEBOOK

One way to impress eggheads and airheads is to bandy about such horticultural terms as "foliar dimorphism." This refers to plants with multiple-shaped leaves. One of my favorite native trees, the sassafras, is a striking example. You'll often see three differently shaped leaves on a single tree—oval, single-lobed (mitten-like), and three-lobed. But that's not the main reason I love this tree. It also develops transcendent fall color in shades of gold, orange, and scarlet. It grows about every place but boggy or strongly alkaline soils. Thanks to a stringy root system, digging one successfully in the wild is harder than finding an on-time airplane. Container-grown trees are the way to go. (Try Woodlander's Inc., [803] 648-7522.) Plant one and soon you'll dazzle neighbors with sagacious pronouncements such as, "Surely no plant is more foliar dimorphic." They'll know for sure you are a grade school graduate. *Steve Bender*

☐ **Birds**—At this time of year, migrating birds need lots of energy. A mixture of suets and seeds provides high-energy foods eagerly consumed at this season. Hang these solid mixtures in racks where they will be easily noticed by the birds.

☐ **Compost**—Cleaning up the garden will yield plenty of fallen leaves and plant debris for compost. In an out-of-the-way corner of the garden, mix green and dry materials with a shovelful of soil and an optional handful of fertilizer (any kind

except a weed-and-feed product). Sprinkle with water weekly if there is no rain. You'll have compost by spring, sooner if you turn the pile.

☐ **Decorative harvest**—Pinecones, grass, wildflower seedheads, grapevine trimmings, magnolia seedpods, bur oak acorns, and other bounty from the countryside and garden should be gathered now for decorative use inside the home.

◄ **Drying herbs**—Because they will soon be killed by frost in the Middle and Lower South, pull up entire basil plants, and hang them intact for use during the winter months. Stems of rosemary, bay, and scented geraniums may also be gathered now while they're in peak condition.

☐ **Perennials**—Now is a great time to divide perennials in the Middle and Lower South. Use a digging fork to lift an entire clump of hostas, garden phlox, heliopsis, Southern shield ferns, or other clump-forming perennials. Many will fall apart naturally; others will have to be pulled apart or cut. Set them back into the soil at original growing depth. ►

☐ **Amaryllis**—Choose red, white, pink, or striped amaryllis for holiday decorations. Blooms appear six to eight weeks after bulbs are planted indoors in containers. Select the largest bulbs, because they often produce two or three scapes of blooms, providing flowers for a longer period. Pot diameter should be at least an inch greater than the largest part of the bulb. Plant with the top of the bulb just above soil level; use a commercial potting mix for best results. In all but North Texas and the Panhandle, amaryllis may be set into the garden permanently after the holidays. Otherwise, they can be kept in pots indoors during the winter.

☐ **Bedding annuals**—Ornamental kale and cabbage, pansies, violas, and snapdragons are mainstays for color displays during winter and spring. Select plants in 4-inch pots, and plant in well-prepared beds that receive at least a half-day of direct sunlight. Bright Lights Swiss chard, with its fine array of colored stems, makes an excellent accent plant.

☐ **Fruit trees**—In the Coastal and Tropical South, if you've lost citrus trees due to the state and federal government's canker control program, consider replacing them with nonsusceptible fruit trees this month. Avocado, mango, lychee, and longan grow to be rather large, up to 30 feet across; star fruit (carambola), jaboticaba, and banana are good possibilities for smaller (10-foot) spaces.

☐ **Herbs**—In the Lower, Coastal, and Tropical South, plant cool-weather herbs, such as mint, thyme, sage, oregano, lavender, and catnip, this month. They will do well in both pot and garden. Several plants with different forms and textures in a large pot can make a pleasant ornament for the patio.

☐ **Lawns**—Continue to overseed lawns with annual ryegrass in the Coastal South this month, and begin overseeding in the Tropical South to keep the lawn green through the winter. Apply the seeds with a broadcast-type fertilizer spreader, and then water them in.

☐ **Onions**—This is a good month to plant onion sets or seeds. For large bulbs, plant a short-day onion, such as Granex hybird. For scallions, any type will do. ▶

◀**Pansies**— When you go to the garden center, look for healthy, green plants with only enough blooms to tell you they are labeled correctly. Avoid plants that are yellowed and leggy. Don't skimp. These are not going to grow into big plants like summer annuals, so buy enough to make an impact. If winter comes early to your garden, consider buying 4-inch pots of pansies, rather than the smaller cell packs that take longer to get established.

☐ **Spring color**—Plan and plant now for color in the spring. Prepare your garden beds by spreading a 2-inch layer of compost or organic material such as sphagnum peat moss or soil conditioner, as well as a slow-release fertilizer (14-14-14, 17-17-17, or 19-6-12) at the rate recommended on the label. Turn it all under. Then set out daffodils or other spring-flowering bulbs. Overplant those with cool-weather annuals, such as pansies or violas, which will bloom in mild winter weather. The bulbs will push up through the annuals in spring for a two-layer garden bed.

☐ **Vegetables**—The Lower South still has time to set out transplants of lettuce and sow seeds of fast-maturing crops such as radishes and cress. Keep harvesting earlier plantings. Cut the center stalk of broccoli, but leave plants in the ground so side shoots can develop.

FERTILIZE

☐ **Lawns**—Fertilize tall fescue and other cool-season lawns in the Middle and Upper South with a quality lawn fertilizer, such as 30-2-4 or 29-3-4, that contains timed-release nitrogen to prevent burn. It will continuously feed your lawn until time for a spring feeding.

CONTROL

☐ **Iron**—If trees and shrubs are showing yellow leaves with greenish veins, they may lack iron. This is particularly a problem in the limestone soils of South Florida. Apply a chelated iron product to the soil at the rate recommended on the label. Ixoras, gardenias, and camellias are especially susceptible, but other landscape plants may also develop this problem.

☐ **Mildew**—Powdery mildew, which looks like a gray-to-white powder on leaf surfaces, appears when nights are cool in the Coastal and Tropical South. Roses, crepe myrtles, grapes, zinnias, mangoes, and papayas are susceptible. Prevent mildew by frequently spraying the foliage with water, or apply a fungicide, such as wettable sulfur.

November notes:

TIP OF THE MONTH

To reduce labor during leaf-raking time each fall, place a curled-up 2- x 3-foot piece of poster board (or thin cardboard) inside a large trash bag. It will hold the bag open and make it stand up straight, so you can toss leaves into it. When the bag is half-filled, remove the poster board. The bag will now stand by itself, and the poster board is ready for the next bag.

PEG HUTCHINS
PORTLAND, MAINE

TULIPS
that come back

I n the garden or in the vase, nothing sings of spring's full-blown finery more beautifully than tulips. If you're in love with this sign of the season but tired of spending time and money on bulbs year after year, it's time you considered species tulips.

It's not too late to plant if you hurry and order bulbs now. These jewels of the spring landscape colonize like daffodils. The majority bloom in April throughout the South, after most of the daffodils have faded. Plants can either grow as high as 12 to 18 inches or be Lilliputian-size, flowering at a mere 3 to 6 inches tall. Flowers cover a range of colors, from bright red to the palest yellow to a pure blush pink. The leaves of many species tulips unfurl into beautiful works of art, striped and mottled in shades of red and purple.

Blossoms open widest on sunny days to reveal detailed splendor, with markings inside the petals that rival the outer hues. Jenks Farmer, curator of botanical gardens at South Carolina's Riverbanks Zoo & Botanical Garden, and the Riverbanks horticultural team plant species tulip bulbs where they will receive full sun. "We suggest keeping them away from the shade of pine trees for the best show," he says, "although they are beautiful when the flowers are closed. The blooms are very elegant and teardrop shaped."

Jenks also recommends that you set species bulbs in beds that tend to be both dry and "not pampered with water and fertilizer in the summer. They do great at the base of spring-flowering shrubs, such as spirea and forsythia."

Cathy Umphrey, a garden designer in Annapolis, mixes species tulips in among perennials. Her beds are hand-watered, so it's easy to regulate the moisture they receive in summer. "For me, sometimes they do just fine in the shade, as long as they don't get too much water," she says.

Mingling tiny species tulips with perennials is a challenge, "because if the tulips aren't placed properly, you lose them in the surrounding foliage," Cathy says. She loves pairing *Tulipa whittallii,* a bronze-tinted bloomer, with the

Apricot Jewel *(Tulipa batalinii)*

Stresa *(Tulipa kaufmanniana)*

BY JULIE A. MARTENS
PHOTOGRAPHY JEAN ALLSOPP
AND VAN CHAPLIN

Lady tulips *(Tulipa clusiana)*

coppery new foliage of Goldflame spirea or with the chartreuse leaves of early spring perennials.

Add species tulip bulbs to your garden this month to enjoy their elegant flower shapes and eye-pleasing colors next spring. Bulbs are tiny; plant no deeper than 4 inches. Mix Bulb Booster Fertilizer (9-9-6) into planting hole.

"Species tulip bulbs are so small and buried so shallowly that they are easy pickings for squirrels," Cathy says. She recommends covering the soil where bulbs are planted with bird netting or plastic strawberry baskets to discourage squirrels from digging and eating bulbs. Water bulbs after planting, and remember to water them in spring when growth emerges. Then simply wait to enjoy a spring performance of perennial color. ◇

(For sources turn to pages 250–251.)

TULIPS WORTH A TRY

Under the right conditions, species tulips come back reliably for years. Unfortunately, discovering which species perform in your area requires a combination of trial and error. Plant different species, taking care to mark planting spots so you can track performance from year to year.

Jenks's picks include plants that are highly reliable:

- Tubergen's Gem *(T. chrysantha)* deep red with yellow center— "Sometimes these bulbs arrive mixed with Cynthia *(T. clusiana)* because they're so similar," he explains. "Cynthia does great too."
- *(T. saxatilis)* rosy pink with yellow center—"This one really needs a summer baking," he says.

Cathy recommends these two:

- Bright Gem *(Tulipa batalinii)* yellow with orange—"This one is so pretty I'd be tempted to try all the *batalinii* cultivars," she says.
- *(T. sylvestris)* clear yellow—"It doesn't come back for me," she says, "but I hate to be without it."

Little Princess *(Tulipa hybrida)*

PHOTOGRAPHS: VAN CHAPLIN

Fruitful Beauty

*One of the most interesting small fruit trees
for the home garden, Oriental (or kaki) persimmon
offers low-maintenance appeal all summer
and delicious, decorative fruit in the fall.*

*These trees supply superb
fall color with vivid fruit and
flaring orange-gold leaves.*

Think of a peach tree hung with giant ripe tomatoes, and you've got the basic idea of an Oriental persimmon. These friendly little trees are dwarf cousins to our native persimmons, but they have much larger fruit.

Oriental persimmons, also known as kaki persimmons from their Latin name, *Diospyros kaki,* grow throughout the South, except for the extreme southern and northern edges. In addition to bearing succulent fruit, these trees have the double virtue of a graceful habit and a multilayered fall color. A valuable addition to the landscape, these low-maintenance, pest-free trees are fast becoming such a hot commodity—and no wonder.

The cool weather of fall and winter is the peak time to enjoy this fruit-laden beauty. It's also the perfect time, after the rains have started and the ground is moist, to plant trees and shrubs across the South. Young Oriental persimmon trees are available this time of year through mail order and at many garden centers. Container-grown trees are perhaps easiest to find and plant, and they usually perform better in the garden.

Because Oriental persimmons don't fall prey to most pests and diseases, there's very little care involved after you've planted them

Oriental persimmons need little care and have a sturdy natural shape, making them a good choice for the garden.

in a nice sunny spot. A light application of fertilizer (either a general-purpose 15-5-10 or a special formula for fruit and citrus) will keep your tree in peak condition. Apply according to label instructions every two months from early spring until early autumn. Usually, the only pruning needed is removing dead wood or crossing limbs.

If you have any doubts about the pleasures of eating a persimmon, you'll be delighted with the rich yet mild flavor of properly ripened fruit. Our native persimmons are all astringent (puckering) until ripe, but Oriental persimmons are divided into astringent and nonastringent types—both absolutely delicious. Nonastringent ones, such as Fuyu Gaki, are sweet and gentle to the tongue. Astringent Oriental persimmons, such as Hira Tanenashi, are probably a little more cold hardy. It's an old wives' tale that astringent persimmons need frost to ripen. What they *do* need is to color up completely and get just a little soft, like a really ripe tomato. Then they are among the tastiest of fruits.

All Oriental persimmons will continue to ripen if left on the tree, but they also will keep well if stored in a cool place. They even make fantastic fall decorations. When you combine decorative, tasty fruits with graceful beauty, you get one of the nicest plants available to Southern gardeners.   *Liz Druitt*

(For sources turn to pages 250–251.)

PERSIMMON PARTICULARS

For extreme climates in the Upper South and Tropical South, we recommend planting the taller, but still very attractive, native (American) persimmon *(Diospyros virginiana).* If you're concerned about the suitability of Oriental persimmons for your area, be sure to choose trees grafted onto native persimmon rootstock.

Plan carefully before planting an ornamental tree that also bears fruit. If you don't pick your persimmons, the dropped fruit can stain a patio, driveway, sidewalk, or deck.

Parsley's bright green hue provides contrast to the pink petals and dark foliage of these snapdragons. Try it with other brightly colored flowers.

PHOTOGRAPHS: VAN CHAPLIN

PARSLEY
At a Glance

Type: biennial usually used as an annual
Light: full sun to partial shade
Soil: rich, moist, well drained
Water: approximately once a week; soil should be moist but not wet
Height: 1 to 2 feet
Range: All South
Season: fall through spring; may last well into summer in cooler areas of the South
Expect to pay: $12 and up per flat

Pretty Parsley

This easy-care herb yearns to add new flavor to the flower border.

ABOVE, LEFT: *When removing transplants from cells, gently squeeze the bottom of the pack to loosen the dirt.* CENTER: *Carefully pull roots apart to encourage spreading once the plant is in the ground. Separate only about the lower third of the root ball.* RIGHT: *Plant in a shallow hole in deeply prepared rich, moist soil, using a timed-release fertilizer such as 14-14-14 or 17-17-17 in the bottom of the hole. Add a few handfuls of composted manure as well.*

Long favored in herb gardens for its fresh peppery flavor, curly parsley *(Petroselinum crispum)* is making the move to the flowerbed. The interesting foliage combines well with many types of flowers, and ease of care makes parsley a great choice for novice as well as experienced gardeners. With bright-emerald color and compact, frilly leaves, this cool-weather herb provides impact all winter long in beds and containers.

"I love to use it in the parterre style," says Jennifer Denslow, owner of Fine Gardening in Columbia, South Carolina. "I create a pattern with the parsley, then fill it in with pansies or violas." She has used the herb as an ornamental in several gardens, including Columbia's famous Riverbanks Zoo & Botanical Garden.

For a container combination, Jennifer suggests planting parsley with red cabbage and large-flowering pansies, such as Majestic Giants. Last year, she edged a client's daylily bed with it during the winter, a pairing she describes as "a really nice contrast, because the dark green parsley against the new growth of the daylilies always looked fresh."

The easiest and quickest way to start parsley is to buy transplants from a garden center and follow the steps as shown above. Do not purchase pot-bound plants. This will cause them to bolt (or flower) early. Parsley also can be started from seeds sown on top of deeply prepared soil that's kept moist. To help seeds germinate, soak them in warm water for 24 hours before planting. A second sowing in late winter often lasts well into the summer.

Once established, plants require only minimal care. If watered too often, they will rot, so moisten just enough to keep the soil from drying out completely—about once a week in most areas. Yellow flowers should appear in early summer. Removing them lengthens the plant's life, but the leaves will be tough and unsuitable for use in the kitchen. Because it is truly a biennial, parsley performs best if you replant every year. *Emily Sollie*

Investing In Silver

These silver plants require little maintenance to add their coolness to a Texas day and their magic to the moonlight.

The wide-open Texas sky brings with it a wide-open blast of sun. Many gardeners focus, with good reason, on plants that can take the resulting heat and drought without wilting, frying, and just folding up. We also tend to focus on plants that look wonderful at dawn or dusk, the times when, let's face it, we're most willing to go out there. To come up with a planting that can cool down a hot noon *and* shine under the midnight moon is a major achievement.

Bill Seaman, a Dallas-based garden designer, worked out a remarkably pretty and functional entry planting that performs this way all year long with minimal maintenance requirements. He chose plants, in consultation with homeowner Barbara Wolin, that would accent and soften the native limestone steps leading from the street to her front yard. "The plants also had to be very forgiving of foot traffic," explains Bill. "Because they are planted into cracks and crevices around the steps and landing, there is definitely opportunity for them to get stepped on."

Barbara truly likes tough plants that perform. "She thinks a lot like I do," Bill says. "We both feel there are so many really good plants out there that don't have to be coddled, why not take advantage of them?" With these sensible guidelines in mind—and the knowledge that drainage would not be a problem—Bill enjoyed developing the basic silver color scheme. "The gray and silver foliage shades are cooling to the eye in the Texas heat, plus they enhance the reflective qualities of the rugged limestone. And," Bill adds, smiling, "the Wolins don't have to use any extra lighting for their pathway at night!"

Bill created planting pockets in and around the stone steps by filling crevices with decomposed granite to anchor the plant roots and a layer of compost for nutrition. "While a planting like this is new, it actually does need frequent watering, just like any

The shimmering foliage of prostrate germander and various thymes softens these stark Texas limestone steps.

PHOTOGRAPH: VAN CHAPLIN

garden bed," he explains. He also suggests the application of a little extra compost to help the plants fill out and get their roots well developed. "Once everything is established," Bill says, "minimal irrigation, an occasional deadheading, and an occasional light top dressing of mulch or compost are all that you need to keep the planting looking fresh year-round."

For extra color, Barbara adds a few annuals, such as violas, to the silver planting every season. And the various perennials in the beds bloom off and on, in cool shades of purple, mauve, and white. "But for the most part," says Bill cheerfully, "the basic planting looks good all year, all by itself, no matter what. It really doesn't have a significant downtime, which is unusual for a perennial bed." Terrific, in fact, especially for a Texas garden. It's a shining example for the rest of us.

Liz Druitt

TOP 10 SILVER PLANTS

- Powis Castle artemisia (*Artemisia* Powis Castle)
- Six Hills Giant catmint (*Nepeta faassenii* Six Hills Giant)
- Crete dittany (*Origanum dictamnus* Crete)
- prostrate germander (*Teucrium chamaedrys* Prostratum)
- horehound (*Marrubium vulgare*)
- lamb's ears (*Stachys byzantina*)
- Spanish lavender (*Lavandula stoechas*)
- common mullein (*Verbascum thapsus*)
- santolina/lavender cotton (*Santolina chamaecyparissus*)
- silver thyme (*Thymus* x *citriodorus* Argenteus)

Tailored to Perfection

PHOTOGRAPHS: VAN CHAPLIN

LEFT: Formal architecture calls for simple planting. The key to success in this design is restraint, keeping the plant palette along the foundation to four species: English ivy, mondo grass, Gumpo azalea, and boxwood.

The most formal clothing is often strikingly simple. Consider the black tuxedo with white tucked shirt or the classic little black dress with a strand of pearls. So it is with a landscape. As this home in Atlanta illustrates, simple plantings combined with formal architecture create an understated elegance.

"It's a very simple, clean design— very tailored," says landscape architect Bill Smith. "Because it is a one-story house, the plantings had to be low. Otherwise, they would have brought the facade to its knees."

Working with only a handful of different plants, Bill sculpted beds that ease the home into the surrounding land. "It looks the same in the winter as it does in the summer," he notes.

Creating surprisingly low maintenance, the evergreen beds require little besides an owner's blowing leaves from the paving, edging the ivy before it creeps onto the drive, and trimming the ivy growing on the house wall before it gets onto the soffit. "I wanted the ivy to look as if it is never quite reaching its goal," Bill explains. "I never want a straight line at the soffit."

Although the plantings give little seasonal variation in color, interest lies in the contrasting leaf shapes and shades of green. The English ivy varies from the bright green of its new growth to the dark green of its mature foliage. The leafy carpet makes a pattern that holds its own against the adjacent brick drive.

Along the foundation, the fine blades of mondo grass provide the dominant texture. Its black-green color complements the dark green shutters. Although their leaves are small, the Gumpo azaleas below the windows stand out by virtue of their rounded leaves and lighter green color. Their placement also emphasizes the windows.

Two black iron urns accent the entry and create an imaginary triangle with the pediment over the door. The urns contrast with the cream trim. Functioning as sculptural ornaments, they remain empty to highlight their classical form.

Because there is no grass to mow, weed, and fertilize, the landscape achieves a true low-maintenance status.

The design is so appealing that the lack of a lawn can be easily overlooked. The drive enters the property with a direct view of the front door, turns right at a generous circle of paving, and continues around the side of the house to the family entrance. Bordered with brick and centered with an antique millstone the circle serves as an entry court.

The drive substitutes for the lawn, creating a simple foreground to the home. The color value of the dyed gray concrete is consistent with that of a lawn and matches the brick used in the house. All in all, this is a design that is timeless in style, with the simplest of needs.   *Linda C. Askey*

ABOVE, LEFT: The entry bricks are set diagonally in a clever basket-weave pattern to give the appearance of herringbone. LEFT: The ivy climbing the wall is periodically pulled away so that it appears to be just filling in.

Gardening on The Wall

Whether you're short on garden space or need to decorate a dull wall, an easy espalier offers big rewards.

Why would anyone take a perfectly nice plant and flatten it against a wall? No, it's not the earmark of compulsive gardeners with too much time on their hands or some strange form of horticultural revenge. Classic espaliers use fruit trees or red-berried pyracantha and cotoneaster, but few take advantage of flowering shrubs and trees. Espalier, especially simple forms such as this gently fanned camellia, is actually beneficial to a flowering shrub and remarkably easy to train and maintain.

Even in partial shade, such as beneath the eaves of your house, thinning and spreading out your camellia allows light to reach every part, not just the outer branches. The classic fan shape also encourages the flow of nutrients along the branches, because there's not quite as much gravity to fight. As a result, the shrub is more likely to bloom from top to bottom and at multiple points along each limb.

If this encourages you to brighten up your own bare walls with a camellia espalier, you'll be pleased to know that this is not a major project. All you need is some nearly invisible 16-gauge galvanized wire and a hammer and nails (for wood surfaces) or, preferably, eyebolts (for wood or masonry) and a drill with the appropriate bit. Eyebolts make the trellis sturdier and hold the wires out from the surface of the wall a bit to allow more air to circulate around the camellia plant.

Set evenly spaced eyebolts into the wall a little higher than you plan for your shrub to grow. You can either measure the width of the space so that the bolts divide it precisely, or simply give it your best guess because the wire won't be obvious anyway. Then set a single eyebolt at the bottom of the wall, below the lowest point where you'll attach a branch of the camellia. This bolt should be roughly in the center of the space to be covered by the espalier. Thread your wire through the top and bottom eyebolts to create a fan pattern, and then twist the ends thoroughly to secure and tighten the wire.

That's all there is to it. You now have a wonderful wire fan trellis. You just need some soft jute twine (available at home or garden centers) to tie the branches to the wires, and you're ready to espalier. Oh, and you do need the camellia, of course.

BY LIZ DRUITT / PHOTOGRAPHY VAN CHAPLIN

Espaliering this camellia's branches exposes more of the shrub to sunlight, increasing the number and effect of vivid flowers.

Plant a young, flexible shrub between 12 and 24 inches from the wall (for growing room and better access to soil nutrients and water), and prune branches that are growing in inconvenient directions or refuse to be bound to the wires. As your camellia grows, continue to clip protruding branches, or secure them to the fan of wires, making sure to allow room in the espalier for good air movement and access to sunlight.

You will be amazed at the abundance of flowers you'll have with this simple training method, and your friends and neighbors will be impressed by your gardening expertise. ◇

Poinsettia combinations (See pages 240–241.)

December

Checklist for December

EDITOR'S NOTEBOOK

Okay, so I like a little color at Christmas. And for holiday color, nothing beats poinsettias. Bet you didn't know that most poinsettias sold in the South originate at the Paul Ecke Ranch in Encinitas, California. I recently visited Ecke's greenhouses to see what's new. I saw bracts of pink, rose, white, salmon, pink-and-white (Marble), red with pink flecks (Jingle Bells), and light pink dusted with deep rose (Monet). I saw Winter Rose, whose short, crinkly red bracts look like corsages. I even saw a purple one (perfect for those festive holiday wakes). But if you think a poinsettia isn't good unless it's red, look for Freedom Red, shown above. Its bright red bracts and burgundy-green foliage last for months indoors. Any other new colors on the horizon? Well, I hear tell the folks at Ecke are working on a blue one. Wouldn't that look great sitting beside your pink Christmas tree?

Steve Bender

☐ **Arrangements**—If you're missing the wealth of fresh material you had in summer for centerpieces, don't overlook the dried seedpods and grasses that offer interesting shapes and textures.

☐ **Cold preparation**—Relocating your container plants to areas where they will be more protected from cold temperatures can save time and work. Putting them closer to your home or under a tree canopy can make the temperature difference necessary to save your plants. Consider using a plant dolly, or place pots on movable casters for easy relocation. ▶

☐ **Freeze protection**—Guard tender plants from occasional freezes by covering them temporarily with sheeting, plastic, or pots (preferably clay) in the Lower and Coastal South. For a more permanent solution, move plants indoors or to a greenhouse.

☐ **Irrigation**—If your automatic watering system stays on year-round, it's time to adjust the amount of watering during each cycle. Many dormant plants require lower amounts of water in the colder months. A good rule of thumb is to reduce station irrigation time by half when night temperatures remain in the 40s or below. Of course, turn the system off in continuously rainy periods to reduce costs and prevent overwatering.

☐ **Mulch**—Try composting or mulching with your deciduous tree leaves rather than bagging them for the trash. Chop and add 2 to 3 inches to the flowerbed, and occasionally rake or fork lightly so water and air can easily move through to the soil.

◀**Poinsettias, narcissus, and amaryllis**—Add color and cheer to indoor holiday decorating. For several weeks of color, select poinsettias that are just beginning to open their small yellow flowers in the center of the colorful bracts. Amaryllis, narcissus, tulips, and other pots of flowering bulbs should be kept cool and moist for longer life.

☐ **Bedding plants**—Add colorful, cold-hardy annuals such as petunias, pansies, sweet alyssum, and snapdragons to the garden. Select plants that are just coming into bloom, and plant early in the month so that they become established prior to arrival of the coldest temperatures. Water well before planting so the root ball is wet and plants are easier to remove from the pot. Check tags for appropriate spacing to ensure beds fill in completely. ▶

☐ **Bulbs**—It's still okay to plant bulbs such as tulips, daffodils, and Dutch iris. By now, many nurseries have put them on sale. Inspect sale bulbs carefully, making sure they are firm to the touch and that the bottoms aren't moldy. If a bulb is lightweight or soft, keep looking.

☐ **Indoor garden**—Many herbs, such as mint, parsley, catnip, thyme, and oregano, will thrive in a well-lit winter windowsill. Select healthy plants from the garden center. Any well-drained soil mixture will work for container-grown herbs. Rotate plants regularly to keep sun exposure even and prevent lopsided growth.

☐ **Roses**—Now is the time to add roses to your garden in the Coastal South. For best growth, select plants grafted on Fortuniana rootstock. Ask the salesperson to be sure.

Plant in an area where they will receive at least six to eight hours of sunlight all year. Cover newly planted bare-root roses with soil, mulch, or a large plastic pot to protect from oncoming frost, and remove cover after danger has passed. When temperatures warm and new growth emerges, begin feeding plants on a regular basis, and keep them well watered.

☐ **Sasanqua camellias**—In the Lower South, these vigorous and hardy camellias are excellent choices for hedges or specimens. They usually bloom from mid- to late-fall. Choose flowering plants to ensure you get the color and blossom form you want. Flowers may be single or double and range in color from white to pink to red. Sasanquas prefer partial shade and acid soil. Mainly useful as outdoor accents, their flowers are also attractive when floated in shallow bowls.

PRUNE

☐ **Perennials**—It's time to trim perennials that have finished blooming in your garden. Cut back Autumn Joy Sedum, Mexican bush Sage, fall asters, and garden mums within a few inches of the crown; then apply mulch for the winter after the night temperatures are consistently below 50 degrees. ▶

FERTILIZE

☐ **Lawns**—Fertilize cool-season grasses during the winter months in the Upper and Middle South. Annual and perennial ryegrass may still be planted and are particularly useful to prevent erosion and stabilize soil. Perennial ryegrass, Kentucky bluegrass, and tall fescue can make beautiful, year-round lawns in these areas, provided you water regularly.

☐ **Lime**—If the soil is acidic, your landscape probably could benefit from an application of lime. The easiest form for homeowner use is pelletized lime. Broadcast using a fertilizer spreader, or apply by hand. Always wear gloves, and distribute evenly. Because lime takes a long time to react with the soil, winter applications help the spring garden. Apply at the rate of 15 to 20 pounds per 1,000 square feet. If you are unsure of how much lime your soil needs, have a soil test performed.

CONTROL

◀**Camellias**—As you cut blooms for decorations, be sure to inspect for tea scale, which appears as white patches on the undersides of leaves. Horticultural oil is good for control. (An effective product is Volck Oil Spray.) Be sure to coat the leaves entirely with the oil. This can be done on a monthly basis, following label directions, while temperatures stay between 40 and 85 degrees.

☐ **Greens**—If frost has not occurred in your area, greens such as turnips, kale, and collards may have aphids. These little green bugs are controlled easily with a jet of water sprayed vigorously on the leaves just before harvest. Follow up with an extra wash before cooking. ▶

December notes:

_____

_____

_____

_____

_____

_____

_____

_____

_____

_____

_____

_____

_____

_____

_____

_____

_____

_____

_____

_____

_____

TIP OF THE MONTH

Don't throw away the wood ashes from your fireplace this year; they make terrific fertilizer for roses. Just spread the ashes around the bases of your roses, and rake gently to mix them with the soil.

SHERRI BROWN
BROOKSVILLE, FLORIDA

petite trees

Decorate creatively with tiny pines and dwarf spruce.

When we bring a tree indoors for the holidays, our senses stir with the memories of tradition—a fabulous Fraser fir, stately spruce, or majestic pine. Loads of lights, ornaments, and a star are all part of the big picture, with a large portion of the room consumed by this seasonal staple. But there are other ways to enjoy the wide variety of conifers available, on a much smaller scale. Bring these tiny trees indoors, and arrange them atop tables, on stairways, or as a centerpiece to spread garden-style holiday cheer throughout the house.

BY ELLEN RILEY / PHOTOGRAPHY JEAN ALLSOPP / STYLING BUFFY HARGETT

Compact conifers rest in festive elegance on a side table. OPPOSITE: *An antique suitcase packs a small forest. A grouping of white flowers works to pull the look together.*

Petite red pots hug the steps, their holiday color contrasting with the walls. Plants this size need water daily; moss helps retain moisture. This grouping requires no other adornment.

CONIFER CARE

The best way to keep conifers healthy is to maintain them outdoors, bringing them in only when company comes. But moving decorations back and forth is not always practical, so try these tips.

Water every two to three days. Indoor heat is drying, and a conifer's soil should never dry out. A finger in the dirt will not give you a good reading on dryness; a moisture meter is more helpful.

Keep them cool. Whenever possible, place your arrangement away from sources of heat. This will lessen drying and diminish insect problems.

Watch out for spider mites. Signs of infestation include brown or yellow needles and small webs. Prevention is easier than a cure, so mist the foliage daily with water.

Once the holidays have passed, gently introduce your shrubs back outdoors. Place them outside on warm days, and protect them—in an unheated garage for example—from frigid nighttime temperatures. Remember to water about once a week. After reconditioning, plant conifers as a group in a large container, or add to your landscape.

First, choose decorative containers. Consider a collection of vessels in graduated sizes, each to hold one small tree. They can be simple and elegant, like the copper pots we used, or as easygoing as galvanized buckets.

Add some surprise to your arrangement by using something that might not ordinarily hold plants at all, such as an antique suitcase or a wooden crate. Wrap a gift box in magnificent paper, and fill it with a miniature forest. Select a simple pot in a striking color, and repeat it across a mantel or down the length of a table. To protect furniture from moisture, line the containers with saucers, plastic, or foil.

Next, peruse the garden shop's shrub stock. Take along your containers to make the perfect selection for each. You're apt to find an assortment of spruce, juniper, cypress, and pine in 1-gallon pots. Some may be pruned into a traditional cone shape, while others may be more free-form or mounding. A combination of shapes and textures will give your arrangement natural appeal.

At home, water all plants well, and allow them to drain before placing them in lined containers. Dress each pot with moss to hide unsightly edges and help retain moisture.

Add flowers to your arrangement for extra sparkle. Snowy-white narcissus and pansies will last indoors for about a week, while petite poinsettias and cyclamen will carry on for several. If space is too tight in the container, place the blooming plants in plastic sandwich bags. They will snuggle easily into the group.

Surround the plant's base with glass balls or pinecones, or use kumquats and cranberries for colorful punch. Add finesse with elegant wired ribbon running through the branches. Incorporate seasonal touches with restraint, so they don't hide these lovely trees. ◇

A little grooming now is all it takes for your water feature to remain an attractive element of the garden.

Winter Care For Water Gardens

Everyone enjoys water features during the warm weather, but don't forget about yours in the winter. A pool can become an eyesore when left unattended. Clean and groom in and around your pool now, so you can enjoy it come spring, instead of working on winter's neglected chores.

Now that most of the leaves have fallen, this is a good time to remove any debris that has settled in your pond. Leaves decomposing underwater give off methane gas, which can create an unhealthy environment for fish. After cleaning your pool, put a thin netting over it to catch any leaves or straw being blown around your yard. Or rake a large area around your water feature to help prevent this.

In warmer regions of the South you may still be enjoying your watery oasis, but in colder areas you could be looking at a frozen ice puck. Cold water makes fish sluggish; with their lowered metabolism, they seem as though they're swimming in slow motion. Stop feeding them once the water temperature dips below 45 degrees. The plant and bacteria growth that breaks down fish waste is not available in frigid water, and the declining water quality can be detrimental to fish.

If you have fish and live in colder regions and your pond surface freezes for more than 10 days, you should make a hole in the ice to release trapped methane. Never break the ice using a hammer; the shock waves can kill fish. Pour boiling water on the pond's edge to melt a hole to release gases.

A submersible pump equipped with a foam jet (bubbler) set to discharge water an inch or two below the surface can be placed in the pool's center to move warmer, deep water to the top. This prevents the surface from freezing. If you leave the pump on throughout the winter, check it periodically to make sure debris doesn't stop up its intake. Also check after power outages to make sure ice hasn't formed over the discharge pipe.

Tropical water lilies will overwinter in warm regions that don't receive killing frost. If your hardy lilies are sitting on bricks or a plant shelf, drop them to the bottom of the pool where they can avoid being frozen solid.

The South is lucky enough to have occasional warm days through the winter months. Use these pretty days to clean your water feature. Although your pond may look lifeless at this time of year, it may be the only source of water for birds and squirrels. Don't turn your water feature into a swamp this winter. The neighbors and the critters will thank you. ◇

The heaviest fruiter of all the hollies, Burford puts on a spectacular show in fall and winter.

Whoa, Nellie! Plant a Burford

The best holly for berries originated not in a nursery, but in a Southern cemetery. Can you dig it?

Cemetery superintendents are usually more concerned with what goes into the ground than what comes out. But Thomas Burford was different. Back around 1900, this particular superintendent planted a number of Chinese holly seedlings in Atlanta's Westview Cemetery. The plants looked just like Chinese hollies are supposed to—kind of gangly, spiny, and unkempt. All except one, that is.

This one grew into an almost perfect ball, 15 to 20 feet high and wide. Its leaves weren't prickly, but possessed a single spine at the tip. Best of all was the show it put on in winter. Large, bright red berries, too many to count and perfect for decorating, nearly hid the leaves—all without the aid of a pollinator. Thus was born Burford holly. It quickly became a Southern standby, thriving everywhere except the Tropical South.

But times change, and not always for the better. Today, it's hard to find Burford holly

(*Ilex cornuta* Burfordii) at many garden centers. A newer holly, Nellie R. Stevens, has dethroned it. With deep-green, spiny leaves and a pyramidal shape, Nellie looks more like a traditional holly tree. It's more cold hardy than Burford, takes pruning very well, and is easier to use up close to the house or in a row as a clipped hedge or screen. But it just can't match Burford for berries.

Burford's rotundity may have caused its fall from grace, but there are easy ways to find space for one. First, grow Burford holly out in the yard as a specimen plant, where it can spread to its trunk's content. Or trim off its lower branches to a height of 3 to 4 feet, and turn it into a multitrunked tree. This way, you can grow grass beneath it or plant it close to the house without blocking lower windows.

Finally, consider planting a compact selection called Dwarf Burford (*I. cornuta* Burfordii Nana). Much like Burford, it sports

When choosing a holly for your landscape, don't overlook alternate selections. While bright red is the usual berry color (above, left), D'Or, a close relative to Burford, features abundant yellow fruit (above).

The berries of either plant are an important winter food source for birds. You'll discover just how much the birds like them if you ever find yourself visiting Callaway Gardens in Pine Mountain, Georgia, on a late winter day. Hungry flocks of robins and cedar waxwings will attack a lengthy hedge of mature Burford hollies that stands about 20 feet high. Luckily, Burford's numerous berries can withstand this onslaught. LuAnn Craighton, manager of Conservation Studies at Callaway, cautions visitors to be wary of these gluttonous birds, as they fly somewhat erratically after consuming a bellyful of sun-fermented berries.

If you want a Burford holly but can't find it at the garden center, it's time for Plan B—get a start from a friend who has one. To start Burford from seed, scrape away a berry's red fleshy coating to expose the seed. Then place the seed inside a zip-top plastic bag filled with moist potting soil. Place the bag in the refrigerator for three months, and then transfer the seed to the garden. You can also root tip cuttings. Just dip the cut end in rooting powder, and stick the cutting into moist potting soil.

This venerable holly merits a fresh, unjaded look. So the next time you visit your garden center, say, "Whoa, Nellie," and buy a Burford. Not only will you be continuing a Southern tradition, but you'll also be correcting a situation that has cemetery superintendents throughout the South gravely concerned.

Steve Bender

single-spined leaves, but it holds its smaller leaves closer together on the stem and does not fruit as heavily. Word to the wise—"dwarf" in this case doesn't mean small. Dwarf Burford can grow 10 feet tall and wide, so plan carefully when deciding where to plant.

When happy, Burford holly is harder to kill than a federal program. It takes heat and drought and adapts to most well-drained soil. It does fine in shade but boasts more berries if planted in sun. Its only serious pests are scales, which form small bumps on stems and leaves. Spraying with horticultural oil according to label directions annihilates the little suckers.

Like many other red-fruited shrubs and trees, Burford has a cousin that bears yellow fruit. A selection called D'Or, pictured above right, looks just like Burford in form, size, and leaf shape, but its berries are gleaming yellow.

Under the Mistletoe: Paradise or Parasite?

Is mistletoe festive and romantic, or a tree-damaging scourge?

Creamy translucent berries sparkle among leathery green leaves. A red ribbon bow suspends the branch of mistletoe from an archway. The stage is set for kisses, and during the social whirl of the Christmas season, opportunity for sneaking smooches is at an all-time high. Green in winter, when all else is sere and brown, fruiting as the autumn ends, living apparently on air—like love itself—mistletoe's right to symbolize renewed fertility and passion in midwinter is clear enough. What isn't clear is how to cope with it.

Mistletoe *(Phoradendron* sp.) is a pest that gets most of its sustenance from the trees on which it grows. It isn't usually deadly to its hosts, but often causes unsightly bulges and warping in a branch where it takes root. And, if enough mistletoe infests a weakened tree, the tree may very well be stressed to death.

"We encourage people to remove it as soon as they find it in their trees," says Bill Seaman, a certified arborist with Arborilogical Services, Inc., in Dallas. "If it's on limbs that can be pruned away without destroying the tree's structure or aesthetics, then remove them back to their point of origin. If that's not possible, cut the mistletoe off at its base. The goal is to not let it seed."

Bill explains that unless you remove the tree limb at least a foot below the point of mistletoe attachment, the mistletoe will grow back from its "roots" (properly called haustoria). "On larger, established trees, it's more practical to focus on managing it. At the worst, you would have to knock it off once a year until the mistletoe finally dies."

Is there any way to prevent it from growing in the first place? "Plant mistletoe resistant trees," says Bill. (For a partial list, see top right.) If you don't have that option, or live in an area with a heavily infested stand of trees nearby, you will always have to keep an eye out for this evergreen pest.

"The most appropriate month for working on control," Bill says, "is obviously December. In fact," he adds with a twinkle, "I always think harvesting mistletoe at Christmas is the ideal use of plant material." *Liz Druitt*

Gardening for the Eye

PHOTOGRAPH: VAN CHAPLIN

Carefully clipped fig vine against a gray wall changes perceptions and makes this cozy garden seem more spacious.

The most prominent visual object in Louis Aubert's new backyard was a glaring white cement-block shed. Fortunately, as an interior designer and colorist specializing in fine-tuning the historic houses in New Orleans, Louis saw his eyesore as an interesting challenge. "This is an urban garden, no larger than 30 by 40 feet," he says. "With this kind of space, I had to put every surface to work."

To give the shed a sophisticated presence, Louis added a few architectural details such as finials, shutters, and an arbor. Then he painted the exterior a dark gray. The new color stopped the glare and allowed the shed to recede, blurring the garden's tight visual boundaries.

"That still wasn't enough to give me a comfortable feeling of space," Louis says, "so I decided to make the area actually look like the far end of a garden by creating a false perspective. I planted creeping fig vine on the repainted shed, behind a border of old bricks and a low hedge of boxwood."

A novel idea fools the eye and stretches this garden's horizon.

FIG VINE
At a Glance

Light: sun or shade
Soil: any
Water: frequently during first year, then as needed
Range: Lower, Coastal, Tropical South. Wintercreeper euonymus *(Euonymus fortunei)* is a good substitute in the Middle and Upper South.
Remarks: reasonably salt tolerant; avoid planting on wood.

He chose fig vine *(Ficus pumila)* for several reasons. "By clipping the vine as a topiary," he explains, "though it's only 1 inch thick, it gives the impression of distant evergreens."

Louis found creating the fig vine topiary remarkably easy. First, he drew pencil lines on the wall where he wanted the vine to grow, and then he simply clipped it with garden scissors. "Once you get the pattern going," he says, "you can pretty much do it by eye."

Maintenance is easy too. "I touch up with a light pruning about every other week," Louis says, "and it takes two or three minutes, no big deal. I clip a little more in the summer, when the rains come. Ficus loves rainwater and responds to it, so I always have to trim it the week following a rain."

This attention to detail might not be for everyone, but Louis feels that gardeners will understand his urge to create the largest garden possible for his little patch of ground. *Liz Druitt*

Easy Ways With
Poinsettias

Plant combinations help put this flower's best face forward.

Poinsettias are an upstanding holiday tradition, with colorful blooms held high on arrow-straight stems. Wrapped in bright foil and flashy bows, they are a challenge to incorporate into your home. They also habitually drop leaves—usually, all of them—when the soil becomes dry. The result is fabulous flowers with naked knees.

Here is an easy approach to showcase this flower to its best advantage and give your seasonal decorating a boost. Combine assorted houseplants with a poinsettia in a pretty pot, and you'll have an arrangement that will help you celebrate into the New Year.

Give your holiday collection a fresh look with an imaginative container. You may have the perfect pot around the house already. A tiny stone birdbath can function as a centerpiece for petite poinsettias, and an old wooden toolbox can do double duty on a tabletop. A galvanized or brass tub will hold large plants and make a big statement in a prominent place.

THINK BIG
For a sizable display, choose a container to hold a 6- or 8-inch potted poinsettia, along with several other similarly sized plants. Line the bottom of the container with foil or plastic, and provide saucers for added moisture protection.

Place the poinsettia as the focal point, and add ferns with soft, graceful foliage

to surround its lanky stems. Asparagus, Dallas, and table ferns *(Pteris* sp.) are good options. Drape a few fronds over the edge to soften the sides. Give short plants a boost: Put these height-impaired additions on upside-down empty clay pots inside the container.

Add more color and interest with decorative foliage. In our arrangement shown at far right, pink fittonia mirrors the poinsettia's color and adds broad-leaved texture to balance the frilly ferns.

Plants such as calathea and dracaena have leaves that match or complement many poinsettia shades.

Place your large arrangement on the floor in a comfortable seating area or on a fireplace hearth. For a grand, colorful welcome, position it on a foyer table to greet arriving holiday guests.

BY ELLEN RILEY / PHOTOGRAPHY JEAN M. ALLSOPP / STYLING BUFFY HARGETT

Poinsettias take on a new look with these combinations. African violets, variegated ivy, and airy maidenhair fern give them a needed boost.

SMALLER SCALE

Use the same approach with poinsettias in 3- or 4-inch pots. Maidenhair fern, variegated ivy, dracaena, peace lily, and fittonia make good companions. Combine lacy and broad-leaved foliage for textural balance, and always choose a draping plant, such as ivy, to cascade over the side.

Add blooming houseplants that work with your poinsettia's color. Dark purple and blue African violets complement most pastel poinsettias, and white kalanchoe adds sparkle to red holiday flowers. Paperwhites, jewel-toned cyclamen, and miniature azaleas offer vivid options.

Snuggle foliage and flowers closely to make your arrangement lush and full. If this is difficult with plants in their original containers, the solution is simple: Place each plant, minus the pot, in a plastic sandwich bag. Without rigid sides, soil can be compressed to allow more plants into the mix. The bags also retain moisture, so roots dry out slowly and require less attention. Tip: When these plants look dry, just use a kitchen baster to drip a small amount of water into each bag.

Silvery Spanish moss is a lovely finishing touch with pastel poinsettias, and green sheet moss makes a rich addition to red ones. Drape it over the edges for a fluid feel. The moss will tie together all the colors and textures. ◇

Step into two homes filled with holiday charm and spirit.

PERHAPS BECAUSE of its history as a resort destination, Alabama's Eastern Shore inspires relaxation and radiates hospitality. The fine old houses edging the water in Point Clear, Fairhope, Montrose, and Daphne often serve as vacation retreats for extended families. Year-round residents bask in the serenity that accompanies their proximity to Mobile Bay; its sound and scent are never far away.

Due to the relatively mild winters, doors often remain open to invite in the crisp December air. The temperate climate means that plant materials such as Spanish moss, camellias, and palmettos are readily available for use in preparing for a season of celebration. When they are combined with fresh fruit, the essence of holiday spirit finds expression simply and beautifully.

BEING NATURAL

BY JULIA HAMILTON
PHOTOGRAPHY JEAN ALLSOPP, SYLVIA MARTIN
STYLING BUFFY HARGETT

THE ROBIN HOUSE

How do you decorate a home for the holidays when it's nearly perfect already, with spacious porches leading to expansive snowy white rooms—all with wonderful views of Mobile Bay. The answer is simplicity. "We want the house to be a pure and simple background with no fuss about it," says Montrose interior designer Candy Murphy as she considers the Point Clear home of Duke Robin.

Candy starts by placing a welcoming holiday tree on the front porch. "We think that with such a beautiful entrance, a simple tree is appropriate," she says. After encircling the fir with tiny white lights and grapevine, Candy hangs spheres covered in cranberries. She adds garlands of red berries from a crafts store, chosen both for their bright color and weather resistance. To finish the festive look, Candy banks the base of the tree with cardboard boxes covered in sheet moss to resemble packages.

Just inside on a table in the foyer, citrus topiaries and pineapples rest atop a blanket of palmetto fronds. The topiaries, which are a cinch to create, use wooden or plastic florist picks to attach lemons and limes to cones of florist foam.

The Robin house offers a sweeping staircase, just perfect for draping with a lush garland of fresh cedar. For a more festive look, an embellishment with lengths of gold ribbons and palmetto fronds (which will dry into papery green fans) is another easy additional step. **Tip:** Insert the palmetto stems into water picks to prolong their freshness.

While this holiday tends to flaunt bold colors, Candy carefully avoids overwhelming the home's neutral palette. Instead, she keeps to natural elements by draping the family room's doors and windows with cedar roping. "Because the room doesn't have window treatments," Candy says, "the cedar makes it seem warmer." The mood extends outdoors, beyond the family room and its enclosed porch, where grapevine balls encircled with white lights hang from ancient live oak trees.

ARCHITECT: ROBERT F. MCALPINE

TOP: *Festooned entry gates beside the garage frame a home beautifully decorated to welcome guests.* ABOVE: *The tall Christmas tree stands opposite windows on the front porch, where it provides a focal point inside as well.* RIGHT: *A sconce sports palmetto fronds, berries, and ribbon.*

ABOVE, LEFT: *Touches of natural greenery, such as the cedar and grapevine wreath on the front door, embellish each room.* ABOVE: *The large enclosed porch, wrapping the house's bay side, presents a spectacular view and is ideal for easy dining and entertaining. After sunset, the house glows like an elegant lantern. Grapevine balls encircled with white lights hang from live oaks, becoming shining spheres in the nighttime sky.* LEFT: *In the family room, yards of cedar roping delineate the door and window openings. Each piece is wired to nails inserted into the molding above the transoms. The tree also features natural materials.*

THE DAHLE HOUSE

Candy takes the natural look in a different direction at Lisa and Craig Dahle's Fairhope home, a two-story brick structure on the site of an old bay house.

The front porch draws its inspiration from the grounds with their extensive plantings of lush camellias. Slipped into water picks, the blooms' light color accents the fresh greenery and white lights around the entry. Delicate Spanish moss, taken from live oaks on the grounds, hangs from the greenery, while a potted ficus tree on the porch twinkles with lights. Wreaths adorn the double front doors, which lead into a wide foyer.

In the dining room, a unique wall piece originated as a shuttered window grate. It acts as backdrop for an arrangement of fresh possumhaw branches rising from a silver wine cooler. More possumhaw, gracefully placed along the console's surface, carries out the motif.

Again, in the spacious family room with its sweeping views of the bay, Candy uses holiday decorations to enhance handsome architectural features. She wires greenery to the banister of the staircase leading to the bedrooms, adding nosegays of soft pink dried roses trimmed with wide ribbon. "Lisa is a gardener, and so we can use both dried and fresh flowers at her home," Candy says. "I always like to reflect a person's hobbies and talents as we decorate."

Lisa enjoys working with the natural materials as well. She creates a festive centerpiece on the breakfast table beside the fireplace by piling oranges, kumquats, pears, and cranberries at the base of small tabletop topiaries. As the season progresses, she can cluster the topiaries in the center of a table or add them individually to accessory groupings throughout the house. ★

TOP: *On the front porch, the Dahles' daughter, Elizabeth, enjoys a crisp December day with Daisy.* ABOVE: *An old shuttered window grate becomes a focal point above a table.* RIGHT: *While building their wonderful home, the Dahles preserved on the property the old camellia shrubs, which continue to bloom profusely just in time for Christmas decorations.*

LEFT: *Lisa and Craig use the handsome staircase in the family room as a gallery wall. Interior designer Candy Murphy embellished the stairway with boughs of greenery, using dried roses and pink ribbon to add accents of soft color. The house maximizes water views, with the family room and kitchen located at the rear.* BELOW: *The spacious screened porch off the kitchen offers a glimpse of the bay through the quintessential symbol of the Eastern Shore, ancient live oaks draped in Spanish moss. The breakfast table beside the fireplace accommodates family meals and also gives a convenient work surface for wrapping gifts or arranging flowers.*

Reblooming amaryllis: *How do you get potted amaryllis bulbs to bloom year after year? All I ever get from mine are leaves.*

MRS. J.E. WALL
RIDGE, MARYLAND

First, buy a bulb that already has a big, green flowerbud showing at the top. That way, you know it'll bloom at least once. After it finishes blooming, put it in a sunny window. Then take it outside to a sunny spot once the weather warms up in spring. Water as necessary, and fertilize once a month with a bloom-booster fertilizer. About the beginning of October, quit feeding and watering. When the leaves turn yellow, cut them off. Bring the pot inside to a cool, dark, dry place. Let the bulb sit there until it starts growing again. Then repot it into a slightly larger container, add fresh potting soil, and water thoroughly.

Mysterious wisteria: *I have a huge wisteria, about 40 years old, that has never bloomed. I want to know why. It's growing in the shade of several tall oaks, but my neighbor's wisterias are also shaded, and they bloomed. One nurseryman suggested that if I pruned my wisteria drastically, it would bloom. I did. It didn't.*

DAVID F. NALEY
ALEXANDRIA, VIRGINIA

Maybe you pruned it at the wrong time. The time to do it is in late winter, before the buds break. Cut back each side branch growing from the main canes to six buds. You should also try rootpruning the vine. Take a sharp spade, and sink the blade into the soil about 2 feet out from the base. Make a circle around the plant. One more thing—never fertilize wisteria. This results in lots of leafy growth, but few flowers.

Last chance: *Are daffodils and other spring bulbs still good if you haven't planted them yet?*

STEVEN CRADDOCK
CLEVELAND, MISSISSIPPI

Yes, provided they're firm and healthy looking, not soft, dried out, or moldy.

But you're really pushing it, so you need to plant ASAP. Don't expect the same show you would have gotten from fall-planted bulbs, though. Some bulbs will bloom late, and some may skip a year of bloom. Tulip bulbs probably won't bloom at all, unless they have been refrigerated.

Trimming azaleas: *When is the best time to trim azaleas? I know the usual time is right after they finish blooming, but someone told me you could also do this from November to February without reducing the spring bloom.*

MRS. LARRY D. NEW
ASHVILLE, NORTH CAROLINA

Well, that's an interesting idea—interesting because it's so completely wrong. Azaleas form their flowerbuds in summer and fall. If you cut them off in fall and winter, you'll have a lot fewer buds in the spring. The best time to trim azaleas is immediately after they finish blooming in spring. Use hand pruners to do this, never hedge trimmers. Prune branches to different lengths to maintain the natural, billowing shape.

Dead as a dogwood: *Last spring, I planted a few dogwoods in a mulched bed in my yard. They put out small, crinkled leaves, made very little growth, and then died. When I examined the roots, I found thick ones sitting atop hard, clay soil and fine ones growing in the mulch. What caused my trees to die?*

SHARON GOLLMAN
LENOIR, NORTH CAROLINA

Two possibilities come to mind. First, it's likely that the trees you planted were balled and burlapped. When these trees were dug from the field, most of their roots were left behind. Next time, try container-grown dogwoods because you can pop the trees out of their pots to check the roots before you buy. A second possibility is inadequate soil preparation. Dogwoods just won't grow in hard clay. For each tree, you need to dig a hole as deep as the root ball and three to four times as wide. Backfill around the root ball with a mixture containing half original soil,

one-fourth sphagnum peat moss, and one-fourth pine bark. Don't apply more than an inch of mulch over the soil surface. If you do, feeder roots may grow into it. These roots quickly die when the mulch dries out, and it's bye-bye to your dogwood.

Bag the beans: *Last fall, we found two "bean pods" on our Carolina jessamine. Is it possible to grow new plants from the seeds inside?*

MARGIE MCKELLAR
BOSSIER CITY, LOUISIANA

Yes, but it's a lot easier and less time-consuming to root cuttings. Just take tip cuttings, 3 to 4 inches long, anytime from late May to October. Dip the cut ends in rooting powder; then stick the cuttings into pots filled with moist potting soil. Like most vines, Carolina jessamine roots quickly.

You're too kind: *I have several clumps of Shasta daisies growing in full sun. They get plenty of water and fertilizer but don't produce a single bloom! What could I be doing wrong?*

GLORIA C. WILL
PLANT CITY, FLORIDA

Maybe you're being a little too nice. You may be encouraging a lot of leafy frowth at the expense of your flowers. Try holding back on the water and fertilizer a bit. Also make sure the fertilizer you're using is a bloom-booster type such as 15-40-15, which contains more phosphorus than nitrogen.

Lawn 911: *I have a big problem with brown patch disease killing off sections of my lawn. I've tried spraying with Daconil 2787. It works for a while, but the disease keeps coming back. Is there anything on the market that will solve this problem for good?*

ALVIS L. GRIFFIN
DEKALB, MISSISSIPPI

Brown patch is a very common disease that often shows up on lawns receiving too much water and nitrogen fertilizer. It appears as an irregularly shaped patch of brown, dying grass that keeps expanding. To get rid of it, do the following. First, water in early morning, never at night, as grass blades that stay wet for hours encourage disease. Second, water less frequently, but always deeply. Third, don't fertilize as much, and use a slow-release fertilizer. Finally, apply Scott's Lawn Fungus Control at the rate specified on the bag. This is a granular fungicide that you apply with a spreader rather than water in. The active ingredient is thiophanate-methyl, a systememic fungicide that controls brown patch. If you can't locate this product, look for another granular lawn disease control that contains this chemical. You'll find additional information about brown patch and many other disease and insect problems in the *Southern Living Problem Solver,* available at most bookstores or on the Web at southern-livingbooks.com.

Rooting boxwood: *There are 100-year-old boxwoods I would like to root cuttings from. How do you do it and at what time of year?*

GARY WASSOM
BLUFF CITY, TENNESSEE

Take tip cuttings in June or July. Stick them in a pot filled with moist sand or potting soil. Cover the pot with a miniature greenhouse made from a clear-plastic, 2-liter soft drink bottle with its bottom cut out. Keep the soil moist. The cuttings should root in about six to eight weeks.

Gophers and moles and voles, oh my: *Some animals are burrowing underground in our garden and eating the roots of our plants. If you see signs of the tunnels, but never see the actual animal, how do you know if you have gophers, moles, or voles? How do you get rid of them?*

KATHY ATTAWAY
AUGUSTA, GEORGIA

We doubt that gophers are the culprits because they leave large mounds of scooped-out soil near the entrances to their tunnels. Voles are probably responsible. They look like moles, but have larger eyes and often travel through mole tunnels. Voles eat plant stems and roots, while moles stick to insects and grubs. One way to control voles is to pull away any mulch from around plants. Voles like to scurry along beneath the cover of mulch. Another strategy is to place a shovelful of sharp gravel around the roots of a plant when you set it in the ground. Voles don't like digging through gravel. Or you can bury some fine-mesh wire along the perimeter of your planting bed.

Going nuts: *Why do pecan trees seem to have a good bearing year followed by a bad one?*

MARGARET RICE
LAUREL, MISSISSIPPI

That's a question that has baffled philosophers, statesmen, and squirrels for many years. All sorts of things can affect pecan production, including bad weather, poor pollination, and disease and insect problems. Also, many trees bear heavily in alternate years. There is nothing you can do about this.

Smoke tree: *Can you tell me whether smoke tree will grow well in my area?*

BRANDON YOUNG
CHARLESTON, ARKANSAS

Smoke tree *(Cotinus coggygria)* gets its name from the lavender-pink seed stalks that top its branches in summer and look like puffs of smoke. It grows about 15 feet tall and wide. Most folks grow the purple-leaved selections, such as Royal Purple and Velvet Cloak. Give smoke tree lots of sun and fertile, well-drained soil, and it will do fine for you, as well as for other readers in the Upper, Middle, and Lower South. American smoke tree *(C. obovatus)* also merits a look. It grows 20 to 30 feet tall and features blue-green leaves that change to yellow, orange, and red in fall. Like its European cousin, it also "smokes" in the summer.

Pruning my ponytails: *I have two large ponytail palms that I take outside for the warm months, then bring inside to a greenhouse for the winter. They've gotten too tall for the greenhouse. Can they be cut back? How far?*

PATRICIA B. WEBB
BAINBRIDGE, GEORGIA

With its bulbous trunk and drooping tufts of leaves, ponytail palm *(Beaucarnea recurvata)* looks like a giant onion sitting atop the soil. Large plants like yours usually develop multiple stalks. You can cut them back up to about 2 inches above the bulbous trunk. Make slanting cuts so that water doesn't collect on the cut ends.

Blueberry blues: *Last year, we transplanted mature blueberry bushes to another spot in the yard. Although they produced berries, they grew very few leaves and look spindly and bare. What should we do to help them? Prune them severly, fertilize, or just wait and see?*

FRANCIS R. SWAIM
SPARTANBURG, SOUTH CAROLINA

Any time you transplant large bushes, you lose roots, which stresses the plants. If the following summer is hot and dry, this makes things worse. It sounds like your plants put everything they had into fruiting and didn't have much left for anything else. It's okay to prune off some of the spindlier growth this fall. But don't prune severely, because blueberries fruit on the wood already formed. Next spring, sprinkle a few handfuls of 13-13-13 fertilizer around the dripline of each plant. Repeat this in midsummer. Water the plants during dry periods, and keep them mulched. They should recover their old form.

Give up on grass: *I live in extreme northeast Alabama and would like to plant a live oak in my yard. Are winters too cold here? If so, could you suggest some other kind of evergreen oak?*

STEVE PERTREE
VALLEY HEAD, ALABAMA

Your location places you in the Middle South, which gets too cold in winter for a live oak to thrive. It may survive there, but it will never achieve the grandeur that it does farther south. However, you can grow Japanese live oak *(Quercus myrsinifolia),* which is evergreen, more cold hardy, and grows about 30 feet tall. Another evergreen oak to consider is laurel oak *(Q. laurifolia),* which does well throughout the South and grows 40 to 50 feet tall.

January

VIBRANT GEMS
Pages 12–13: **Jewel orchids** available from Dowery Orchid Nursery.

February

PAINLESS LOVE
Pages 24–26: **Thornless roses** available from The Antique Rose Emporium, Chamblee's Rose Nursery, www.southernliving.com.

BLOOMING BEAUTIES
Page 31: **Orchids** available from Carter and Holmes Orchids.

March

SPRING'S BASHFUL BEAUTIES
Pages 44–45: **Wildflowers** available from Woodlanders, Inc.; Sunlight Gardens; Missouri Wildflowers Nursery.

BETTER BLACKBERRIES FOR YOUR GARDEN
Page 46: **Blackberries:** Arapaho, Navaho, and Kiowa varieties available from Simmons Berry Farm; Arapaho and Kiowa varieties available from Raintree Nursery.

April

NO STING TO SCORPION WEED
Page 73: **Scorpion weed** *(Phacelia bipinnatifida)* available from Native Gardens.

GOOD OLD WEIGELA
Page 75: **Weigela** *(Weigela florida)* available from Forest Farm.

A GARAGE IN KEEPING
Pages 82–84: **Architecture** by Stephen Feller. **Landscape design** by Bob Heath, Garden Arts Design, Inc.

May

LOW STRESS & COLORFUL
Pages 100–101: **Lilies** available from Dutch Gardens. **Japanese iris** available from Plant Delights. **Flower Carpet rose** available from Lowe's. **Foxglove** and **daylilies** available from Andre Viette.

VIRGINIA SWEETSPIRE
Page 103: **Virginia sweetspire** available from Woodlanders, Inc.; www.southernliving.com.

A SILVER LINING
Page 110: **Lavender** available from Goodwin Creek Gardens.

SIMPLY SMASHING, Y'ALL
Pages 112–113: **Exbury azalea hybrids** available from Pushepetappa Gardens.

SHUCKS, IT'S GOOD
Pages 114–115: **Corn** available from Park Seed, Burpee.

June

NOT YOUR MOTHER'S ABELIA
Page 127: **Chinese abelia** *(Abelia chinensis)* available from Niche Gardens; Woodlanders, Inc.

VIVE LE FRENCH HOLLYHOCK
Page 129: **Zebrina** *(Malva sylvestris)* available from White Flower Farm.

PLAYFUL POTTED GARDEN
Pages 134–135: **Metal frog** available from Christopher Glenn, Inc.

July

A PLACE TO GROW
Pages 156–159: **Architecture** by Lou Kimball Architect, Ltd. **Landscape design** by Eleanor McKinney. **Water sculpture** by artist Beverly Penn. **Studio lighting fixtures** available from Lighting Incorporated. **Exterior lights** available from Maxim. **Interior lights** available from Forcast. **Table and chairs in the studio and wicker furniture in gazebo available** from The Greenhouse Mall.

August

THIS FERN WON'T BURN
Pages 168–169: **Southern shield fern** *(Thelypteris kunthii)* available from Woodlanders, Inc.

ROOM FOR QUIET, ROOM TO PARTY
Page 176: **Trellis** available from Country Casual.

LATE-SUMMER ARRANGEMENTS
Page 177: The **book** *Flowers Are Almost Forever* available from www.amazon.com; www.garden.com; Brandylane Publishers, Inc.

CASTOR BEAN, AN AGE-OLD BEAUTY
Page 179: **Castor bean** available from Henry Field's Seed & Nursery Co.

September

SALAD DAYS
Pages 188–190: **Seeds for cool-weather vegetables** available from Johnny's Selected Seeds, The Cook's Garden, Nichols Garden Nursery. **Transplants** available from most nurseries, garden centers, feed stores.

FALL FOR FLOWERS
Page 191: **Jindai aster, hardy begonia,** and **Autumn Joy sedum** available from Niche Gardens. **Jindai aster** and **hardy begonia** also available from Woodlanders, Inc.

WASTE NOT
Page 194: **Compost bins, pitchforks,** and **compost thermometers** available from Peaceful Valley Farm Supply, Gardens Alive!

A SAGE CHOICE
Page 197: **Salvia greggii selections** available from Yucca Do Nursery, Heronswood Nursery.

October

TAKE SHELTER FROM THE COLD
Page 207: **Storage equipment** available from Charley's Greenhouse Supply, Lee Valley Tools.

VINE TIMES OF FALL
Pages 210–211: **Cypress vine, black-eyed Susan vine,** and **Spanish flag** available from Park Seed. **Cypress vine** and **black-eyed Susan vine** available from J.L. Hudson, Seedsman.

November

FRUITFUL BEAUTY
Page 222: **Oriental persimmon trees** available from Edible Landscaping, Louisiana Nursery, TyTy Nursery.

December

BEING NATURAL
Pages 242–247: **Architecture** for Robin house by Robert F. McAlpine, McAlpine Tankersley Architecture. **Interior design** for both houses by Candy Murphy and Julie Martin, i.e. Interiors.

SOURCES

Andre Viette (O), (800) 575-5538.

The Antique Rose Emporium (O), Brenham, TX; (800) 441-0002.

Beverly Penn, Austin. Represented by James Gallery, Houston, TX; (713) 942-7035; and Heriard-Cimino Gallery, New Orleans, LA; (504) 525-7300.

Bob Heath, Garden Arts Design, Inc., Winter Park, FL; (407) 645-4644.

Brandylane Publishers, Inc., (800) 553-6922.

Burpee (O), (800) 888-1447.

Carter and Holmes Orchids, P.O. Box 668, Newberry, SC 29108; (803) 276-0579; www.carterandholmes.com.

Chamblee's Rose Nursery (O), Tyler, TX; (800) 256-767; www.-chambleeroses.com.

Charley's Greenhouse Supply, 17979 State 536, Mount Vernon, WA 98273-3268; (800) 322-4707; www.charleys-greenhouse.com.

Christopher Glenn, Inc. (R), Homewood, AL; (205) 870-1236.

The Cook's Garden (O), (800) 457-9703.

Country Casual (R,O), (800) 284-8325; www.countrycasual.com

Dowery Orchid Nursery (O), 4000 Dowery Lane, Hiwassee, VA 24347; (540) 980-0817; shipment begins mid-March; free list of Jewel orchid species.

Dutch Gardens (O), (800) 818-3861.

Edible Landscaping, P.O. Box 77, Afton, VA 22920; (800) 524-4156; www.eat-it.com.

Eleanor McKinney, ASLA, Austin, TX; (512) 445-5202.

Forcast (M), model #F50737-460.

Forest Farm (O), (541) 846-7269; catalog $4.

Gardens Alive! (O), (812) 537-8650; www.gardens-alive.com.

Goodwin Creek Gardens (O), (541) 846-7357; www.goodwincreek-gardens.com.

The Greenhouse Mall (R), 9900 Ranch Road, 620 North, Austin, TX 78726-2203; (512) 250-0000.

Henry Field's Seed & Nursery Co. (O), (800) 235-0845; www.henry-fields.com.

Heronswood Nursery (O), (360) 297-4172.

i.e. Interiors, 308 Woodbridge Road, Daphne, AL 36526; (334) 626-1628.

J.L. Hudson, Seedsman, Star Route 2, Box 337, LaHonda, CA 94020.

Johnny's Selected Seeds (O), (207) 437-4357.

Lee Valley Tools, P.O. Box 1780, Ogdensburg, NY 13669-6780; (800) 871-8158.

Lighting Incorporated (R), Austin, TX; (512) 491-6444.

Louisiana Nursery, 5853 State 182, Opelousas, LA 70570; (337) 948-3696; www.louisiananursery.org.

Lou Kimball Architect, Ltd., Austin, TX; (512) 494-1055.

Lowe's (R).

Maxim (M), model #8723.

McAlpine Tankersley Architecture, 644 South Perry Street, Montgomery, AL 36104; (334) 262-8315.

Missouri Wildflowers Nursery (O), (573) 496-3492; catalog $1.

Native Gardens (O), (865) 856-0220; www.native-gardens.com.

Niche Gardens (O), Chapel Hill, NC; (919) 967-0078; catalog $3.

Nichols Garden Nursery (O), (541) 928-9280.

Park Seed (O), 1 Parkton Avenue, Greenwood, SC 29647; (800) 845-3369; www.parkseed.pointshop. com.

Peaceful Valley Farm Supply (O), (916) 272-4769; www.grow-organic.com.

Plant Delights (O), (919) 772-4794.

Pushepetappa Gardens (O), (504) 839-4930.

Raintree Nursery (O), (360) 496-6400.

Simmons Berry Farm (O), (501) 369-2345.

Stephen Feller, Architect, Winter Park, FL; (407) 647-8778.

Sunlight Gardens (O), (800) 272-7396; free catalog.

TyTy Nursery, Box 130, TyTy, GA 31795; (800) 972-2101; www.tyty-ga.com.

White Flower Farm (O), (800) 503-9624.

Woodlanders, Inc. (O), 1128 Colleton Avenue, Aiken, SC 29801; (803) 648-7522; available October 1; catalog $2.

www.amazon.com (O).

www.garden.com (O), (800) 466-8142.

www.southernliving.com.

Yucca Do Nursery (O), (979) 826-4580.

(M) Contact the manufacturer for a retail source near you. (O) Mail order. (R) Retail store. Unlisted items are one of a kind or unavailable.

Index

Plant Hardiness Zone Map

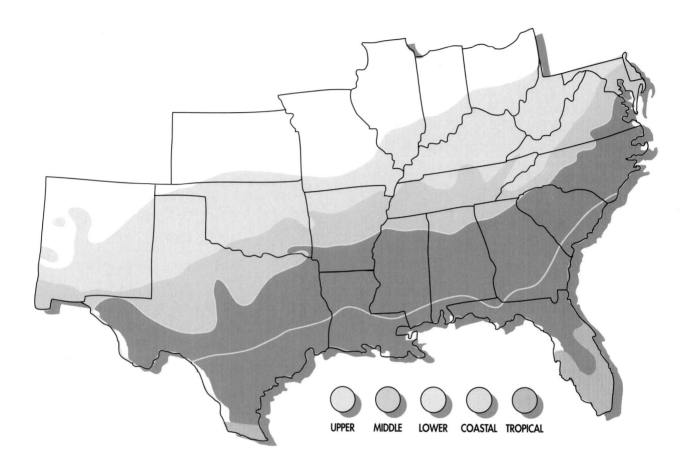

UPPER MIDDLE LOWER COASTAL TROPICAL

The United States Department of Agriculture has charted low temperatures throughout the country to determine the ranges of average low readings. The map above is based loosely on the USDA Plant Hardiness Zone Map, which was drawn from these findings. It does not take into account heat, soil, or moisture extremes and is intended as a guide, not a guarantee.

The southern regions of the United States that are mentioned in this book refer to the following:

Upper South: -10° to 0°F minimum
Middle South: 0° to 5°F minimum
Lower South: 5° to 15°F minimum
Coastal South: 15° to 25°F minimum
Tropical South: 25° to 40°F minimum